RAM   July 2016

Before Action

For Smiler, JDU, Nibby, Iscariot, Inchy and friends

Before Action

William Noel Hodgson
and the 9th Devons

A Story of the Great War

CHARLOTTE ZEEPVAT

Pen & Sword
MILITARY

First published in Great Britain in 2015 by
PEN AND SWORD MILITARY
an imprint of
Pen and Sword Books Ltd
47 Church Street
Barnsley
South Yorkshire S70 2AS

ISBN 978 1 78346 375 6

Printed and bound in England by
CPI Group (UK) Ltd, Croydon, CR0 4YY

Typeset in Times by CHIC GRAPHICS

Pen & Sword Books Ltd incorporates the imprints of
Pen & Sword Books Ltd incorporates the imprints of Pen & Sword
Archaeology, Atlas, Aviation, Battleground, Discovery,
Family History, History, Maritime, Military, Naval, Politics,
Railways, Select, Social History, Transport, True Crime,
Claymore Press, Frontline Books, Leo Cooper, Praetorian Press,
Remember When, Seaforth Publishing and Wharncliffe.

For a complete list of Pen and Sword titles please contact
Pen and Sword Books Limited
47 Church Street, Barnsley, South Yorkshire, S70 2AS, England
E-mail: enquiries@pen-and-sword.co.uk
Website: www.pen-and-sword.co.uk

Contents

Introduction

There was a time when William Noel Hodgson was one of the most celebrated poets of the Great War, named alongside Brooke, Sassoon, Graves and Owen. Letters in the archive of his publisher and newspapers of the 1920s and 1930s bear witness to the number of times his poems were reprinted, broadcast – especially on Armistice Day – even set to music (they lent themselves to music rather well). He wrote about places that mattered to him, hills most of all; about ideas and dreams and hopes, sometimes about sadness. He had a neat touch with comedy too, though few of his funny poems ever saw print. When war came his voice was distinctive, setting the crisis of the day into the long perspective of history. He was no fan of war, but accepted that particular war with resignation as something that must be faced and fought, and this was an attitude his contemporaries understood. Most shared it. His poems touched readers, none more than the last, 'Before Action', a prayer for courage in the face of death which he wrote shortly before he was killed on the Somme.

It was in the 1930s that things began to change. A generation too young to have fought and tired of hearing about the war would gladly have cut war poetry altogether. In a *Times Literary Supplement* article in December 1943, the playwright and critic Charles Langbridge complained of war poetry's exclusion from Yeats' 1936 *Oxford Book of Modern Verse*. He singled out three poets who should have been included: Charles Sorley, Wilfred Owen and William Noel Hodgson.

At the same time, as the sorrow and pride of the early post-war years gave way to a deepening bitterness, fuelled by the political divisions of the day, so the poets who had expressed anger and bitterness at the war began to take precedence. By the 1960s this had become a matter of definition: war poetry was supposed to be about protest. Mud, blood, tears and futility. To be worthy of consideration a poem had to be 'on message'. Those that were not – most of the poems published during the war, in fact – were dismissed as being at best irrelevant, at worst, part of the mindset that had come to be blamed for the war itself. In the meeting of these two strains of thought, Noel Hodgson fell from favour.

But history stepped in to keep his name alive. Whatever the literary world might say of his poetry, his last poem made him one of the best-known casualties of the opening hours of the Battle of the Somme, a tragedy which has never ceased to haunt the British imagination. Interest in the story was revived in the 1970s thanks to a powerful and successful book, Martin Middlebrook's *The*

First Day on the Somme. Middlebrook described how Hodgson's battalion had known that their advance that morning would be exposed to fire from a particular German machine gun, thanks to a relief model made by Captain Martin, one of their company commanders. But Martin's warning was dismissed by his superiors; Middlebrook saw Hodgson's 'Before Action' as moving proof that he and others believed Martin and knew they faced certain death. The story has been embellished down the years and much of it does not stand close scrutiny, as this book will show, but thanks to its existence Noel Hodgson became a name at once known and unknown, familiar to both camps, literature and history, but with almost no attention paid to his life. In common with so many of his generation he was remembered for dying, and for knowing that it was likely to happen.

And that is a shame, because in life Noel Hodgson was cheerful, sociable and easy-going. He enjoyed hill-walking, rugby, cricket, hockey, tennis, running – anything active – and was good at them too. He had an intensely private side which he kept for his writing; few of those round him were even aware of it. But he was not content to keep his writing a private hobby; he wanted to write for publication. War gave him a subject and it made his name. It also took away whatever chances he may have had.

This is his story. And because, for reasons that will become apparent, there would be no story without his family, the book is their story too. His experience opens a portal into the worlds he knew: of family life before the war; of school and university, most of all, of a 1914 volunteer battalion, in training and in France; their experiences – good as well as bad – brought back to life in their own words. Hodgson's life is the thread that links these lost worlds. Through them, the book becomes a story of the Great War itself.

Acknowledgements

Before Action has been over thirty years in the making and several people who helped in the early days did not live to see the end result; I hope they would have approved.

The most significant 'missing piece' in Noel Hodgson's story is his parents' papers. No one knows what became of them. His sister's papers proved invaluable. This book could not have happened without the help of Henry and Penelope Hodgson's descendants, especially Christopher and Adam Balogh, Susan Ashmore, Christopher Hodgson and Tirril Harris. All the family members I have contacted over the years have my heartfelt thanks for their willingness to help, their knowledge and their patience. I'm particularly grateful to Christopher Balogh and Christopher Hodgson for permission to use photographs and documents in their possession. In the same way, it would have been impossible to describe the experiences and characters of the 9th Devons without the generous help of William Upcott – his grandfather JDU really deserves a book in his own right – Paul, Martin, Richard and Patrick Wollocombe; Paul, John and Russell Freeland. Paula Richardson kindly shared her grandfather Alan Hinshelwood's photograph album and gave permission for the use of his sketch; Dorothy Parr shared her memories and Geoffrey Mason allowed me the use of three letters to Robert Parr that he found in a second-hand book.

I am also grateful to the following for permission to quote from material in their collections or to which they own the copyright: the Provost and Fellows of Worcester College Oxford [Oxland]; the Special Collections Research Center, Morris Library, Southern Illinois University, Carbondale [Inchbald Brothers Collection]; the National Library of Scotland [John Murray Archive]; the Westminster School Archives [George Hodgson]; Leeds University Library, Liddle Collection, [Pocock and Wide]; The Keep Museum [W.J.P. Aggett's *The Bloody Eleventh*]; Clara May Abrahams [May Wedderburn Cannan's *Grey Ghosts and Voices*]. While every effort has been made to trace copyright holders, in some cases this proved impossible. The publisher and I would welcome information from anyone who believes their material has been used without due credit.

For information on Thornbury, I'm grateful to Leslie Hawkins and Canon John Cornwall, who enjoyed describing his and Noel Hodgson's childhood home. Also thanks to Sandra and Chris Doig of the Thornbury Roots Website. At Berwick, the memories of Miss M.C. Cowen and Mrs Frances Donaldson set me on the path, and more recently my thanks go to Linda Bankier and Anne Moore of the Woodhorn Trust, to Judith Nicholson and James McDougall.

Durham School mattered to Noel Hodgson and the school still remembers him. Bill Surtees (past) and John Malden (present) school archivists have been immensely helpful and Robert F. Kirby and Frank Youngman were generous in sharing their memories. I also wish to thank the school for permission to use three photographs from the archives. As for Hodgson's Oxford, thanks to June Wells and Judith Curthoys at Christ Church, Emma Goodrum at Worcester College and Julie Blyth at Corpus Christi. School and college archivists have been a mine of information: Elizabeth Wells at Westminster School; Angie Edwards at Pocklington; Jerry Rudman at Uppingham; Paul Stevens at Repton; Penny Hatfield and Roddy Fisher at Eton; Viola Lyons at Trinity College School, Port Hope, Ontario; Adam Green at Trinity College, Cambridge; and the archives at the Rossall School. Other archives that provided help include the Shrine of Our Lady at Walsingham; the Hudson's Bay Company; and the archives of the publisher John Murray.

Then the Regiment. I'm grateful to the old museum of the Devon and Dorset Regiment in Exeter and to Helen Jones and Colin Parr at its successor, the Keep Museum. Also to the staff of the Imperial War Museum; Pamela Hackbart-Dean at the Special Collections Research Center, South Illinois University; Sharon Maxwell, the Shepard Archivist at the University of Surrey, Richard Davies and Matt Durrant at the Brotherton Library, University of Leeds; Father David Macdonald and the library at Sarum College; Darren Jones and John Carter.

Geoffrey Dearmer, the last of the war poets, was a joy to write to and a great encouragement. Nigel Sisson, John Lewis-Stempel, Chris Warwick, Tim Kendall and Stephen Cooper, all nudged me in the direction of publishers. Henry Wilson of Pen & Sword listened: I'm grateful to him and to my editor, Irene Moore. My thanks also go to Graeme and Julie Skinner, Mary Freeman, Mark and Jeremy Banning, Paul Reed, Gordon Shaw, Robin Schäfer, Geoff Darrall, David Oakley, Mary Wilson, Lee Richards, Chris Baker, Elizabeth Vandiver and so many helpful friends, for variously, ace research skills, superior knowledge, encouragement, brainstorming, photography and, in one case, a website. Thank you.

Prologue: The Last Morning

The Somme, Saturday, 1 July 1916. In the early hours of what promises to be a fine summer morning, three officers of the 9th Battalion, The Devonshire Regiment, are standing on the firestep of their assembly trench, scanning the horizon. But this is no ordinary morning. As they watch the bombardment of Mametz village on the hill facing their position, the noise level is beyond imagining. The air around them screams and vibrates from the shells passing overhead, and the ground throbs beneath their feet. Enemy shells are falling too in retaliation, but the three are safe for the moment. The incoming shells are ranged precisely on their front line, some 250 yards from where they now stand, every sense tuned to the trenches across the valley. If the bombardment does its work they might stand a chance. If not, in less than an hour's time they must advance at walking pace across open ground swept by enemy machine guns from two, maybe three sides. Less than an hour.

They have anticipated this moment for weeks. Two days ago Lieutenant William Noel Hodgson's acceptance of his own imminent death was voiced in a poem, 'Before Action', published in Cecil Chesterton's weekly paper *The New Witness*. He used a pen name, but those close to him at home will know that the words are his. And Captain Duncan Martin beside him on the firestep, scanning the German trenches through field glasses, knows every hill and fold and danger point as only a man can know who has shaped the landscape in plasticene with his hands, making a relief model to be used in preparation for the battle. For the last week all the officers of 7th Division have pored over the model at Brigade Headquarters. Now Martin can only hope he was wrong in predicting that his own battalion will have to cross no man's land at its most dangerous point. Too late now, though, to worry. Time to lead. So he and Hodgson and Second Lieutenant Freeland jump back into the trench and sit on the firestep eating the sandwiches they were issued with last night. It will encourage the men to see them look so unconcerned.

They are still there, talking and laughing, when a runner comes from headquarters: the CO has sent for Mr Hodgson. So he leaves his friends and makes his way up the crowded trench. Before long the others also make a move. Time is ticking on now and there are things they must do.

He will see Rowan Freeland once more after he leaves headquarters. He asks him for help when he finds that the rum ration has been handed out and his bombing sections have missed it. Have Freeland's platoon any to spare? No, their ration was short, but Freeland goes round the other platoons in his company, then the other companies, trying to scrounge some rum for the bombers. Disappointed, he returns to his platoon. He and Noel Hodgson will never meet again. With Duncan Martin, Freeland will be in the first line to go over, Hodgson and his bombers in the second. At precisely 7.27am, three minutes before the advance begins on the rest of the British front line, the whistles blow and the 9th Devons climb out of their assembly trenches and begin to move forward.

And the machine guns open fire.

Chapter 1

From God's Hills to Gloucestershire

'In the train, Liverpool Street,
Dearest Star,
. . . I am writing my letter now, as tomorrow may be very full, while we
sit in the dining car waiting for the train to start. We have been most
favoured in every way: never missed any train or connection, and had
two good cross Channel passages; never at all crowded in the carriages,
the only trouble was the crowd on and off the boats. . .' [1]

Four years on from that blood-stained Somme morning, Noel Hodgson's father, Henry, settled into his seat on the homeward train, his mind full of memories of an extraordinary journey. After four years of patient grief, four years of trying to reconcile themselves to a bereavement on paper, shorn of all the normal funeral rites, he and his wife had at last been able to visit the place where their youngest son died, to spend time by his grave. And in the interval of stillness before the train moved off, Henry began to set down his impressions of the journey in a letter to their daughter. He had no need to write to her. He had already sent a telegram and expected to see her before long; in the event, she was waiting for him and her mother when they arrived home. His letter would not be finished until the next day, and posted after that. But the experience was too important to be trusted to conversation. It needed ink and paper to hold it fast, fresh and vivid for years to come. It marked the family's personal crossing from war towards peace, and a deeply felt moment of closure.

Less than two years after the fighting ended, the physical scars of war were everywhere. *'Up to Amiens,'* Henry continued, *'the country looked much as it always did except for the remains of Camps and hospitals at Etaples, and two large cemeteries, but after leaving Amiens we soon came into the devastated area and that word cannot depict: it came as a kind of shock to catch the first view of trees, long rows, dead and gaunt, almost branchless, standing grim and horrid along the roads; all destroyed by gas, or shock of explosives, and the poor country, one desert of long brown tangled grass and weeds. . . .'* His wife Penelope had written much the same in a letter from France a few days earlier.

'It is impossible to speak of the ruins of this place, but I think the sight of the trees was almost the worst.'[2]

After the fighting ended it was the scale of the devastation that most appalled. In the Somme department of France alone about 477,000 acres – an area larger than the whole of Buckinghamshire – had been blasted by years of high explosives, poison gas, disinfectants, and all the detritus of mechanised warfare. Whole villages were reduced to brick dust and rubble. Many places were unrecognisable, leading to fears that the wounds war had inflicted on the landscape would never heal. Topsoil was torn away, livestock had been killed or scattered and roads destroyed; fuel was short, food was short. Yet people had lived there once and they were intent on returning. As their determination became apparent, so schemes were devised to help them. Individual gifts of sheep were sent from Britain, and a whole breeding flock transported to the departmental farm at Boves, south of Amiens, to produce future generations of lambs for local farmers. British towns and villages were encouraged to adopt their ruined French counterparts, and the first glimmerings of normal life returning to the former battlefields seemed to promise so much more. A report in *The Times* on 8 June 1920, two months before the Hodgsons' visit, celebrated *'the supreme message of the battlefields in the new era of peace – the love of home, the power of hope, the consciousness of the dignity of labour, and the proud confidence of humanity in its destiny.'*[3]

These were the prevailing feelings immediately after the war. Sorrow and pride. Gratitude. A sense of wonder that humanity had come through so much and survived. There was also reverence. Men had died on the battlefields in numbers almost impossible to comprehend. Some graves were known, others had been lost in later fighting, and some bodies would never be found at all. Their presence transformed the way people felt about the land. A special correspondent to *The Times*, writing in the autumn of 1919, described the pull of the landscape:

> *'One is drawn to it as it were by hands invisible. . . . And in great silence one finds here, as in old sanctuaries, the sweetness of a man's life and its power. For the air is quick, if you will believe it, with the spirits of those who died. They are about you, touching, welcoming; they move with your steps on the light sward; they beckon to you from the slopes of the upland.'*[4]

Reports like this urged visiting the battlefields as a duty the living owed to the dead, but the spirit of their visits was all-important. Mere curiosity, tourism for its own sake, seemed inappropriate. The word 'pilgrimage' came to be used for the 'right' sort of visit; a century on, it still is.

Henry and Penelope Hodgson may have read some or all of *The Times* reports, or similar ones in other papers. In the months leading to their visit advice to would-be travellers was everywhere. Go soon, because the battlefields are changing so quickly: *'in a year or two's time many of the keys to this great store of history will have been lost for ever.'* Go in an organised group, because of the shortage of resources, accommodation and transport. The South Eastern and Chatham Railway Company, for example, offered daily departures from June 1920 on two- or three-day packages costing 13 or 15 guineas. A committee was formed in Parliament to liaise between groups working to help bereaved families, and to make visits possible quickly at a reasonable cost. The Salvation Army, Church Army and YMCA, all began to cater for the needs of visitors as once they had catered for the troops.[5]

But the Hodgsons had the means and the confidence to travel independently, disregarding at least some of the proffered advice. Organised groups based themselves in Amiens, where decent hotel accommodation could be found; Henry and Penelope Hodgson wanted to be nearer the battlefields. They chose Albert, a town Noel and his fellow 9th Devons knew well. But its post-war state was distressing. *'Though one had seen pictures,'* Henry told their daughter, *'only one's eyes could really help to take in what war had meant.'* He saw just one complete house and that was new, *'all the others are heaps of ruins; and so is the Cathedral; [where] the Virgin's Statue stood; yet in this awful scene . . . there are 3,000 inhabitants, out of 8,000 before the War, living in wooden and tin huts, and working with wonderful diligence from dawn to dark. Our hotel was an erection of wood and corrugated iron: one bedroom <u>and bed</u> very small . . . as for sanitary arrangements, you know what France is; and this was <u>more so</u>! Except for this we were all right; and the cooking quite good; and everything was spotlessly clean.'* In any case, these things were unimportant. What mattered was <u>*'to be there*</u> *in the very areas of suffering and conflict: with the hideous traces of war on every hand: never to be forgotten.'*

This was in August 1920. The couple had arrived in Albert on a Wednesday evening after twelve hours of travel. In their luggage they had rose bushes – no easy things to transport – and, presumably, the tools they would need to plant them. A car was booked for the next day to take them to the hillside facing Mametz, where their son and his friends had watched the bombardment that July morning and where, in the old front line trench where the German shells had been falling, he, Duncan Martin, and 159 other Devons were buried. But let Henry take up the story:

'Our visit to the Devonshire [Cemetery] was all we could wish: we had little difficulty in finding it: and we spent four hours there, from 11.30 – 3.30. The grave plots are in two rows; about 8 or 9 lie in each plot: and a wooden cross in the centre has their names punched on tin tape – our Boy lies with one fellow Officer, W. Riddell, and eight private soldiers. We planted our rose bushes and hung on the cross a tiny crucifix of

mine. We felt so glad that this graveyard was <u>not</u> one of those huge cemeteries with thousands of graves; he lies with his own comrades around him, in this tiny close, on the top of a hill "looking out" over miles of open land; where great winds blow! and in the very heart of the land for whose deliverance they all contended to the death. Just behind lay the remnants of the old British lines, and trenches: with bits of bombs, and harness, and wire tossed about here and there. You could hardly have a more fitting environment: so different from the smug respectability of the normal Town Cemetery.'

'Where great winds blow.' Visitors to the Devonshire Cemetery in more recent years, who see it nestling behind the regrown trees of Mansel Copse, a hidden, sheltered place, may find Henry's description hard to recognise. In 1920, though, the thicket of broken stumps, wild flowers and brambles that was all the war had left of the copse did nothing to disguise the height and openness of the site. For Henry, this meant everything. He was quoting from one of his son's poems, *'Where fell tops face the morning, and great winds blow,'* and with it evoking a love they shared, which ran deep in Noel's character and his writing. It was a love for the high places of earth, most particularly the Cumbrian fells; a love that stretched back into the roots of their family history.

The Hodgsons belonged to Cumbria; they never doubted it. The family believed its origins lay in the Viking settlements of the eastern fells. In the more recent past, Henry's grandfather William Hodgson was a lawyer, Clerk of the Peace for the county of Cumberland and five-times-elected Mayor of Carlisle. While still in his twenties and single, William had a large house built in open countryside to the north of the city. Houghton House took eleven years to complete and by the time it was built, he was married with a rapidly growing family. Three of his six sons became lawyers, two clergymen (the other died in childhood). His five daughters married professional men or, unmarried, were provided for by their father and fitted in where the family needed them, as housekeepers, companions, carers. These were the Hodgsons: practical, earnest and hard-working, bound to one another and to Cumberland. Thomas, the eldest son, followed his father as Clerk of the Peace and held the position for over half a century; later it passed to his brother Charles, later still to their nephew.

When work took them further afield, the Hodgson men remained staunchly Cumbrian. William Henry, the second son, spent his working life in London as a Treasury barrister, but he retired to Carlisle. When he died he was buried at Houghton with his parents and brothers. This homing tendency of the Hodgsons resonates through Noel's wartime poems. In 'God's Hills', written on the Somme in the spring of 1916, his thoughts turned as they often did to the high fells, to the clouds and the mist and the peculiar quality of the light; then to the people of

Cumberland and to generations long dead. He contrasted their lot with the new, wartime reality, that *'on some stifling alien plain/ The flesh of Cumbrian men is thrust/ In shallow pits, and cries in vain/ To mingle with its kindred dust.'* Not for him the certainty of Rupert Brooke's soldier, whose death would take England itself to *'some corner of a foreign field'*. Thomas Hardy imagined much the same in the Boer War poem 'Drummer Hodge'; *'Yet portion of that unknown plain/ Will Hodge forever be.'* For Hodgson the field, the plain, remained alien places. The dead needed their own soil for the cycle to be complete.

The Hodgsons were committed to their county: practical, earnest, and, in the memory of later generations, unfailingly kind. Henry's father, the Rev George Courtenay Hodgson, was the fourth son and a well-known figure in the north. When he died suddenly on Easter Sunday morning in 1886, in his vicarage at Corbridge on Tyneside – he suffered a heart attack while dressing – an obituary in *The Carlisle Patriot* praised him for turning his back on well-paid livings to serve in poorer parishes where he saw a need. Before Corbridge he had spent twenty years as rector in the tiny hamlet of Barton, between Penrith and Pooley Bridge. Henry was born at Barton and grew up in its high, open spaces. From the end of the church lane a short ride on the coach from Penrith led to Ullswater, and Henry and his brothers learned to row on the lake and climbed the surrounding fells. In 1878, three years after the family left for Corbridge, he and his brother Charlie returned to Ullswater to spend three days climbing with two younger boys. Henry kept a detailed diary of the holiday, which foreshadows a similar account Noel would write over thirty years later. Henry's diary is a handwritten notebook with photographs carefully pasted in; Noel's, scribbled on the backs of a handful of postcards, but there was much in their minds and attitudes that was similar, and Henry's diary illuminates his son's passion for climbing.

Henry considered himself *'an experienced mountaineer'*. He led the party along Thirlmere and up to the summit of Helvellyn, coming down on the far side to Patterdale and Ullswater. He had climbed Helvellyn three times before, he said, which does not sound very many, but he knew every feature of the landscape by name. When a thick mist descended while they were on the summit, Henry had the skill and confidence to find the way down. He was a good leader too, constantly watching the younger boys to make sure they were coping. Later, the boys he led on climbing expeditions would be his own sons. He also felt the emotional pull of the landscape. From Patterdale the party sailed up Ullswater on the steamer – a new boat Henry had never seen before – and he was struck by a feeling of dislocation. His father had given up all this for Tyneside, and it hurt Henry to be back in the place he loved, yet no longer part of it: *'it was difficult to persuade ourselves that we were not a few miles only from home, and that the coach would not drop us within an hour or two at the end of the church lane. And all the time while we felt so different, while there had been such changes among ourselves and our friends, the lake lay calm, and the great hills stood round unchanged to guard it as in past days.'*

The hills endured and Henry drew comfort from them, just as his son would in the trenches. Henry had just graduated with a double first from Oxford that summer, and was preparing to follow his father into the church. The next year saw him ordained deacon. He also took up his first job in 1879, very far from Ullswater, as chaplain and Classics master at Elizabeth College on Guernsey. It was on Guernsey that he and Penelope met. The census of 1881 finds them both living in St Peter Port: he in lodgings a few minutes' walk from the College, she in a house near the Upper Candie Gardens with her widowed mother and siblings. They probably met at church or through the College, where her teenage brother was a pupil. Or perhaps, one winter evening at the weekly entertainments at Castle Vaudin, where Henry's comic readings were always enjoyed. He was popular on the island, but in their society a man thinking of marriage needed to have a reasonable income and a home to offer. So Henry returned to the mainland later in 1881 to become vicar of Staverton, a small village to the west of Daventry in the east Midlands. Penelope's family left Guernsey around the same time to join her eldest brother Pelham. He was on a rare period of extended home leave from the China Consular Service, with his wife and three children his family in England had never seen.

And on 1 June 1882 Henry Hodgson and Penelope Maria Warren were married in the church of All Saints in Leamington, where his father had once been curate. George Courtenay Hodgson performed the service assisted by his elder son William, also a clergyman. This was a family habit: with so many priests and lawyers among their number, the Hodgsons were self-sufficient when it came to weddings, funerals and wills. Back in St Peter Port the local paper, *The Star*, reported:

> *'The bride wore a cream brocaded satin dress, trimmed with Brussels lace and orange blossoms, and Brussels lace veil. The bridesmaids, five in number. . . wore cream cashmere and brocaded silk dresses, cream straw hats, trimmed with ferns and mignonette, and carried lovely bouquets, the gift of the bridegroom. The wedding party returned to breakfast at the residence of the bride's mother.'*

Penelope brought a very different strain of character and influence to her children. While the Hodgsons were firmly rooted in the north and in a stolid, local tradition of life and work, the Warrens belonged to the Empire. Beyond being broadly southern, they had no attachment to a particular place. Penelope's parents were first cousins, grandchildren of the society doctor Richard Warren, who was physician to King George III in some of his most distressing periods of illness. Of the doctor's reputedly eight sons, Pelham, another doctor, was Penelope's maternal grandfather. Pelham's brother Frederick entered the navy while still in his teens and rose to the rank of vice admiral; his elder son, Richard Laird Warren, was Penelope's father.

It was the navy and the world view that went with it, coupled with the wealth and social standing of the royal physician, that defined Penelope's branch of the Warrens. Like his father, Richard Laird Warren joined the navy as a boy; for a time he served on the most famous ship of all, HMS *Victory*, under Sir Robert Stopford. He was flag lieutenant to his father at the Cape of Good Hope and captained ships on voyages to the West Indies and North America. His third command, HMS *Trincomalee*, is still afloat as the centrepiece of the Historic Dockyard in Hartlepool. Richard Warren sailed her to the Caribbean, where her duties included providing hurricane relief to colonists and searching for illegal slave traders; then to the St Lawrence estuary, Newfoundland and Labrador. He captained HMS *Cressy* in the Baltic during the Crimean War. He rose steadily in rank, and in the meantime married his cousin Eleanor Warren and fathered eleven children. Penelope was the ninth, born in St Saviour's on Jersey in 1861. The tenth, another girl, was born in Montevideo while their father was commander-in-chief of the South American station, a post he held for three years.

In 1870 Richard was promoted to full admiral, a matter of immense pride. When the next census was taken he listed Eleanor's profession as 'Admiral's wife' and each of the children still living at home save one, already a naval sub-lieutenant, as 'Admiral's daughter', 'Admiral's son'. What all this meant for Noel and his siblings, who would never know their grandfather, was a sense of how vast the world was and a wealth of stories. A sense too of Britain's place in that world and the opportunities it offered. One of their Warren uncles emigrated to Australia. Two served in the navy and the eldest, Pelham, was in the Consular service in China throughout Noel's boyhood. In 1900, during the Boxer Rebellion, Pelham Warren sent a telegram to the Foreign Office which played an important part in resolving the crisis. In recognition of this, he was made consul-general in Shanghai in July 1901. The following year he was knighted. He retired in 1911, a few months before Noel left school.

So alongside Cumbria and its legends, the imagination of the Hodgson children fed on stories of the sea, the Caribbean and the Far East. Of sailors and adventurers; of 'Cooking Pot Warren', who sounds like a very unfortunate missionary but turns out to have been one of the naval Warrens, who invented a sort of pressure cooker. Mrs Beeton described 'Captain Warren's Cooking Pot' and it was praised in several Victorian recipe books. According to the *Nursing Record* of April 1890, Captain Warren also invented a 'Batchelor Frying Pan', which again has unintended echoes of the cannibal. In his last year at school, Noel wrote a story about smugglers, piracy and romance in Far Eastern waters; his fascination with pirates and smugglers stretched back into childhood and lived on in his published work:

> *'We trafficked in Baghdad and Samarcand,*
> *Or handled ankers in the smugglers' den,*
> *Or came at evening to an unknown strand*
> *Where each man gripped his cutlass in his hand.*
> *For magic ruled the whole earth over then.'* [6]

The Warren heritage also brought an edge of social awareness – snobbery, the Hodgson children called it, with a mischievous glint. While Henry was restrained, principled, and rather serious, at pains to communicate with everyone in his parish, Penelope was much more keenly aware of the absurdities in people and situations. The middle son Hal surely had his mother in mind when describing the rector's wife in his 1930s novel, *Heats of Youth*, with *'her faintly enigmatic smile'* and, in her eyes, *'a hint – a gentle hint – of mocking, the faintest, the most delicate suggestion of irony'*. His daughter remembered Penelope as *'charming, petite and utterly indomitable, her biting wit sometimes made her sound uncharitable, but my grandfather had enough charity for both of them.'* [7] Always quiet in public and supportive of her husband, in private Penelope supplied the drive and ambition in the partnership, and viewed their life with an amused, critical eye. Henry was the steady, encouraging presence, *'with his darling smile or whimsical expression, & always understanding'*. [8]

Their eldest child, Arthur, was born in the vicarage at Staverton on 1 July 1884 – thirty-two years to the day before his brother's death on the Somme. Staverton was a very small parish which took the young couple to its heart; over twenty years later their daughter visited for the first time and found herself welcomed and recognised. *'It is just a tiny village, but very picturesque, & such jolly people. They, one & all, declared me to be exactly like Mother!!'* [9]

Henry had been vicar of Staverton four years when their lives seemed poised to take a very different turn. He was chosen as headmaster of Birkenhead School. This was an achievement for a 29-year-old with very little experience of working in a school, but if it suggested a change of heart about his career, that change was to be short-lived. He moved to Birkenhead to take up the appointment at the start of the autumn term and the term was barely over before his next move was sealed. The living of Staverton, left vacant on his resignation, was taken by an older man who could no longer cope with his large parish; that parish, Thornbury in Gloucestershire, passed to Henry. So in the spring of 1886 a new headmaster was appointed for Birkenhead and the Hodgsons moved on.

Noel Hodgson was born in Thornbury vicarage on 3 January 1893, in one of the coldest spells anyone could remember. Not as cold overall as the winter in which his sister Stella was born two years earlier; their brother Hal, four years her senior, was also a January baby. But the turn of the year 1892/3 was cold enough to paralyse normal life right across Europe. Temperatures as low as nineteen degrees below freezing were recorded daily. In London, the public parks were thrown open for skating, with lamps to illuminate the scene until late into the evening. There were even refreshment tents, and extra police and volunteer 'icemen' standing by in case of accidents. On the day Noel was born, 30,000 people skated in London according to *The Times; 'Viewed after dark last night from the bridge, the Serpentine looked like a country fair at night. Naphtha and other lamps threw a glare over the polished surface of the ice, and men with torches were scudding along rapidly upon skates.'*[10] Similar scenes were repeated all around the country.

The cold set in just before Christmas Eve with a dense hoar frost. This, and closeness to her time, did not prevent Penelope Hodgson from supervising the church Christmas decorations; she had a real flair for it and her work was always admired. She also had visitors at the vicarage, but Henry's unmarried sister and brother, Marion and Charlie, would have been a help to her, and could keep the children amused when the baby arrived. *'My aunt is 'nice', awfully holy and overpoweringly energetic,'* Stella wrote some years later, visiting them in Carlisle. *'They are awfully good to me & I daresay I could have the moon if I really wanted it and it could be got.'*[11] On the evening Noel was born, 'Uncle Charlie' was entertaining Henry's parishioners in the popular farce *Poor Pillicoddy*, in aid of the Parish Sick and Poor Fund. The local paper reported on a programme of charades and songs performed by friends and neighbours with *Poor Pillicoddy* as its climax: *'There was a large and fashionable audience by whom the entertainment was thoroughly appreciated.'*[12] The birth of the vicar's youngest son, meanwhile, slipped by unnoticed.

Thornbury, in the Vale of the River Severn, was quintessentially English, a small market town in gentle, managed countryside; safe, confident and comfortable, busy with its own concerns and those of its neighbours. The population when Henry took over the living was perhaps 1,500 to 2,000, with more in the outlying hamlets of Sibland, Gillingstool, Crossways and The Hacket to the east, Buckover, Upper and Lower Morton to the north, Kington, Kyneton and Duckhole; all these were part of his parish. Bristol lay some twelve miles to the south, Gloucester to the north; the road to Thornbury branched off the main road between the two by the Ship Inn at Alveston, descending Marlwood Hill and rising slightly into the town. Then the High Street sloped gradually downhill to The Plain, where the markets were held, on down Castle Street to the gates of the Tudor castle – home, at that time, to Edward Stafford Howard, his wife Lady Rachel, and their three children. A prominent figure locally, Stafford Howard was another native of Cumberland. Born at Greystoke Castle near Penrith, he had represented East Cumberland in Parliament for nearly ten years, and would have known the Hodgson family.

The vicarage lay west of the castle gate. Jokes about *'the rich man in his castle, the poor man at the gate'* were a favourite with Thornbury's vicars, though in fact there was a very good relationship between castle and vicarage. Stafford Howard was an active member of the church and a patron of its many causes. He supported the vicar on innumerable committees, provided him with a horse, and welcomed the vicarage children into the castle grounds, allowing them to use his outdoor swimming pool and indoor tennis court, amenities few people enjoyed.

On the east side of the castle gate was the medieval church of St Mary the Virgin. Opposite lay the glebe field, where the vicar kept his pony and trap and where, behind the stable, a kitchen garden grew potatoes for his table. The vicarage had its own large garden too, with a gravel path and flower beds at the front, bordered by a low hedge and gate. At the back was a croquet lawn, framed by a shrubbery and a stand of old, clipped yew trees; to the south of them, a grass tennis court, a shed, and a long walled garden for fruit and vegetables. Apple and plum trees grew there, and cherry and fig trees were trained on the wall above beds of strawberries, raspberries and currants. A raised mound of large stones at the intersection of three paths was a focal point for the children's games; they called it 'the castle'. Beyond the garden wall the fields fell steeply away to the Severn, two miles distant. In winter or spring the river could be seen at high tide, and beyond it, blue in the far distance, the hills of the Forest of Dean.[13]

Vicarage, castle, church and glebe field; this corner of Thornbury was the hub of the Hodgsons' life for eleven years, and the first home Noel and his siblings knew – all but Arthur, and he was little more than a baby when their father accepted the living.

But idyllic as it sounds, life was not without problems. In Noel's early months, long-standing concerns about the state of the vicarage reached crisis point. Henry had first raised the issue around the time Stella was born, writing to the Dean and Chapter of Christ Church, who owned the living, to tell them the house was beyond repair. Two successive surveys confirmed it: the second, when Stella was a few weeks old, found that the vicarage had been built badly with inadequate drainage. But two months later, on the night of the 1891 census, the building still held thirteen people: Henry, Penelope, the three children, her unmarried sister Eleanor Warren, (known to the children as 'Baba' because she sang 'Baa Baa Black Sheep' so often); their nurse, the cook, the housemaid, a general servant, and three male students in their late teens. Clergyman often took in students, 'cramming' them for university entrance or scholarships. It was an extra source of income, but fitting everyone under the one roof must have taken a miracle of domestic management, and it placed increasing strain on the building.

At the end of Noel's first year the vicarage was condemned as *'insanitary and unsuitable for the accommodation required of it'*. The Bishop gave permission for the house to be pulled down and a new one built for just under

£1,700; this included £75 to cover the family's removal expenses and the rent on temporary accommodation. A few months later Henry thought of a different plan, writing to the Dean and Chapter to suggest that instead of building a new house, the vicarage and part of the glebe field could be sold and an existing house bought from the proceeds. He was probably trying to speed things up and save his family the trauma of two moves. But his scheme fell through in May when the owner of the house he wanted raised the asking price by £800.

So, later in 1894, the Hodgsons moved to a temporary home while work on their new vicarage began. The parish had undertaken to cover the cost and most of the money was pledged by individuals and charities; the rest had to come from fund-raising events. In June 1895, Stafford Howard opened the grounds of Thornbury Castle to a three-day bazaar in aid of the new vicarage. His sister, the Countess of Carnarvon, travelled from London to open proceedings, and Henry made the opening speech. He was on the planning committee and Penelope helped organise the stalls. The bazaar was a major event locally with attractions including a conjuror, a display of Morris dancing by local children, concerts, open-air theatre, and music from the Bristol City Band.[14] Visitors would have seen the building work in progress on their way in, and Arthur, Hal, Stella and Noel would surely have provided an eye-catching reminder of the reason why the vicar needed a new house.

Vicarage families were always on show, known and observed by the whole community, and the children were expected to play their part from an early age. In 1890 the local paper spotted Arthur scattering flowers in the path of a newly married couple as they walked down the aisle of St Mary's; he was five years old.[15] They would have attended Sunday school and special children's events, like the flower services their father held, when children brought flowers and toys for the Bristol Children's Hospital. The chemist in Thornbury, Spencer Palmer, was the local dentist and the family's illnesses were treated by Dr Lionel Williams in Castle Street. The other doctor in Thornbury was E.M. Grace, a celebrated cricketer and a brother of W.G. Grace, one of Victorian England's great sporting heroes. The Graces had their own cricket club which played on the Castle Ground, two fields below the vicarage, and watching their matches occupied many a Saturday afternoon.

The age gap between Hal and Stella divided the children naturally into two pairs; the older boys, then Stella and Noel, who were always very close. Echoes of their early childhood linger in their later writing, like the small boy in Stella's novel *Old Mrs Warren*, who announces over his breakfast egg that he means to be a poet. There are hints of remembered mischief too. On the Somme in 1916, arranging for the income from his published work to be set aside for Stella's unborn child, Noel remembered a time when they would have found it useful to have money. *'By the way send along the cheques for endorsement; I mean what I say about them; just think if we'd been started in life with a bank balance, even a few quids like that – we could have indemnified Peadie for that check dress!* '16 There was a Pead family living not far from Thornbury. The story of the check dress is lost but the children seem to have been forgiven; a Miss Pead appears in Stella's 1912 wedding present list. She gave a lace handkerchief.

The family spent at least a year in rented accommodation. Then came the upheaval of packing and moving, but the new house was a handsome modern building designed around their needs. A photograph of Noel and Stella around this time shows them perched uncomfortably on a small polished table in a wide area of open grass. Noel looks very solemn. Perhaps he was fighting to stay on the table, or wishing the man with the camera would go away and someone lift him down. He was between three and four years old and instantly recognisable from studio photographs taken during the war; it brings home how short a time would elapse between the two. But in 1896 he was just the tail-end of the vicar's children, the small boy Thornbury knew and remembered years later, when the town's list of men and women serving in the forces was published in the local paper. The Hodgsons had moved away long since, but Thornbury still counted Noel Hodgson as one of its own.

> *'Now men there be that love the plain*
> *With yellow cornland dressed,*
> *And others love the sleepy vales*
> *Where lazy cattle rest;*
> *But some men love the ancient hills,*
> *And these have chosen best.'* '17

No one reading Noel Hodgson's poems would guess that his life began in this gentle, rural setting, so far from the rugged mountain landscapes he claimed as his own. Perhaps the first hills that stirred his imagination were the blue hills on the horizon, seen from the vicarage garden. In the spring of 1916, when Stella was expecting her baby, and took refuge in Worcester to escape German air raids, he told her, *'I hope when the BIT arrives he will be made to look often to the Malvern hills, so that a true strain of hill blood may be developed in him.'* '18

Chapter 2

Berwick-upon-Tweed

In 1896 Henry Hodgson turned forty. For a decade he had devoted himself to Thornbury; the local papers of the day bear witness to an extraordinary workload. In addition to the day-to-day running of the parish – which at that time included two services on a Sunday and sometimes three, with visits, more services in outlying chapels, christenings, weddings, funerals and administrative work – he was in demand to speak at meetings of local societies and charities and to arrange special services for them. He gave public lectures and commented in newspapers on everything from the state of roads to the disestablishment of the Welsh church. He helped the children of the Band of Hope perform the popular (and very moral) story *Dick's Fairy* at their Christmas party. On one memorable occasion he took a service in the dairy shed of the Bath and West Show, choosing, 'The Lord is my Shepherd' as his text.

Some of his work related to the vicar's social position. He was on the Parish Council and took a keen interest in local schools, campaigning regularly on educational issues. He was an external scholarship examiner. He served on the committee of the Horticultural Show and judged exhibits. Once he joined in, entering (and winning) with his petunias. But none of this was enough. Deep in Henry Hodgson's soul ran a determination to improve life for his whole parish, not just the churchgoers. He wanted to make a difference. The Church of England's failure to reach large sections of the population worried him, and he tried to bridge the gap by giving weekly Bible classes for working men during the winter; these were said to be very popular. He was adamant that the Parish Sick and Poor Fund should help anyone, regardless of creed, and he suggested that it should employ a nurse. In a world with no state provision, the idea of individual responsibility was woven into the fabric of life and Henry encouraged his parishioners to give as far as their means allowed. Charity bazaars and amateur concerts performed by friends and neighbours in aid of local causes were a staple of his family's social life, and for him they were the only entertainment anyone needed. Years later he would be baffled by Penelope and Stella's decision to go to a professional concert: *'there's no one we know performing!!!'*[1]

He had earned Thornbury's affection, but at heart, Henry Hodgson was still a northerner. So when a letter came from the Bishop of Newcastle in the spring of 1897, inviting him to take over England's most northerly parish, Berwick-upon-Tweed, it must have felt like a summons home. He said that the pain of parting was *'very keen and very severe'*, but the question of refusing the invitation simply did not arise. [2] His father's memory still acted as an inspiration and a spur, and in leaving rural Thornbury for Berwick he was echoing his father's move from Barton to Tyneside. In the north, George Courtenay Hodgson was still remembered, and it was as his son that the bishop recommended Henry to the people of Berwick.

But what of Penelope and the children, comfortably settled in their new house at last after all the upheaval? Noel was very young and would soon adapt, but Hal and Stella had had time to put down roots in Thornbury. Both would later write novels woven round their memories of the town, and in time Hal married a Thornbury girl – his sister's friend – and settled there. Arthur, on the other hand, had left home already in term time. At twelve years old he was sent to the Elsted Rectory in Sussex, where the Rev J.K.S. Paget-Moffatt ran what amounted to a small school, coaching boys for scholarships. In the summer of 1897 Arthur's success in the scholarship exams of the Rossall School in Fleetwood was reported by the local paper on Guernsey. The decision to leave Thornbury came hardest for Penelope. Rural Gloucestershire was a perfect setting for her, providing the kind of society she was used to, a good standard of living in a beautiful new house and, above all, the vicarage garden. Penelope Hodgson loved her flowers. She would accept Henry's decision. Her existence revolved around his, but for her, life in Berwick was never quite the same.

The appointment was made public in the spring of 1897, and in the first week of September the Hodgsons arrived in their new home. They may have visited the town before: at some time during the Thornbury years Henry at least had been to Berwick, standing in while the vicar was on leave. The Hodgsons' holidays often took the form of vicarage exchanges and this may have been one. But in September 1897, as the train brought them through Tweedmouth on its way to the Royal Border Bridge, which carried the line into the town, and they glimpsed the pinkish-grey stone vicarage across the broad river estuary, they had come to stay.

A few days later, on the evening of Friday, 10 September, Henry was formally instituted and inducted Vicar of Berwick, by the Bishop of Newcastle and the Archdeacon of Lindisfarne. The church was crowded, and the service had a more public aspect than such things usually do thanks to a peculiarity of the building. At the end of an induction service the new incumbent tolls the church bell, as a signal that he has taken over the parish. But Holy Trinity, the parish church in Berwick, has no bells. So at the end of the service, Henry, the bishop, the archdeacon and a flock of local clergy, the churchwardens, and representatives of the town corporation, trooped in procession through Berwick to the Town Hall. A crowd had gathered in the streets, as Henry climbed into the bell loft and tolled the Town Hall bell. After this, everyone made their way back up Church Street to the Girls' School in the Parade for a social gathering. The Bishop recommended Henry as *'a north countryman'*, whose *'father had been a clergyman in the Newcastle Diocese,'* and Henry shook hands with everyone present.

His speech included a revealing glimpse of the state of things at home:

> *'I should like also to say one word on behalf of Mrs Hodgson. We have made a long journey, and have got only partially settled in our new home. If any of our friends should intend to call upon us I hope they will bottle up their kindness for a few days so as to give us a few days to feel our feet and brush down the cobwebs before they arrive.'*[3]

Everyone laughed, but for Penelope, surrounded by packing cases, children, and cobwebs – the house had been empty for five months – it might have been rather soon to see the funny side.

Berwick was a different kind of parish in a very different setting. Built on a narrow strip of land between the Tweed and the North Sea, the town had a population over four times that of Thornbury, and most of their homes were clustered within the safety of the Elizabethan wall. An outlying group of buildings to the north came within the medieval grass rampart, both sets of defences recalling a time when the possession of Berwick was hotly disputed between England and Scotland. Captured decisively for England in 1482 by the future King Richard III, the town was still treated as an English outpost on Scottish soil: hence the building of the Elizabethan wall, with large projecting bastions on the landward side. Even after the union of the crowns in 1603, Berwick could still find itself on the front line. According to local tradition, the parish church owed its lack of bells to Cromwell, who stopped in the town on his way to fight the Scots. The church was just being built, and he is said to have forbidden the addition of a steeple. For a boy with an active imagination there were stories in the stones of Berwick, and the town's long turbulent history and exposed setting gave it a grandeur all its own: bleak, impressive, and a world away from the gentle Gloucestershire farmland of his early years.

Daily life was very different too. Unlike Thornbury, where the church and vicarage were separated only by the castle gate, in Berwick the parish church was at the north end of the town, under the wall. The vicarage was in the south, built directly on the wall itself. It would have been possible for the family to commute to the church by horse-drawn cab: for the most part, though, they seem to have walked. The most direct way to reach Spittal, across the river, was by ferry, a small rowing boat which stopped at points along the way like a bus. Exposed to wind and weather, it could be a hair-raising journey, particularly if a certain one-legged boatman was on duty. On one occasion, Stella described how her mother had used all her charm (and not a little native cunning) to persuade another passenger to help him with the rowing: *'"We waited for you, Mr Parkes, because we thought we should get back quicker with two to row"! So tho' I'm sure he had never intended to row'*, Stella wrote, *'he felt bound to, & nearly expired trying to make the boat move against the tide!'* [4]

The vicarage itself, 2 Wellington Terrace, was the centre of a block of three stone houses facing out across the Tweed, on a section of the ramparts that was extensively remodelled in the 1700s to protect the river estuary, with lookout towers and artillery batteries along its length. Smaller than Thornbury vicarage, it had a modest back garden (modest in comparison with what the family was used to) leading into the street behind. There was no front garden. A small flight of stone steps led down from the door to the walkway circling the top of the wall – all that separated the houses from a thirteen-gun saluting battery directly in front, pointing out across the river. Beyond the houses on the seaward side the wall turned a corner, marked with a lookout tower and a flagstaff; beyond that, nothing but the estuary and the open sea. When the east wind blew it was vicious and the wall was a forbidding place to be.

All the fortifications surrounding the vicarage were more than just reminders of a martial past. Berwick was still a garrison town. The eighteenth century barracks, depot and headquarters of the King's Own Scottish Borderers, stood hard by the church, and Henry's Sunday congregations were used to hearing the call of the sergeant from the parade ground, the marching feet, louder as they drew nearer, and the clatter of the officers' swords as they took their places in the pews. Members of the garrison joined in with church socials and charitable events, and in a town so closely associated with the military there were also several volunteer regiments. A few months after his induction, Henry became chaplain to the 1st Berwick-upon-Tweed Artillery.

The Hodgsons had been two years in Berwick when war broke out in South Africa. They had a personal interest: Henry's youngest brother, the Rev Joseph Lowther Hodgson, was headmaster of a school in Johannesburg. And remote though the conflict was from the Scottish borders, it also had a special resonance in Berwick. Week on week the local papers carried news of individual men leaving or returning from the town or the barracks, of lucky escapes and not-so-lucky casualties. Flags were flown in the streets to cheer the breaking of the agonisingly long sieges of Ladysmith and Mafeking. When it was known that a detachment of six men from the Berwick-upon-Tweed Volunteer Rifles would be coming home together in the spring of 1901, a huge party was planned, with a parade, a service, and a civic reception, at which the men would be given the freedom of the borough. The flags and bunting were brought out again as they had been for Ladysmith and Mafeking, and the shops closed. The Volunteers paraded and crowds built up in the streets. There was a slight hiccup when news reached the town that two of the men had been kept in hospital on arrival in England, and the remaining four had missed their train at Newcastle. The shopkeepers opened their doors and the crowds dispersed, but they gathered again a few hours later, '*pent up enthusiasm . . . only a little conserved*', to celebrate the homecoming.

A procession formed at the station led by the mayor's carriage, and more people joined at the Town Hall. The bands played, and the sun shone on cheering crowds – a cine film was taken, for the first time in Berwick. Henry and his curate Oswald Owen met the procession at the church and led them in for a service of thanksgiving – Henry gave a gentle reminder in his sermon that the war was not yet over. Then the procession reformed, complete with clergy, and made its way back to the Town Hall for the main ceremony of the day, followed by a civic dinner.

And somewhere in the crowds, in the church too most likely, taking it all in, there was surely an eight-year-old Noel Hodgson. His generation often recalled the flag waving and parades that marked the end of the Boer War as their first encounter with war in the real world. For him there was a deeper dimension to those memories, beyond the colour, the excitement, the popular songs and the carnival atmosphere. When his father spoke people listened, and his father described the war that day in terms which prefigured the war that was to come. Henry traced its history through initial enthusiasm, through military disasters into a struggle which seemed endless, in which the soldiers were still having to fight on, '*doing their steadfast, uttermost duty. . . . day in day out, to stand the strain of constant petty perils; the hourly call to some sordid service; the endless round of paltry skirmishes; foraging, sentry go; scouting; with the prospect of being knocked on the head some dark night, and bundled into a nameless grave as the end of all.*'[5] His approach helped give his son a clear view from the start of what the Great War might mean.

Henry Hodgson seemed to have an instinctive understanding of the ordinary soldier's lot as he did of the lives of his beloved working men – in Berwick too he ran his winter Bible classes for them. But Berwick also faced him with challenges he had not met before. A dedicated campaigner against the abuse of alcohol, Henry belonged to the Church of England Temperance Society, which emphasised moderation and education rather than total abstinence. His temperance work in Thornbury only involved speaking to the committed. But in a large urban parish with a garrison and a transient population from ships anchored in the harbour, alcohol abuse caused real social problems. Henry became part of a much larger campaign, shared with the civic authorities and the other churches in the town. He also campaigned with the town's doctors on the dangers of smoking for the young. His life was busier than ever, but the parish was large enough to support two curates to help him.

Penelope was able to be more involved too as the children grew older and she played an active part in several local organisations. The children helped as well. One Tuesday afternoon in April 1901, the local paper noticed Noel helping his sister to run the toy and sweet stall at a church mission sale.[6] For decades the parish church had provided a supper for the 'aged poor' on Old Year's Night (New Year's Eve), and the young Hodgsons were drawn in to that too. Each year 150 or more guests sat down to a feast of roast beef and rabbit pies, plum pudding, coffee and cake, with an amateur concert to follow; this was Edwardian charity at its most open-hearted. Henry, his curates, and prominent men from the congregation, carved the roasts, and were said on one occasion to have been kept hard at work for an hour. Penelope and the other ladies hosted the tables, and a team of soldiers from the garrison and older boys did the serving. Arthur was among the helpers in 1901 and sang a solo in the concert. For the next few years Hal joined him (in the serving but not the song); later it would be Noel's turn.

This was his family's life: gas-lit, homespun, played out in a close-knit community where the same families shared church, good works and recreation, in events they organised for themselves. Their world could be narrow and insular and it was very sharply divided. Clergy families counted as minor gentry, ranking alongside other professionals and the better-off and better-connected people in the area. There were parishioners with whom Penelope and the children would not have mixed socially. But Henry belonged to everyone. A lovely instance of their dynamic as a couple emerges from accounts of a meeting held in the autumn of 1904 to celebrate Henry's appointment as Archdeacon of Lindisfarne. The parish had decided to present him with a gift and nearly 350 people subscribed, raising almost £60 – an enormous sum in those days. It paid for an engraved gold watch for Henry, with so much left over that the organisers decided to buy a gift for Penelope; a silver rose bowl was duly bought and engraved.

When the gifts were presented, Henry turned to Penelope to speak first. She rarely did this, she said, *'having lived all, or rather nearly all, her life, with a man who had been able and willing and ready to do the talking for her. . . . Of course, she knew that on this occasion she shone with a reflected light. . . . but still, she did think that it was so kind of them to have made her a separate person. (Laughter.) Husband and wife were one, but she was certainly of the opinion that in the matter of presents they should be counted as two'*. Henry followed, joking that he had clearly been keeping her from her proper place for years. He then launched into a serious talk on the role of the archdeacon which ended with a touching snippet of personal history. He told his audience he had never owned a gold watch before and *'would treasure it as a token of their love and kindness'*. But the silver watch he must now lay aside *'would still have a place in his heart, as he bought it in the year he had made the acquaintance of Mrs Hodgson.'*[7]

In a world in which the father's word ruled, Henry's rule in the vicarage at Berwick was tempered by his kindness and by a subversive undertow from his compliant but slightly mischievous family: *'Dad is interviewing a female in the hall. To judge from his voice she is deaf & if she isn't she soon will be!'* They played their part in public, but it was not in their nature to take things too seriously, unless they were so serious there was no other way to take them. *'Be sure & look at the Spittal news in the P*[arish] *M*[agazine]. *There is a large heading: <u>Notable Event</u> – Miss Pringle has gone home at the age of 92! We laughed over that at breakfast this morning till we nearly cried. Poor old lady, she had a long night 'out' didn't she?'*[8]

The Hodgsons were not particularly well off. In comparison to the large vicarage staff in Thornbury, in Berwick they employed a maid and a cook. At home their amusements were simple. They did jigsaws, played patience, draughts, chess, and bridge. All were keen readers and, given the importance that recitation and acting had within their social circle, and the fact that three of the four children went on to become published writers, it seems likely that they wrote their own poems and stories and performed plays at home. Henry and Penelope were patrons of the Border Children's Club, which was associated with one of the local papers, the *Berwickshire News*. The club ran essay and letter-writing competitions for its young members, published short stories, and encouraged them to collect pennies for charity. Its section of the paper always included a quotation from Dean Farrar: *'The Children of a Nation are its dearest, its best, its most inestimable treasure. . . . Its Children will be Men of England in those Dark and Perplexing Days which seem to lie before another generation'*. This has a grimly prophetic ring, but the club armed its children for the darkness to come in the gentlest of ways. Four of its five rules were about treating pets and wildlife properly; the fifth, *'to be helpful, loving and kind to everything and everyone'*.

Beyond the home there were various 'suitable' entertainments not connected with the church. Henry was a keen golfer. Arthur played for the town cricket team. Both he and Hal were part of a mixed hockey team captained by the junior curate, while the younger ones would have watched their matches. Noel and Stella were close friends of Mary and Francis Cowen, the children of a local businessman who lived not far from the vicarage, and Noel was also friendly with Henry, Frank and Ingram Smail, whose father owned the other local paper, the *Berwick Advertiser*. And occasionally there were real treats from outside. In July 1904 Buffalo Bill's Wild West Show came to Berwick, and December that year saw the arrival of the 'Mafeking ape'. Trained by an officer during the siege to ring an alarm when the Boers started firing and then run for cover, the ape had never failed in his duty. Now he was a crowd-puller for Bostock and Wombwell's Menagerie. But events like these were all the more special because they were rare.

Family holidays were often spent in Scotland. Once, the Hodgsons stayed a month in 'Milsey Bank', a hillside cottage overlooking the Bridge of Allan. They visited Callander, the Bracklinn Falls and the Wallace Monument, climbed in the hills and, as Stella remembered, *'we caught the fishing craze but no fish. Though we used to sally forth, Father, Arthur, Noel & I, all armed with rods etc & stand patiently waiting for bites, but the only bites I ever got were midges!'*[9] In other years they went to Crieff and Castle Douglas in western Scotland. But the move to Berwick had also brought them 200 miles closer to Henry's old home in Cumberland, and it was surely in the years following the move that Noel learned to love the fells and to identify them as his place, though he would never live there.

Until her death in 1902, his grandmother Elizabeth Hodgson lived in Keswick. His uncle Charlie worked with his great-uncle Charles Bernard Hodgson as a solicitor in Carlisle; another uncle, Henry's elder brother William, was Rector of Distington, not far from the Cumbrian coast. William married in 1886 – with Henry taking the service – and their children were close in age. Mary, eldest of the Distington cousins, was Hal's age, then came George; Florence, who was Stella's age; Charles, a week younger than Noel; and the youngest, Eldred, born in 1896. Their home was a gateway to the fells: one of Stella's letters captures a soggy outing to an agricultural show at Threlkeld in the autumn of 1908:

> *'Yesterday it was a glorious morning & we started off to the show. Seven of us – very gaily. However our joy was soon turned to sadness & we arrived at Threlkeld in pouring rain. . . . We had to go into a minute tent & sit amongst the burly farmers & shepherds and whenever it cleared for a moment we made hasty dashes for the field where the sheep-dog trials were going on. We had to give it up in the end & return by an earlier train. You would have laughed if you'd seen us returning through the mud. We must have looked very comical. Tonight the curate is going to bring his gramaphone up and we are going to dance to it!'*[10]

The Distington Hodgsons were much better off than Henry's family. This was thanks in part to William's inheritance of Houghton House, which he rented out. It was also thanks to his marriage, which linked the family to a colourful character who is still remembered in Cumbria, and to a story which had a permanent effect on the landscape. William's wife Catherine Mary Harrison was a barrister's daughter from Penrith; the story and the wealth came from her maternal grandmother Mary Jackson, a young heiress who inherited a substantial estate in the Thirlmere valley. Mary married Count Boris Ossalinsky, a Polish nobleman. She had been widowed for some years when the Manchester Corporation, seeking water supplies for the city's rising population, chose Thirlmere as the site for a new reservoir. This meant flooding the valley; Parliament approved and the corporation began buying the land. But there was understandable resistance locally and Mary was one of the last landowners to give way. Her case had to be taken to arbitration where, to the horror of the corporation, she was awarded £70,000, almost three times their offer. A very wealthy woman, Mary moved to Kensington. Her Hodgson great-grandchildren were regular visitors, and it seems likely that Mary's fortune helped to pay for George, Charles and Eldred to be educated at Westminster School, paying full fees.

But if Henry's children were to have the education he wanted for them, they needed scholarships. Arthur started as a scholar at the Rossall School a week or so after the family moved to Berwick. In the autumn of 1899, Hal went to his uncle Charlie's old school, Pocklington in Yorkshire. That left Stella and Noel. Their earliest lessons probably came from their parents. Henry was a gifted teacher and took special interest in local schools, visiting the Church School in Berwick every day. His curates may have helped teach the children too, and Stella learned to play the piano from the church organist. In 1901 there was a governess, Jessie Pears, living in the vicarage, but the census identifies her as 'governess (school)' – a schoolteacher – and as a boarder, so she is more likely to have been a paying guest than an employee. And by the school year of 1902/3, both children were attending a local school.

The Avenue School in Berwick was one of a small cluster of private schools in the streets below the vicarage. It occupied two adjoining houses, numbers 6 and 8, Palace Street East, at the end of the Avenue, which gave the school its name. Locally it was also known as St Duthus, the name of one of the houses. At most it could have taken about twenty pupils, and the Hodgson children joined just as it came under new ownership. This was probably no coincidence. Henry had a good working relationship with the school's new owners, the Misses Macdonald, who took over from Miss Margaret and Miss Augusta Batters in the summer of 1902. He acted as an external examiner for them and regularly spoke and officiated at prize givings. With his interest in education and strongly held views, it seems likely that Henry approved of the Macdonalds' plans for the school and wanted to support them. Their advertising laid stress on the qualifications of their teaching staff; within eighteen months of taking over they had a mathematics department, run by a university graduate who was also trained in foreign languages, and a music department. It sounds extremely ambitious for so small a school. A sergeant from the Royal Garrison Artillery was employed to organise physical drill until a teacher could be found: Henry spoke with particular enthusiasm at the first school concert about *'this new element of education'*: exercise, he said, was good for mental as well as physical development.[11]

Henry liked the school and entrusted his children to it, but for his son there was a catch. The Avenue was a school for 'young ladies'; Noel was the only boy until his second year, when a kindergarten was added. This was rather progressive of Henry. There were boys' schools close by that he could have chosen: Noel's friend Frank Smail went to the Grammar School, just a few doors down, but Noel began his school life among the girls. At the end of his first year one pupil from the Avenue School passed the Oxford Local Preliminary Examination in the First Division: W.N. Hodgson. He was ten years old.[12]

In those days the idea of a State-regulated education system for every child was in its infancy. Schools had always been run privately by individuals, institutions or charities, along whatever lines the owners chose. Most were small – the Grammar School had forty-seven pupils in 1902 and that was said to be doing well. And if the Hodgsons were content to choose a girls' school for their son and the school was willing to take him, there was nothing to stand in their way.

Noel seems to have flourished. At the school concert in November 1903 the local paper was impressed with the whole school's achievements:

> *'Judging by the excellence of the concert given in the Queen's Rooms on Thursday afternoon, the Avenue School, Berwick, must be in a prosperous condition. The very high standard of the programme, in elocution even more than in music, speaks volumes for the Misses Macdonald and their assistants.'*

Henry presented certificates to Noel and an older girl for success in the Oxford Locals; then to Stella and seven other girls for passing Royal Academy of Music exams. There were displays of ribbon drills, singing and recitation, but one performance stole the show. It was a scene from *Julius Caesar. 'The two characters, the passionate Cassius and the stoical, honour-loving Brutus, were well taken by Miss Hodgson and Master N. Hodgson respectively,'* the *Berwickshire News* reported, adding that their acting *'was really splendid'.*[13]
The quarrel between Brutus and Cassius is a substantial piece of Shakespeare for a ten-year-old and a twelve-year-old to have learned by heart, but Noel and Stella must have relished the tit-for-tat dialogue, *'I am – "I say that you are not" –You did – "I did not"'*; for a small brother and sister that would have been very familiar ground.

So far they had done almost everything together, but the time was coming when each would embark on a separate course. Stella remembered setting out for the first time to St Mary's School in Scarborough: *'Dad said when I was going in for my scholarship, "If God means you to get it you will, & all you have to do is trust & do your best.'*[14] This would have been in 1904. A year later it was Noel's turn.

Chapter 3

Durham

At twelve years old Noel Hodgson was his father in miniature, slight in build and brown-eyed, his most noticeable feature a pair of very prominent ears. In the rough-and-tumble of the boys' boarding school he was about to inhabit these quickly earned him the nickname 'Lugs', but he seems not to have minded. He was quiet but not shy, preferring to assess people and situations in his own time before letting himself be known. This was a Hodgson trait which always amused his sister. *'I have developed into a true Hodgson & hardly ever speak now,'* she wrote, years later, *'merely smile when the occasion demands.'*[1] The smile too was characteristic.

Noel was very close to his father. Friends remembered them holding long conversations in Latin – conversations rich in the word play and teasing that was part of the family's shared existence. Watching his youngest son grow, Henry cherished the hope of seeing Noel follow him into the church, as he had followed his own father. The elder boys would not. Arthur had left school in 1902. He returned to Berwick at first, but did not settle there. In the early 1900s emigration to Canada was promoted heavily through public lectures and newspaper advertisements, and some time between 1905 and 1908, Arthur was lured away. He tried his hand at several jobs: the Canadian Census of 1911 found him in Dauphin, Manitoba, keeping the accounts in a store. Later he worked for the Hudson's Bay Company. Hal was about to enter his final year at Pocklington. A talented painter, Hal played football and cricket for his school and had an outstanding academic record. He was a prefect and a librarian, edited the school magazine, and dominated the debating society, where the side he supported always seemed to win. One report gives a glimpse of his technique: the proposition was that educating the lower classes would be bad for the country. Hal destroyed it with his *'usual talent for hidden sarcasm'.*[2]

So on the subject of education, Hal was his father's son. But he showed no sign of wanting to be a clergyman, and that left only Noel. It is hard not to see Henry's ambitions for his youngest son in his choice of school. Durham School had close links with Durham Cathedral, one of the most beautiful places of worship in the country. The school, founded in 1414 by Thomas Langley, Bishop of Durham, had occupied a site close to the Cathedral until the mid-nineteenth century, and it was still governed by the Dean and Chapter. Unusually for a boarding school there was no chapel; the school attended Cathedral services, and if ever a setting could fire a love for the aesthetics of the church, then surely it was Durham. A more cynical mind might have wondered if compulsory church attendance among a pack of schoolboys would be more off-putting than inspiring, but Henry Hodgson was no cynic. His brother Joseph had attended Durham School for two years in the 1880s before winning a scholarship to study theology, so the portents were good.

There was also a practical advantage. The school offered generous financial help to clever boys whose parents could not afford the fees. About five of the eighteen King's Scholarships (the king in question being Henry VIII) fell vacant each year, with awards varying from 16 guineas to £50. These scholarships lasted four years, but boys who held them were free to compete afresh each year until they were about to turn fifteen, to improve their award and win extra years of funding. If they failed, their existing scholarship was unaffected. The examinations were held each spring and would-be new boys sat them alongside existing scholars, staying overnight in the school. Candidates had to show ability in the Classics, translating from Greek and Latin without a dictionary and composing Latin prose and verse, and in mathematics, answering questions on arithmetic, algebra and geometry. There were also papers in French and English. These last were less important, though a boy who was unable to offer Latin verse could make up for it with excellent French. It says a lot for the Misses Macdonald and for Henry that Noel was able to hold his own against older boys and win a £20 scholarship on his first attempt. In subsequent years he managed to raise it to the full £50, lasting until he left school.

Scholarships were awarded in June. In September 1905 Noel left home on the journey that would become familiar, watching the vicarage recede into the distance before the train headed south, down the coast past Holy Island and on through Newcastle and Chester-le-Street to Durham; these days it takes about an hour and a half. The last leg was horse-drawn, with boys and luggage ferried from the station to the school buildings, facing Durham Cathedral across the deep gorge of the River Wear. Noel was one of an intake of sixteen boys that September and among the youngest of them; there were two other twelve-year-olds and one aged eleven but, unlike Noel, all three were day boys. He would not see home again until Christmas.

The school rapidly became his world; an enclosed world with its own quirks of language and its own customs. In the autumn of 1905 there were ninety-one pupils in all: no great size, though it would have seemed large to him, and very far removed from the ladylike classrooms of the Avenue. Most of the boys boarded and they were split between two houses: the Headmaster's, 'School House', and the Second Master's House. Decades earlier, School House boys had christened their rivals 'Caffinites' after the then Second Master, the Rev Caffin. Second Master's House retaliated with 'Bungites', from the nickname of the Headmaster, the Rev Holden. By 1905 the masters and boys concerned were long gone, but the names lived on; Noel Hodgson was a Bungite and proud of it.[3]

There were initiation rites. Other boys who joined the school in the early 1900s recalled being made to sing or to box; at first an older boy would have been assigned to introduce him to the school and its ways. The accommodation was spartan and privacy unknown. He would have shared one of four dormitories with up to a dozen other boys. They slept on plain iron bedsteads and the rooms were lit by gas jet burners, each with an iron pipe coming down from the ceiling and branching into two arms, a shaded flame at either end. With a good leap from a bed it was possible to swing the whole contraption; this was strictly forbidden but a constant temptation to the adventurous spirit. The studies – four in School House for the monitors (Durham School's prefects), one more for all the rest – had gas brackets which posed their own temptations and dangers. A small saucepan balanced on a bracket would certainly heat, offering the promise of hot milk and cocoa, but the balance was precarious and scalding accidents not unknown. Not surprisingly, perhaps, the school had its own volunteer fire brigade.

Snacks in the study supplemented a diet that was adequate but unexciting. All the boys had tuck boxes and a tuck shop operated from the front room of a house in a nearby street. The housemaster gave out weekly pocket money: 1/- [5p] for senior boys, 6d [2½p] for juniors. For his first two years at least, Noel would have been expected to perform simple duties for one or more of the monitors: lighting fires, making tea and toast, cleaning shoes, tidying rooms. He would also have had general duties around the school and on the games field. In a system designed to train the country's future leaders, 'fagging' – serving older boys and taking orders – was seen as an essential part of the process, allowing those who would one day give the orders a taste of life on the receiving end. The brighter a boy was, the sooner he escaped the obligation.

Academically the school divided into two groups. The 'Classical Side' studied a traditional curriculum based on Latin, Greek and ancient history. The 'Modern Side' substituted German for Greek and placed more emphasis on mathematics and science. Noel was a classicist and began his school career in the Classical Remove. In schools that took boys from the age of nine, the Remove was an intermediate stage between the junior and senior forms. Until 1910, when Durham School admitted younger boys, it was often the entry class, with progress to the upper forms dependent on results rather than age.

Daily life for the boys was strictly organised with little free time. Early morning service in the Cathedral was optional; the day began with prayers and a roll call, breakfast and classes. After morning school, boys were allowed into Durham for an hour from noon. Those who went had to wear their house caps or straw boaters and to follow one prescribed route, crossing the river gorge by Prebends Bridge, a superb viewpoint which most probably took for granted.

Lunch followed, then compulsory games, with half an hour afterwards to wash and change for afternoon school, forty boys managing as best they could with one full-sized bath and two hip baths between them. But games were something most enjoyed; Sunday, by contrast, was a day of gloom. All games and sports were banned. In the morning the whole school walked to the Cathedral – always referred to by the boys as 'Abbey'. Once there the King's Scholars, Noel included, went to the Chapter House and donned white surplices, to process behind the clergy and choir and take their allotted places in the choir stalls. The rest of the school sat out of sight in one of the transepts, making their presence felt through the service by stubbornly failing to keep pace with the organ and choir.

If the sermon was short, boys would be back at school in time to change for dinner into best black suits with striped trousers. A long sermon obliged them to go straight into lunch and change later, ready to walk back to Abbey for Evensong. Meantime letters home were written in the afternoon, and the day was rounded off with half an hour's preparation for Divinity classes. This was the routine, and it hardly varied from week to week, year to year. Sunday apart, added interest came in the form of clubs and societies, and sometimes there would be lectures, illustrated with lantern slides, readings and recitations. The school had a drawing master, a music master and a choir, so culture was not overlooked, but it did not rate very highly in the scheme of things. A Christmas concert at the end of Noel's first term earned only a terse comment in the school magazine; *'the concert also began and finished punctually and was not long enough to be tedious'.*[4]

For the first few years Noel blends into the crowd, just another boy, stiff white collar, hair slicked down, jostling, laughing, fitting in with the rest. His results at the end of his first term were middling, neither good enough nor bad enough to mark him out. But by the end of the first year he had climbed to the top in most subjects and had won his first school prize – the first of many – *The Complete Works of Shakespeare*, presented for Grammar by the Dean and Chapter of the Cathedral.

By chance, the headmaster who presided over Noel's first two years at Durham occupies a unique place in the literature of the Great War. The Uppingham School Speech Day of 1914, described by Vera Brittain in her classic memoir *Testament of Youth*, has become a defining image of the public school culture on the brink of war. In his address to the assembled ranks of boys and parents the headmaster – Uppingham boys called him 'The Man' – quoted the precepts for boys laid down by the Japanese general Count Nogi, whose name had become familiar after Japan's surprise defeat of Russia in their war of 1905. Most memorable was the climax, *'If a man cannot be useful to his country he is better dead.'*[5]

The date was 11 July. Two weeks earlier, the heir to the throne of Austria-

Hungary and his wife had been assassinated in the streets of Sarajevo by a Bosnian Serb. Little more than three weeks later, Britain and Germany would be at war. If a man cannot be useful to his country he is better dead. The searing irony of those words, spoken by a schoolmaster to boys whose usefulness to their country was about to lead them to death, has engraved the scene on the collective memory of generations. And the man, 'The Man', who uttered them, the Rev Harry Ward McKenzie, was Noel Hodgson's first headmaster at Durham.

We might fear for Noel, enclosed from the age of twelve in the house of a man who made such uncompromising demands on his boys. Vera Brittain remembered McKenzie as an intimidating figure, so it is something of a relief to learn that the quality most noted by his contemporaries was his humour. Appointed Head of Durham in 1905 after ten years as Second Master, McKenzie was a solid business manager, stern and formal in manner and in many ways rather dull. His saving grace was humour, and it was said to be genial and warm, untouched by sarcasm. There were no personality clashes under McKenzie's rule. He got on well with his staff and he read boys with ease. They liked him too. His signature humour was present even in the famous Uppingham address, though Vera never noticed: a detailed account in the school magazine shows McKenzie playing his audience skilfully by making them laugh. He even used Count Nogi's precepts for comic effect, save the last, which was not quite as she remembered. The exact quotation is, *'Be a man – useful to your country; whoever cannot be that is better dead.'*[6]

A subtle difference, but the emphasis here is on living, not dying, and usefulness defines what it means to be a man. McKenzie was indeed echoing the prevailing culture of the public schools, but there is no sense that he or anyone present suspected that the shadow of imminent death hung over the boys. Three weeks before Armageddon the sun was shining and the diplomatic standoff in the Balkans merited only a few brief sentences in *The Times*.

When parents chose to send a boy to public school they were looking for two things: a sound education that would open doors to university or the professions, and a training in character. That was the word. Character. Most valued it above academic success. Public schools were supposed to produce gentlemen, whose status was not defined in the eighteenth century way, by property, but by a shared moral code. The new gentleman understood the importance of duty and service: he wanted to be useful. He was honourable, brave and loyal. He told the truth. He was stoical, bearing pain without complaint. He kept his emotions rigidly in check and was self-effacing, placing the needs of others before his own. He protected the weak, and kindness was an essential part of his make-up. He made a natural leader simply because he was worth following, and he cared for those he led.

> *'Free in service, wise in justice*
> *Fearing but dishonour's breath;*
> *Steeled to suffer uncomplaining. . . .'*[7]

That was Noel Hodgson's definition of the type, from one of his early war poems. Kipling's famous poem 'If', first published in 1910 and still regularly voted the nation's favourite poem, was another. The ideal had grown through the nineteenth century, fed by Christianity, by the reforming work of Dr Arnold at Rugby School, by the Victorian cult of chivalry (which Arnold detested), and by the philosophies of Greece and Rome, familiar to all educated men. It was popular, not least because it did not depend on birth. With the right education, anyone's son could become a gentleman. The boys who shared Noel Hodgson's schooldays were not the sons of the aristocracy. They came from homes much like his own. Of the fifteen boys who started at Durham with him, four were the sons of clergymen, two of architects and two of men with medical qualifications; it was a typical mix. Except at the leading schools – Eton, Harrow, Charterhouse, Winchester, Westminster, and Rugby – the overwhelming majority of public schoolboys had fathers who were either professional men like Henry, who valued education, or they were self-made men who had built fortunes in commerce or industry and could afford to make gentlemen of their sons.

The public school education relied on the Classics with 'modern' options added, as at Durham, and on sport. When it came to building character there was nothing like sport, and many rated it above academic work. Competitive sport was valued not only for creating physical fitness, desirable as that was, but for developing a whole list of less tangible attributes. The ability to think quickly, plan strategically, react to the unexpected, gained on the sports field would be useful skills for the country's future leaders in whatever work they chose, either at home or as administrators in far-flung corners of the Empire. Courage and endurance could be learnt through sport, while team games were seen as training grounds for loyalty and unselfishness.

Coming from a girls' school, Noel's earlier sporting opportunities must have been limited, and in his first year at Durham he tried swimming and sculling. Durham had an outdoor swimming pool and, being so close to the river, its own boathouse. From the mid-nineteenth century its crews were a strong presence in the Durham Regatta. In his first summer Noel was cox to the School House team, then to the school's second crew, though this may not have been his choice. A few years later an anonymous letter to the school magazine complained of the way small boys were picked to cox the school crews simply because they were small, and they were then blamed for any failure: *'three people are chosen and hammered into something like shape, whether they show promise or not. If more people were tried, no doubt better people would be found, in accordance with what the Senior Maths Master calls the "Law of Averages".* [8] Noel may have been among the 'chosen and hammered', but as an active boy who liked to succeed he did do rather well as a cox (unlike his cousin George, who built a reputation for running boats into river banks). After the first two years, though, Noel abandoned the river altogether.

But he did write a rowing song for the school. It was one of a suite of three songs, rowing, cricket and (rugby) football, published as sheet music by Novello & Co in London, with settings by the music master. The imagery, particularly in the rowing song, is striking:

> *'Though breath come scant and thin,*
> *And hearts beat loud and fast,*
> *Though seems no chance to win,*
> *Have courage to the last.*
> *Until the race is ended*
> *The victory is not won,*
> *There's nought that can't be mended*
> *Until the fight is done.'*

He could be writing about a battle, and in a sense, he was. Sport is a kind of sanitised warfare without the killing, and the physical and mental skills it developed were equally useful on a battlefield. This was an undeniable part of the public school education. The ideal gentleman knew how to fight. In everyday life he fought his own demons: the destructive power of emotion, and the temptation to luxury, idleness, or anything else that might prevent him from being the man he was meant to be. In the outside world he was supposed to fight injustice when he found it. If war did come, he would play his part in that too.

Public school was a very male environment. With only the occasional master's wife and the matron on hand to provide any female influence, and that only in domestic matters, life could be harsh. Discipline was strict and corporal punishment an accepted part of the system; even the monitors were allowed to use the cane on other boys. 'Lamming', they called it, and though each instance had to be recorded in a book for the housemaster's inspection, it still gave selected older boys a degree of power which could easily be abused. Those who knew Durham School in Noel's time or soon after remembered a lot of rough horseplay, though no actual bullying. But whatever abuses a modern reader might anticipate in such a system, when Noel Hodgson wrote about the school, these things seem not to have touched him at all. The language he used of the school's influence was gentle, loving even. For him the school itself became the female influence which on the surface appears so lacking. The school was a mother – foster mother, at least – offering nurturing and care. *'From her full*

breast we drank of joy and mirth/ And gave to her a boy's unreasoned heart'.
So sheltered, he and his friends could grow and learn in safety, *'In the infinite compassion of thy fashioning enfolded.'*[9] He addressed these words to Durham School, not the Almighty.

By contrast, as a true son of the North-East, when he wrote about his schoolmasters he drew imagery straight from the Newcastle shipyards:

The Master-Smiths

See the silent smithy where,
On the noiseless anvil laid,
Day by day and year by year
Souls of men are forged and made.

Ceaslessly the hammers fall,
Making ties and rivets fast,
Till the perfect ship is found
Ready for the seas at last.

Trial and temptation strong
Beat upon the hardening steel,
Love and trust and self-control
Rivet it from truck to keel.

Loud though wind and waters roar
In the caverns of the sea,
Unafraid we launch our ships
Builded for eternity.

Hammered into shape, and loved; that was the school experience as he saw it.

The autumn term of 1907 brought a new wielder of the hammer into his life, and one who would have immense influence on him and on the school. Harry Ward McKenzie had left for Uppingham that summer and Durham gained a new Headmaster, the Rev Richard Dutton Budworth. Seventeen years younger than McKenzie, Budworth was a former England rugby international. A tall, powerfully built man with fair hair and distinctive, heavy-lidded eyes, his coming intensified the bluff masculinity of the school and its spartan atmosphere. As a proven sportsman, Budworth raised the profile of competitive sport even further. He took exercise himself most days, playing Fives (a sort of hand tennis), coaching in the nets, playing rugby with the boys, or even sawing logs. Later it would be digging, extending the playing field in person, spade in hand. One of the countless stories the boys told of him – he was the sort of man around whom legends gather – described a boy asking, 'Sir, do you think we could have tennis-courts sometime?' to which his reply was, 'You can't get killed playing tennis.' This was probably apocryphal, but it gives the flavour of the man.

Famously taciturn, Budworth's remarks were brief and blunt and he did not make conversation. He was shy with women, mothers most of all, though on paper he could be charming. A copy of the school register for 1912, inscribed in his hand to a Mrs King, reads, *'from R.D.B. as a small pledge of a friendship not all, he hopes, on one side.'* But with a book in his hand he was transformed. His reading would hold an audience spellbound, and there were times, particularly at the end of term, when he liked to read to his School House boys, or perhaps to the whole school. Kipling was a favourite on these occasions.

Younger boys were in awe of Budworth while their elders held him in great respect. McKenzie had been a married man with a son, but Budworth never married. The school was his life and his commitment absolute. He worked long hours and had no secretary, writing his own letters in longhand while standing at a reading desk surrounded by piles of books; he rarely sat down during the day. His influence on his boys lasted for life. In the 1980s, men who attended the school during Budworth's time still enjoyed talking about him and retelling the old stories; *'he was a great Headmaster and a real influence for good on the boys who passed through his hands. A sixth former, asked why his Headmaster was so popular, replied, "Because he never thinks of himself".'*[10] All shared the same respect, tinged with affection. All agreed that Noel Hodgson was a particular favourite with their headmaster, almost the son Budworth never had.

Asked after the war for a memoir of Hodgson's time at school, Budworth wrote:

> *'From the first it was evident that he possessed ability, but its extent was, I fancy, not suspected until near the end of his time at school. The impression one now has, looking back, is that he very seldom gave his powers full play. He kept them in reserve until the real occasion presented itself.'*[11]

This is striking because the written record shows that after the first term, Noel's academic results took him consistently to, or close to, the top of his form. In his second year he was moved up to the Vth form and at the start of his third to the Classical VIth, the top form in the school, placing him at fourteen alongside boys four and five years his senior. Even in their company he was able to do well. But Budworth may have been thinking of abilities other than academic success, which was never his first priority. The records also show a steady rise in Noel's confidence and in the range of his activities and interests as he moved up the school.

The acting talent young Hodgson had shown at the Avenue found an outlet on Speech Day in 1907, when he took part in an extract from Aristophanes' comedy *The Acharnians*. He played one of a pair of sisters disguised as pigs, traded by their father for garlic and salt. This was a part rich with comic possibilities and he must have made a success of it. For the rest of his school career he was invariably in the handful of boys who acted a comic scene on Speech Day, save only in 1910, when the King's death led to a postponement of the event and a shortened programme. There was no acting that year. But Greek and Latin plays and Shakespeare were always on the curriculum, so there was ample opportunity for a boy who enjoyed performing to test his skills. In 1909, 1910, and 1911, Noel won prizes for recitation.

He had to work harder sometimes to succeed at sport, the ability closest to the headmaster's heart. But he was a hard worker, and by his third year he was beginning to do very well in athletics, Fives and gymnastics; the summer of 1908 found him in the School House cricket team. The school magazine praised *'good and plucky innings by Ward, Brown and Hodgson, the three youngest and smallest members of the team,'*[12] and a photograph was taken of the boys in cricket whites with their house tutor, Mr Wilkinson. It has the inescapable poignancy that shadows team and school photographs taken in the years leading up to 1914: of the boys shown at least four, Hodgson himself, Alan Brown, Francis Adamson and Hugh Dingle, would be dead before the war ended.

In the autumn and winter months the school had a debating society, and the brief – all too brief – mentions of its activities provide the first hints of what was to become the most important friendship in Noel Hodgson's life, with another future war poet. Nowell Oxland was two years older than he was and had been at Durham since 1903. He came from a Devonshire family, with long connections in and around Dartmoor, and, like Noel, he was a clergyman's son. Despite the age gap, the two boys had a great deal in common.

Nowell Oxland was born in December 1890 at Compton Gifford, near Plymouth, and he also had three older siblings, though in his case they were so much older that he might as well have been an only child. His parents were in their forties when he was born; he was four when his only brother and closest sibling left home for university, nine when the younger of his two sisters died. The elder sister, Colette, was more than eighteen years his senior. Their father, the Rev William Oxland, was a naval chaplain; after a lifetime of service on board various ships, in 1897 he became chaplain to the Royal Dockyard and the Naval Hospital in Chatham and moved the family to Kent. In 1901 he left the navy behind him, accepting the living of St Augustine's Church at Alston in Cumbria, high in the North Pennines.

For Nowell, then ten years old, the remoteness of this new home excited his imagination. A solitary boy and very independent, young Oxland explored the moorland landscapes, drank in their history and legends, and became a keen climber and bird-watcher. The Cumbrian fells quickly became his own place, an identification he felt so deeply that his southern roots were forgotten – and it was this love of Cumbria more than anything else that bound him and Noel Hodgson together.

Of Nowell Oxland's early education there seems to be no surviving record. At twelve years old he sat the King's Scholarship examinations at Durham and was successful, and his school career began the following autumn in Form IV Modern. He too was in School House. By the spring of 1905 when Noel Hodgson arrived in Durham to try for the scholarship, Nowell Oxland was fourteen years old and well-established at the school, as good at sport as he was in class. He too sat the exam that spring. This was the first time their paths would have crossed, but the gulf between a self-assured fourteen-year-old who knew his way around and a twelve-year-old outsider was probably too wide to bridge. September brought them together again, living under the same roof and, more significantly perhaps, both King's Scholars. That bond was forged afresh every Sunday, setting the eighteen boys who wore the surplice just a little apart from the rest. But it is not until 1907, and the debating season of Noel Hodgson's third year, that there is clear evidence of the two enjoying a shared interest.

In the first debate of the season Nowell Oxland opposed the formation of a cadet corps in the school. Later that season Noel Hodgson spoke against House of Lords reform. Sometimes the two took opposing sides. In the autumn of 1909 Hodgson proposed a motion calling for the abolition of censorship in the theatre. Oxland led the opposition and scored a resounding victory, forty-two votes to three. He was a force to be reckoned with in the school by this time, a monitor and, from 1908, Head of School, the highest position of trust a boy could reach. Unusually, he was to hold it for two school years. And in the autumn of 1908, having risen though the school on the Modern side, he changed to the Classical VI – the same form as Noel Hodgson; until he left school the two were consistently well placed in the form order, their results running neck and neck except in Greek, which Oxland being a 'Modern' had not studied. No reason is given for his move to the Classics; most likely it was related to university entrance, perhaps also to some changed plan for his future.

So little evidence survives of Nowell Oxland that his character is something of an enigma. Slightly shorter than Hodgson when both were full-grown, and stockier in build, he was a talented rugby player who went on to play for the Rosslyn Park Club. His skills on the rugby field are analysed frequently and in detail; his character has to be pieced together from the shadows and hints in the factual record. Photographs show him to have been attractive, with a confident air. He must have stood out as a natural leader, and have been considered a good influence on other boys, to be made Head of School. But his views are hard to pin down and he appears at times to have delighted in taking a provocative stance in argument, as teenage boys will. He was certainly another aspiring writer, though when the ambition came to him is impossible to say. And of his side of the friendship with Noel Hodgson almost nothing remains.

Boys with literary leanings were often outsiders at school, but there is no hint of this about Oxland and Hodgson. Both fitted in, both were popular. Among Noel Hodgson's other friends was Robert Parr, who was also a vicar's son, in School House and a King's Scholar. He was a year younger and entered the school in September 1907. Less athletic – his eyesight was poor and at school he concentrated on rowing – Robert Parr was another keen actor who became a regular performer on Speech Day. Ingram Smail, the youngest of Noel's three Berwick friends, entered School House at the same time as Robert Parr. And yet another School House boy, Francis Fisher, would later describe Noel Hodgson as, *'one of the truest and most loveable of those who will always live in our schoolday recollections'*.

Fisher sent one of Noel's poems, 'Dunelmia Mater Nostra' [Durham, our mother] to the school magazine in 1916. It was written in 1913, he said, and had never been published. In fact, Noel had submitted a revised version of it to the *New Witness*, and it appeared in 1915 under a different title. It paid tribute to their school years and celebrated their friendships:

> *Oh Durham's three tall towers,*
> *Behold the tides of men*
> *Flow from their silent waters*
> *To seas beyond our ken;*
> *They gazed on us, my brothers,*
> *And we were happy then.*
>
> *Our footsteps, oh my brothers,*
> *In pleasant paths were set,*
> *With pleasures to remember,*
> *And sorrows to forget;*
> *Deep draught of love and laughter*
> *A cup without regret. . . .*
>
> *Time is the strong destroyer*
> *Of much that heaven sends,*
> *And cherished treasures daily*
> *Draw to their destined ends;*
> *But youth shall live for ever*
> *In the trusty grip of friends.*

Fisher remarked, *'They are just such lines as all of us would wish to have been able to write.'*[13]

Chapter 4

'We Learned and Grew'

In his mid-teens Noel Hodgson begins to emerge from the sheltering presence of family and school as a person in his own right. One early sign of independence was a change of name; around the age of sixteen he started to call himself Bill. His sister adapted quickly. Their mother took longer, and would revert occasionally to his childhood name. On formal occasions he still used it too, signing himself 'Wm Noel Hodgson'.

He also started to take his writing seriously. The earliest surviving manuscripts date from 1909 when he was sixteen. They were carefully copied by him into a black notebook with the title 'Prose and Poetry and all Fiction', beginning with a list of contents on the inside cover. In time this list would extend over another page, but the first entries were probably made at the start of 1910: the 1909 work is dated but not in strict date order, suggesting that he began by copying earlier pieces that he wanted to keep. From February 1910 the dates are in order. There are no workings out and few corrections: the notebook was meant to be a fair copy book and it may have come to him as a Christmas or birthday present. It was not a school book, though some of the many verse translations from Classical authors may have started as classroom exercises.

Poetry was woven into the fabric of everyday life then, from the recitations and songs learnt in childhood and performed in family and community entertainments, the verse translations from and into Latin and Greek set at school, the frequent use of poems in newspapers and magazines, and, Sunday by Sunday, the familiar cadences and language of *Hymns Ancient and Modern*. There seems to have been a handful of aspiring poets at Durham School who shared their efforts and encouraged one another. They saw themselves as a subversive underground, championing an activity the system repeatedly failed to recognise. In the summer of 1911, Noel's final term, the school magazine published an anonymous letter appealing for a poetry competition:

> *'There are at least three poets in the school at present, perhaps more. I know that two of them have spent considerable time & trouble over the composition of attempts which the authorities never even desired to see.'*

The writer signed himself simply *'one of them'*; it might have been Noel; after he left, the magazine began to include his poems.

His notebook includes a tremendous variety of work, bearing witness to his interests and the breadth of his reading. The Latin verse translations show an intense delight in language, and in playing with language for its own sake. He translated anything and everything, from Tennyson's epitaph for the tomb of the explorer Sir John Franklin in Westminster Abbey, *'Not here: the white north has thy bones,'* to poems by Robert Louis Stephenson and Walter Scott, to the hymn 'Abide with me' and the chorus of the music hall song 'I'm following in father's footsteps', which Vesta Tilley recorded in 1906. The title of this probably amused him, given his father's ambitions for him.

He did not limit himself to poetry. The book begins with 'The Elephant,' a humorous take on H.G. Wells-style science fiction, in which a narrator describes visiting his friend 'the Professor', who shows him a bizarre invention. It is the body of an elephant, re-animated with a series of cylinders turned by clockwork. On their sensitive surface the *'passions and feelings'* of living elephants have been recorded. These recordings are played as the cylinders turn, and the body moves in response. But when the Professor attempts to demonstrate his *'wonder of the century'* he inserts the wrong cylinder. Instead of simply walking a short distance, the elephant runs amok, pitching the Professor into a very smelly dung heap before smashing the yard, then taking off across country with the two friends in pursuit – until the clockwork runs down.

Apart from translations, the 1909 work includes a number of original poems. One describes moonrise over the coast, another is a short 'drinking song':

> *Here's to the gallant that's quick with his blade,*
> *Here's to the man that can manage a maid,*
> *So up on your feet with a glass*
> *Drink life to the sword & the lass*
> *And death to the man that's afraid.*

Knowing Henry Hodgson's untiring support for the Temperance movement, the number of poems in which his son mentions or – more usually – celebrates alcohol is hard to miss. Like his change of name, this was probably a gesture of independence. Later in the notebook he includes a cheeky 1910 parody of 'The Tide River' from Kingsley's *The Water Babies*:

> *Clear & cool, clear & cool,*
> *When playing pyramids, snooker or pool,*
> *Cool & clear, cool & clear*
> *Is Pilseners Golden Lager Beer.*
> *In the Savoy where the diamonds flash*
> *Or the lowdown pub where the glasses clash,*
> *Bitter & mild for the bitter or mild,*
> *Drink me, rejoice in me father & child.*

But the most striking of the 1909 pieces is 'Asgard', a verse play based on the stories of the Norse gods from the *Prose Edda*. The play is in three acts, takes fourteen pages in verses of varying length, and he describes it as a fragment, so either more was written and discarded or he planned to write more. This was an ambitious undertaking for a sixteen-year-old. It also sets his imaginative development into a wider context. The remoteness of Norse myth provided inspiration for many writers in the nineteenth and early twentieth centuries, none more than J.R.R. Tolkien. Tolkien's image is fixed now as an older man, a don in 1950s and 1960s Oxford, just as Noel Hodgson's is inextricably bound to the Somme. But in the early 1900s both were clever schoolboys – in fact they shared a birthday one year apart – and Tolkien was equally fired by the mythology of the north. The writing of *Asgard* was something the schoolboy Tolkien would have understood; he had ambitious writing plans of his own.

The last 1909 poem in Hodgson's notebook, dated for Boxing Day, 26 December, is 'The English Flag':

> *The negro on the Niger's bank has seen it flowing free;*
> *The Eskimo has seen it 'mid the ice of a frozen sea;*
> *The lonely gull has seen it in the grip of the Ocean gale,*
> *Ragged and rolled in ribbons lashed fast to a creaking rail.*
> *It has flown at the mast of a warship, unstained & bright & proud*
> *It has flown at the head of a liner swallowed up by the storm-rent cloud.*
> *It has flown at a whaler's taffrail that has sunk in the trackless main*
> *It has been round the world on a cruiser & returned to its own again.*
> *I have seen it fly on a tiny fort far south on a sandy shore*
> *I have followed it far 'neath the burning sun from Natal to Singapore*
> *I have seen it cast on a dead man's bones to be his winding sheet*
> *I have seen it supreme and untainted wherever the true hearts beat.*

The poem is patriotic in its opening and ending, but the real pleasure in the writing seems to have been in conjuring all those images of ships and the sea. This probably owes something to his Warren ancestry and more to a childhood spent on the bank of the Tweed, watching the ships sail right past the vicarage on their way in and out of the harbour. Adventure and a sense of distance is the imaginative spark, and it is easy to picture him at home for Christmas, seeing a ship pass by and wondering where it had come from, where it was going, and then beginning to write.

He gives no sense – in this poem at least – that the Empire needs to be defended. The warship's flag is 'unstained', the 'tiny fort' appears inactive, and the dead man might have died of old age. Only the ocean gales cause any injury to the flag. But in the world outside the vicarage there was a niggling sense of unease about Britain's future which deepened as the new century progressed.

The country no longer felt as secure as it had in the past. There was a growing expectation that war would come and that when it did, the enemy would be Germany. The first concerns had been voiced in 1871, when the defeat of France in a war engineered by the Prussian Minister-President Otto von Bismarck opened the way for the King of Prussia to be proclaimed German Emperor in the Hall of Mirrors at Versailles. Prussia's rise had been achieved through earlier wars between the German-speaking countries, now France had been humiliated. Where would it end? *The Battle of Dorking*, a short story which imagined the possibility of England being invaded, was published in *Blackwood's Magazine* that same year, and was so popular that it inspired a wave of invasion stories in the decades that followed.

By 1903, when Erskine Childers' classic novel, *The Riddle of the Sands*, was published, in which two friends stumble across a secret German invasion plan, the idea of a war with Germany was commonplace, appearing in everything from political speeches to Punch cartoons. This co-existed, rather uncomfortably, with a longstanding friendship between the two countries. Their royal families were closely connected, King Edward VII being a descendant of the kings of Hanover and uncle to three reigning German princes (one of whom was the Kaiser). For those who could afford to go, Germany was popular with holidaymakers, and ordinary Germans had lived and worked in Britain for years – the same being true in reverse. Yet none of these friendly ties could dispel the growing shadows, and the early 1900s saw a series of diplomatic crises when war seemed only a whisker away.

Even schools were not immune. The military potential of the well-educated, well-motivated young men in public schools, all trained to lead, had long been recognised. Early in the nineteenth century the threat of French invasion stimulated the formation of volunteer units, and in many school and colleges they lived on when Napoleon was a distant memory. Some schools had close links with the army or with a local regiment, and the country's mixed fortunes during the Boer War increased calls for a reserve of men equipped to become officers at need. In 1907 Lord Haldane's army reforms included the establishment of the Officers' Training Corps (OTC), with a junior division in the public schools and a senior division in the universities. Almost all public schools had an OTC and many made membership compulsory.

Durham did not. The school had no military tradition and in the past had probably produced more clergymen than anything else. It was too small to sustain a cadet force or OTC; the only nod made in that direction was a rifle range, which opened in 1906 in what had been the School House lavatories. But rather than seeing this as a shortcoming in the education the school offered, there seems rather to have been pride in the fact that Durham took its own line. In *The War Record of Old Dunelmians*, published in 1919 as a tribute to those who served, the authors, both former pupils, explained:

'Durham School is not, and never has been, what is known as an "Army School"; rather it has been the aim of the authorities to prepare boys for the Universities and professions with a view to fitting them to practise the arts of peace.'

But they went on to outline the response of former pupils to previous wars; the idea of war as the ultimate call on a man's loyalty and duty was too widespread to be denied.

When Nowell Oxland opposed the creation of a cadet force in 1907 in the debating society, he was surely speaking in response to the Haldane reforms. His argument may have followed the line expressed in the *War Record*; unfortunately neither his speech nor the result of the debate is recorded. At the first meeting of the debating society in the autumn term of 1908, soon after the outbreak of a diplomatic crisis brought on by Austria-Hungary's annexation of Bosnia, Oxland opened another debate, proposing the motion, *'That in the opinion of this house a war between England & Germany in the near future is inevitable'*. This was clearly prompted by the crisis, which underlined once more how nervous Europe became when anything threatened to alter the balance of power. Neither Britain nor Germany was directly involved, but the Austrians were greatly encouraged by German support. Boys at Durham School had access to *The Times* and could have followed what was happening; the mere fact that the debate happened shows that some were concerned. Not many though, according to the school magazine. The debate was said to have lacked interest and once again, neither speeches nor result were reported. The second debate, *'This house believes in the existence of ghosts'*, sparked far more interest. Noel Hodgson was one of those who opposed the motion, arguing that ghosts were creatures of the imagination which people saw only because they wanted to or because they misunderstood some natural phenomenon. This time he was on the winning side, helping to defeat the motion by just one vote.

At home too changes were afoot. Hal had left school in 1906 with an open scholarship to read history at Brasenose College, Oxford. He graduated in 1909 with a third class degree – a tongue-in-cheek comment in the school magazine he had once edited was unsigned, but surely came from him:

'Harry Courtenay Hodgson took a third in History. Did this result represent [his] fine capabilities? If a penny stamp is enclosed [he] will answer all queries at considerable length. Harry Courtenay Hodgson will also be cast upon the world by the time this letter is published. May it use him gently is his fervent prayer.'[1]

He tried teaching but did not enjoy it and opted for a career in the colonial service.

Stella's school life ended in the summer of 1908. In early November, her father's junior curate, Bernard Tower, asked her to marry him. This did not come as a surprise to her because they had been exchanging letters during her last term at school and she was obviously attracted to him. But when she told her parents that evening, her father was not happy. He felt that at seventeen and just out of school, Stella was too young to think of marriage. He was also rather hurt that his curate had not spoken to him first; more so when he discovered that Tower had confided in the senior curate. Henry was too wise and too shrewd a parent to refuse his permission outright; in any case, he liked Bernard Tower. So he told them they must wait a year before he would allow them to be engaged. In that time, no one else must know about the proposal except Tower's parents. While they waited, they were not to look for opportunities to meet, or to meet alone at all outside the vicarage. They may write to one another, but he trusted them not to write too often, and to be careful with their language, writing only as friends.

Stella wrote almost every day. It becomes apparent that her parents knew she was writing and, beyond letting her know that they knew, they made no attempt to intervene except in play:

> *'I have to stop this at intervals because Mum wanders in & says "Oh dear! think of the postman"! and things like that which interrupts the train of thought. We've just had a fight because she came in & tried to wrest this pen from me & I refused to give it up!'* [2]

Penelope Hodgson was less surprised by the proposal than her husband and, quietly, more indulgent. She knew more than he did about the life of a teenage girl at home once her education had finished. For Stella, the 'secret' correspondence enlivened an existence that was far more restrictive than that of her brothers. She went back to Miss Macdonald for occasional literature lessons; otherwise her life revolved around the church, helping her mother to arrange the flowers and change the altar cloth, teaching Sunday school – *'my boys behaved like little fiends!'* [3] She was close to the senior curate Oswald Owen and his wife, and helped with the regular massage prescribed for their little girl, who had difficulty walking. She made social calls with her mother – *'Mum & I are both nearly 'wore out' from sheer exhaustion brought on by gallantly maintaining conversation!! And if when you see me on Sat I 'moo' at you, don't be surprised . . . the cause is VEAL'* [4]

During the early months of 1909 she was encouraged to travel further afield on her own, staying with relatives and friends of her parents. In February she was taken to the State Opening of Parliament: *'I know I shall have an insane desire to yell "Votes for Women"!!'* [5] She visited the family's former homes in Staverton and Thornbury and spent nearly two weeks with Tower's family; by April she was back in the vicarage and her life back to normal.

Her brothers flit through her letters. Hal talking nonsense to the dog, 'Bill' going out on his bicycle; *'Bill having mended a puncture with liquid indiarubber*

& many curses has gone off to Heathery Tops. Personally I think the tyre will blow up on Sunnyside!' This was only the second time she called him Bill, and she slipped back to Noel once after, dating his change of name quite precisely to the summer of 1909. The brothers were not supposed to know about her relationship with Tower: in August she told him:

> *'Hal asked plump out at breakfast whether I <u>had</u> been to stay with the Towers in Yorkshire (After <u>all</u> our 'diplomacy'), in our anxiety to deny my having anything to do with your family, Mum, Dad & I all <u>shouted</u> 'No' simultaneously!'*

But Noel knew. He and Stella had always been so close that he probably knew all along. The vicarage was ideally placed for watching trains go by on the far bank of the Tweed, though the river was too wide for it to be possible for someone on the train to pick out a face at the window, or a waving hand. When Tower left Berwick that summer to visit his family Stella found a novel way to give him a send off, and a willing ally. *'Did you see us waving? I caught up Mum's white Dressing-gown & flourished it & Bill had a shirt.'*[6]

The family holiday in September 1909 was a two-week house exchange with the rector from Kelso in Scotland and his family. For the first few days Noel had a friend staying; when he left, the Hodgsons were on their own, walking or going for longer outings in the day and playing bridge in the evenings. Hal and Noel went climbing in the Eildon Hills while Henry fretted over his *Spectator*, which was supposed to be sent on from Berwick, and took Sunday services in the church. *'We had Royalty in the Church yesterday morning! Princess Victoria & then some wicked sounding German names!'*[7] Noel had to leave early to return to school. Before he did, Stella darned his socks and mended the holes in his clothes.

He was returning to his fifth year at Durham, a year that began uneventfully. The autumn term saw the debate on censorship, which he lost and Nowell Oxland won, and in his notebook more verses translated into Latin, the 'Drinking Song', and 'The English Flag'. In the spring he found a new subject, writing a passionate twelve-verse ode on the death of Joan of Arc:

> *Great was the throne of France , she knew,*
> *And great the King that sate thereon;*
> *Glorious the lilies of his shield,*
> *And wide the lands o'er which they shone.*
>
> *But well she knew that not for her*
> *Were destined lands, or King or throne;*
> *Not she by them, but they by her*
> *Must rise – & by her death alone.*

Death seemed to be on his mind at that time, prompted perhaps by news that the King, who was taken ill in March, did not have long to live. But there was nothing of King Edward in a short poem on the subject which he wrote later in April:

> *Once more, dear heart, once more*
> *– The end is nigh –*
> *Kiss me once more dear heart*
> *Ere that I die.*
>
> *Life with its toils is past*
> *Life, with its pain;*
> *I am lost in the dark, dear,*
> *Oh kiss me again.*
>
> *Ah, Jesus has come to me*
> *In kind arms I lie.*
> *The darkness has fled away*
> *Goodbye, dear, goodbye.*

Poetic melancholy apart, though, he was full of life and up to no good. Ascension Day that year fell on 5 May, and it was a fine morning with a light mist. Breakfast was at 9am, timed for the school to attend Matins in the Cathedral, and he and Nowell Oxland had a plan. Before sunrise they were up and, climbing from the window of the lower study, which Oxland occupied as Head of School, they made off across country on a bird-nesting expedition. They forded the river, going waist deep in water – from the map, this must have been the small River Browney, to the west of the school. They had found several nests before some gamekeepers, *'the slaves of the rich'*, he called them, spotted and gave chase. Escaping that danger – they were young, after all and keen athletes – they found refuge in a cottage where they were given an early breakfast of bread and lemon curd. This was interrupted by the sound of a clock striking eight, a warning to them to hurry, in order to be back in school and smartened up in time for the morning roll-call. This demanded the cross-country run of their lives but they made it. The other boys, who knew what they had been doing, were full of admiration, and Noel remembered falling asleep during the service.

But the adventure did not remain a secret and once found out, the pair were in real trouble. Breaking bounds (leaving school premises without permission) was crime enough, never mind the trespass which had alerted the gamekeepers, if that was known. And there may also have been more to the story. The only account is Noel's, written on the Somme in 1916 in the glow of reflected memory, and it does raise questions. The cottage especially: why would someone take in two obviously misbehaving and sopping wet schoolboys and feed them – unless perhaps they knew the boys, and one or both of them had been before. In any case, for the Head of School to do something like this and take a younger boy with him was unprecedented, and it posed the headmaster with a dilemma. How to punish him. Nowell Oxland was nineteen and weeks away from leaving school; he would turn twenty before the year's end. For him the cane would be as inappropriate as it was meaningless. So the Rev Budworth sent him down: a step short of expulsion, but one that denied him the chance to take his final examinations. If he wanted to go to university, which he did, he would have to take responsibility for arranging it himself. His position as Head of School was given to one of the senior boys in Second Master's House until the term ended.

Noel Hodgson was two years younger and therefore easier to deal with. Boys in their middle years at school did misbehave at times, and clergymen's sons were known for it. They came under so much pressure to be good. It was probably the cane for him, and that would have ended the business. He did exceptionally well in the summer exams, coming out top of the Classical VIth in Latin, Greek, English, Divinity and History. He collected seven prizes on Speech Day. His notebook contains no hint of how he felt about what happened except perhaps one poem, a second and more melodramatic lyric on death:

> *Come death, my only friend! Dim gentle Queen*
> *Embrace me now. None other brings me love.*
> *But thou with cool-enfolding arms outstretched*
> *Receive me. On thy bosom let me lie,*
> *And sleeping fall in sweet oblivion,*
> *And kiss my weary lids & make them close*
> *So let me quite forget the troublous world*
> *And soundly slumber, life's hard voyage o'er;*
> *As once I slumbered on a mother's breast.*
> *Mother! I have no mother. Oh to see*
> *A mother's eyes again & feel her breath*
> *Upon my cheek, & all my cares confide*
> *To her. It cannot be. Come then, smooth Death*
> *And be to me both sister, mother, sire,*
> *Yes, all to me. And in thy cool embrace*
> *Let me for ever part from hence. O come!*

This was written a week after the bird-nesting expedition. It would be tempting to make it part of the story ('I just want to die; I want my mother') but as he was playing with poetic melancholy before Ascension Day it may be completely unconnected. It is striking, though, that he uses the image of death as a lover so freely here. Love had not featured in his notebook before, but he wrote two more poems on the theme that summer: a lament on remembered love and 'To My Love':

> *The stars are shining clear and bright*
> *But I know of eyes that are brighter still;*
> *The wave's beat sounds from beyond the hill*
> *And I feel the deep calm of the night.*
> *But I know of a heart with a truer beat,*
> *And a soul with a calm that is deeper far;*
> *And I turn my back on the sea & the star*
> *And I throw myself at my true love's feet.*

But again, physical love is a natural enough preoccupation at seventeen, and he may have been exploring ideas he found in books and other men's poems, or thinking of the change that was coming into his sister's life; her engagement had finally become official at the start of 1910.

Noel returned to school in the autumn to begin his final year, and was made a monitor. He seemed to be in high spirits at first: his parody of 'The Tide River' dates from the autumn term, and another on income tax: also an ode to the Roman poet Horace, which becomes a hymn to poetic immortality, ending:

> *Great have been sackers of cities,*
> *Great have been leaders of men,*
> *Great have been sailors of vessels,*
> *Greatest the god-guided pen.*
> *For vessels are sunk & the sailor & soldier are naught but a name,*
> *But Time cannot blot out the poet, <u>his</u> glory is ever the same.*

He was writing more of his own verse, fewer verse translations. Two poems of the autumn of 1910 are particularly interesting in the context of war, and his developing attitude to it. 'Fortes creantur fortibus et bonis' (a title taken from Horace, meaning 'Brave sons spring from the steadfast and good') is a tub-thumping call to a country too reliant on past achievements:

> *But what do <u>you</u> know of fighting*
> *Of trenches, big guns and shells!*
> *Did the Nile and Corunna help you*
> *On the brown South African fells?*
> *Did the slouch-hatted, keen-eyed burghers*
> *Shoot any more loosely at you,*

'Cause they knew that your great-grandfathers
Were the victors of Waterloo?
Then give up your pride & your lazing;
It's all right to be proud of your race
But the pride that you're always wrapped up in
Is a little bit out of place.
For the nations you think are beneath you
And believe to be worshipping you,
Are mocking the obsolete nation
That's living on Waterloo!

So preparing, training to be ready to meet war if it came, was something he believed was important. But what of war itself? A few weeks after that poem he wrote another, with a Greek title, Πόλεμος ακήρυκτος [Unheralded War]:

The brazen-throated bugles shrill
The trumpets call to war;
The rolling summons of the drum
Bids every patriot soldier come
To cut, to stab, to maim, to kill
To face the cannon's maw,
To climb a bullet-spitting hill
To charge the trenches belching shell
To wait the lyddite-carried hell,
    To fall, to die,
    Untended lie,
In foreign lands where none shall know
His vines are fattened by the gore
Of soldiers buried long before,
Unwitting shall the farmer sow
His seed among their bones
And yet they come in spite of all,
Prepared to fight prepared to fall,
And with their dying tones
Will boast in joy their victory
And revel in a splendid glee
That they have set another gem
In England's world wide diadem.

This is the first appearance of a theme he would return to in 1914 – the irony of war. The fighting is ugly and vicious; his language makes that clear. The soldiers in the poem believe they are achieving something glorious and lasting, while in fact it is their fate to be forgotten entirely. He had come to see war as a fact of human existence. It happened, so it was important to be ready for it, but ultimately it would not achieve anything. The dead would return to the soil and life would carry on, oblivious to them and their cause.

His mind seemed to be very much on endings and beginnings. He wrote a lengthy prose sketch, 'Fire Pictures', which returned to many of his early ideas: Valhalla and the Norse gods; Joan of Arc; and the dead lover, ending with an untitled poem:

> *There's nothing new in all the earth*
> *Its all been done before…*
> *And yet the race is only begun*
> *So play your part as best you can*
> *And try to act up to the role of a man*
> *Altho' it may cost you sore.*

In the light of what happened to him later those lines sound prophetic, but when he wrote them 1916 was still a world away. Outside the covers of his notebook he was as energetic as ever. He represented the school in Fives and rugby: according to the magazine he weighed 10st 7lb [66.7kg] and *'improved greatly towards the end of the season. A nice dribbler and is learning to tackle'.*[8] In mid-December he was in Oxford, trying for a scholarship in classics at Christ Church, his father's college. While away from Durham he visited his uncle and aunt, Sir Pelham Warren and his sister Mary, in Daventry; his tiny copy of Fitzgerald's *The Rubaiyat of Omar Khayyam* is inscribed 'Daventry, Northants', with the date and his other addresses, at school and at home. He was obviously afraid of losing the book, which must have been a favourite. Several passages are marked or underlined, and his tiny marginal notes add explanations – *'The Persians believed that the healing power of Jesus resided in his breath'* – or link particular lines to quotations from Tennyson, Herrick, Shakespeare, Horace and others.

Small enough to fit in a pocket, the book was a practical companion on a journey. Its themes – the shortness of life, the need to snatch at every moment before darkness closed in – and its agnosticism seemed to resonate with him. *'One Moment in Annihilation's Waste,/ One Moment, of the Well of Life to taste –/ The Stars are setting and the Caravan/ Starts for the Dawn of Nothing – Oh, make haste!'* was one of the verses he marked. Lively and sociable, and mischievous as he was, he seemed to have a shadow of foreboding which came out in his reading and his poems. Perhaps the imminent end of his time in Durham was making him uncertain. But the result of his trip to Oxford was a triumph. In January he learned that he had won an open exhibition to Christ Church worth £45 a year, the payment of his tuition fees and free dinners in Hall. On the last day of the month the whole school had a half holiday to celebrate.

Spring came and summer, and he was one of the heroes of the cricket team, pulling off a famous catch against at team from the Northumberland Fusiliers: *'Captain Morrison played well and looked like staying when he was magnificently caught, with one hand, by Hodgson at cover.'*[9] He wrote more poems than ever: long and rather heated descriptions of Semele, priestess of Zeus – *'The iridescent robe/ In filmy silkiness embraced her waist/ And lower limbs, soft & voluptuous'* – and of a tree goddess; a rousing call to abandon the books and spring into action, in the same vein as his earlier 'Drinking Song'; and a handful of love poems, most of them more cheerful than his previous efforts:

> *Today she smiled. I wonder why*
> *The heavens seem so bright.*
> *Why sings the lark so tunefully?*
> *Why is my heart so light?*
>
> *On every bush the spiders hang*
> *Their necklaces of gems*
> *And every field of buttercups*
> *Wears countless diadems.*
>
> *Naught's wrong in all the world today*
> *The air is fresh as wine,*
> *There is no sorrow anywhere,*
> *And all the world is mine.*

Almost all the love poems are about an unnamed 'she', one about love for a man. *'He smiles, the world is full of light,/ He frowns, the world is wrapt in night.'* He seemed to be exploring ideas of love. In February 1911 he embarked on two short stories written on alternate pages of a school exercise book, with the title 'Greater Love Hath No Man'. The first asks what might happen if friendship and love were to clash, describing the consuming jealousy a young man feels when he finds that his best friend has a girlfriend and wants to spend time with her. At the story's melodramatic climax the young man sacrifices his life in a mining accident to save the lovers. The second tells of a sea captain in the Far East, who falls in love with an American woman he rescues from a lifeboat. When she is taken by pirates, then shot, he throws his life away trying to be revenged on her killer.

Setting love aside, Noel wrote a narrative poem about a drunken serf and, unusually for him, a fairy poem. Fairies were a fashionable subject then, but his version is so unbearably cute that he was surely poking fun at the whole idea. The poem ends:

But when you're really happy
And have helped your friends a bit
If you sit alone and listen
Before the lamps are lit
You may hear the dainty footsteps
And the notes of fairy bands
And the quaffing of fresh dew-drops
And the clap of fairy hands.
And if you're drefful, drefful good
The little pixy girls
Will come & kiss your eyes to sleep
And dangle in your curls.

The last of the summer's poems are dedicated to Durham School; one to the school itself and the idea that its community lived on in its former pupils, scattered round the world, the other a short rowing chorus. He did exceptionally well in his Higher Certificate Examinations, passing Latin, Greek, Divinity and English with distinction. The Dean and Chapter of the Cathedral awarded him a second scholarship, a three-year leaving exhibition, to supplement the exhibition he had already won at Christ Church. On Speech Day, 2 August, he collected seven more prizes, and he, Robert Parr and Alick Todd, also of School House, performed a scene from Aristophanes' comedy *The Frogs*. And with that it was over, and Noel Hodgson's school days had come to an end.

Chapter 5

Oxford, 1911–1913

In 1911 Christ Church College was no longer the fashionable centre of the University's social life. That was in the past, when Henry Liddell was Dean, his wife managed the guest list and his daughters, once the bewitching children who inspired *Alice in Wonderland*, entranced a generation of undergraduates. In 1911 the fashionable world had moved on to other colleges. The Deanery at Christ Church was home to the Rev Thomas Strong, an intensely shy man with a brilliant mind who had worked hard to build up the intellectual level of the House. ('The House' was the college's own name for itself, from the Latin *Aedes Christi*, the house of Christ.) Dean Strong was unmarried and had no interest in lavish entertaining, preferring the company of a few friends or his undergraduates. It was said that he knew every one of them by name, year and course. He was noted for his extraordinary memory, also for his knowledge of music, his efficient business management, and for a quiet charm and good humour which shone out at times from behind his outward reserve.

Christ Church, largest of the Oxford colleges, was unusual in being an ecclesiastical foundation. Created by Cardinal Wolsey on the site of an earlier Augustinian priory, and taken over by Henry VIII after Wolsey's fall, the college was attached to Christ Church Cathedral. It was governed by the Dean and canons of the Cathedral and, from the mid-nineteenth century, the Students. (Students with a capital 'S' at Christ Church are graduates and members of the teaching staff, equivalent to the Fellows in other colleges.) And when Noel Hodgson was about to go up for the first time, in October 1911, the ecclesiastical grapevine swung into action on his behalf. One of the Students, the Rev George Kennedy Alan Bell, was approached by Canon Robert Ottley, Regius Professor of Moral and Pastoral Theology, and asked to look out for him. *'I was asked by Dr Ottley to make friends with him,'* Bell recalled, *'for his father's sake, and also because of the hope his father had that he might become a clergyman. It was not hard to get on terms with him, but one felt at once that his character was one of those vastly firm characters that are well able to look after themselves.'*

Does this suggest that Henry Hodgson feared his son might be led astray, or was he just being a concerned parent? It is impossible to tell. What is clear between the lines of Bell's account, is that Noel was not open to being steered towards the ministry. He received Bell's approach equably, but would make his own decisions:

*'Most men come up to Oxford mentally and morally less formed than
Hodgson. He had got a good line always and kept to it. . . . He was
growing steadily, justly and freshly, but the roots were deeper than you
will ordinarily find them. He had not to find his balance or even bother
about trying to keep it. His balance was natural and he was true to it.'[1]*

For the first year Noel was allotted rooms on the eighteenth century Peckwater
Quad. The panelled first floor rooms on 'Peck' were much sought after for their
size and decoration. His rooms, staircase 1, room 7, were on the third floor, with
no view at all from the living room and a bedroom overlooking the buildings
on Blue Boar Street. But unlike school it was at least private and offered a
degree of comfort, looked after by the hard-working college servants. Their day
began at 7am, lighting fires in the rooms, and did not end until fourteen hours
later when the college closed for the night. Prince Serge Obolensky, a Russian
aristocrat who was assigned ground floor rooms on 'Peck' the following year,
remembered the Quad as crumbling and dilapidated, its stonework falling prey
to the effects of wind, weather and undergraduate high spirits, yet still possessed
of an indefinable charm.[2]

Noel Hodgson matriculated on 13 October and settled down to study
'Greats', with Sydney George Owen as his tutor. The 'Greats' course consisted
of Latin and Greek literature for the first five terms, leading to Classical
Moderations, then ancient history and philosophy. 'Greats' had long been the
bedrock of an Oxford education, seen as the finest possible training for the mind
because it offered complete objectivity, and had no function beyond pure study.
Once a man had qualified in 'Greats', it was said, he could adapt to any practical
or intellectual task.

Life at Oxford was, for the most part, centred on study. The majority of
undergraduates were at university because they needed a degree or because they
enjoyed academic work, and scholars in particular were expected to do well.
Mornings were given over to lectures, tutorials and reading, with men working
in their rooms, alone or with friends. Early afternoons tended to be for sport
and games, with the last couple of hours between tea and dinner providing more
useful study time – in that respect, the routine was very similar to the one he
had known at Durham. Dinner was a semi-formal affair in Hall for which
academic gowns were worn, and after dinner men would return to work in their
rooms or socialise with friends. At five past nine the bell rang in Tom Tower,
over the main gateway to Christ Church, and the gates of all the Oxford colleges
were locked for the night. Anyone not safely inside at a given time would be
'gated' (confined to college) as a punishment.

University life was much freer than school and undergraduates were trusted
to organise their own time and develop their own interests, but there was still
discipline. Attendance at Cathedral services was expected, and noted. There

were roll calls, dress codes for formal occasions. There were also conventions to be observed. J.C. Masterman, who was an undergraduate at Worcester College and became a Student at Christ Church in 1913, recalled a world in which it was 'not done' to advertise the amount of work you did, so that even those who worked very hard put up a pretence of not working. Discussion of religion was generally avoided, as was discussion of sex: according to Masterman, there was an unwritten understanding that female company was best saved for the vacations. There were female students at the four Oxford women's colleges, but they were fiercely chaperoned and unreachable. So for Noel and others like him Oxford was both like and unlike school, an enclosed male world with its own language and a new set of rules and customs to be learned and followed.

Leaving Durham had been a wrench. He had been so happy and seemed haunted by the fear that nothing could ever be the same. But the school community did embrace former pupils if they chose to stay in contact; the break did not have to be absolute. The Rev Budworth kept in touch with any Old Boys who wrote to him, as Hodgson certainly did, and took a genuine interest in their well-being, appearing to find communication with them easier once they had moved on. There were Old Boys' teams for cricket and rugby too, and the ODs (Old Dunelmians) at Oxford and Cambridge sent newsletters to the school magazine. Noel would have found several familiar faces at Oxford too. Another School House boy, Stephen Hodge, had entered Christ Church as an Exhibitioner a year before him: at Keble were James Dingle, the boy who took over as Head of School after Nowell Oxland was sent down, and James Tombs, whose father was the Durham School VIth form master. Another School House boy, Anthony Allwork, was at Queen's. And October 1911 saw the arrival at the University of someone Noel Hodgson would have been even more pleased to see again.

Nowell Oxland had taken up the challenge the headmaster threw down and found his own way to the university. This meant spending time at a crammer; the census of 1911 found him living in Tingewick Rectory on the Oxfordshire-Buckinghamshire border, as one of the Rev Phillip Raynor's three pupils. Being within easy reach of both Oxford and London, he made contact with friends of his year who had gone straight from Durham to the university. He also joined the Rosslyn Park Rugby Club; both he and James Dingle appear in a match report in *The Times* in November 1910 against Harlequins, and both continued to play for the club. But Oxland did not let rugby get in the way of his studies and in the summer he passed the examinations necessary for Oxford entrance. On 15 July he wrote from Tingewick Rectory to the Bursar of Worcester College:

> *'Dear Sir.*
> *As I have just passed Responsions I should be obliged if you would kindly give me some information about college expenses and rooms for next term.*
> *The Provost told me to write to you about work to be done during the*

vacation. I want to read for Honour Moderations, and with this end in view have started on the Odyssey, Cicero's Philippics, the Aeneid, the Annals of Tacitus, Thucydides, Books I and II and Horace, Satires I. For "portions of authors specially offered" I should like to take two Latin books and one Greek (Horace, Tacitus and Thucydides). I should be obliged if you would tell me whether I should continue with the books I have named during the vacation.'[3]

In September he was back home in Alston helping to organise a mixed hockey club at his father's church, which he would return to in the vacations. And in October, when Hodgson went up to Christ Church, he matriculated at Worcester College.

Spread around the Oxford colleges, the Durham boys were able to maintain contact while building new circles of acquaintance and friendship. Christ Church was home to an eclectic mix of undergraduates. Most came from the public schools and had similar backgrounds to the boys at Durham, being the sons of professional men, like Noel, or sons of rich men with fortunes from industry or trade. In 1911 the presence of these last made Lord Derby advise the King that Christ Church would not be suitable for the Prince of Wales – too many *nouveaux riches*.[4] But though the British elite may have moved on, to Balliol, New College or Magdalen (the college actually chosen for the Prince in 1912), the *nouveaux riches* and their old school fellows rubbed shoulders on the staircases and landings of the House with a clutch of far more exotic characters. Men like Serge Obolensky, Prince Paul of Serbia, who also had rooms on Peckwater Quad; princes from India and Thailand and the sons of foreign ambassadors added a cosmopolitan thread to the social and intellectual life of the House.

Undergraduates moved in different circles depending on their backgrounds, the schools they had been to, and the depth of their pockets. Noel would not have mixed socially with the princes but he could hardly have been unaware of them. In 1912 and 1913 the Prince of Wales was a frequent visitor to Serge Obolensky's rooms, and if the House was celebrating they joined in by blowing hunting horns in the Quad and making a bonfire of other men's furniture.[5] Among other notable names, Noel would surely have known Gilbert Talbot, at least by sight. Gilbert, younger son of the Bishop of Winchester, was reading 'Greats' a year ahead of him and was one of those characters who stand out effortlessly from a crowd. A powerful speaker, he was the elected president of the Junior Common Room, was successively secretary, treasurer and president of the Oxford Union, and a leading figure besides in many Oxford clubs. He became more widely known after his death at Hooge in 1915, when his name was given to Talbot House in Poperinghe, the original home of the TocH movement.

The Michaelmas term of 1912 also brought two future war poets to Christ Church. Geoffrey Dearmer, who survived the war, dying in 1996 at the age of

103, did not know Noel at Oxford, but was at school with his Distington cousins, George and Charles Hodgson, and in later life became very friendly with Stella. The other Christ Church poet, Alan (E.A.) Mackintosh, who was killed in action in 1917, may have known Noel; they had rooms not far from one another on the Great Quadrangle, 'Tom Quad', in the last year before the war, and they shared a tutor in their final term.

One friend Noel certainly made was John Warwick Nind Smith, the son of a county judge in Madras. They were neighbours on Peckwater Quad in their first year and Smith was also an aspiring writer. In a later memoir he recalled:

> *'What I know of Bill Hodgson at Christ Church, was almost entirely confined to our personal friendship. We never belonged to the same clubs and rarely met, except in the evenings, when we met in his rooms or mine after Hall, and sat hour after hour reading Classical texts and discussing the latest books and each other's writings. Few subjects remained undiscussed, from football to social reform, and then frequently we would clear the chairs on one side and have a spar without gloves, my weight compensating for his skill . . . . Himself simple, fearless, and wonderfully alive, he enjoyed every instant he lived, and his games were one with his scholarship.'*[6]

Smith's memories have the afterglow that inevitably followed death in the war. No one enjoys every instant of life, and the first term seems to have been emotionally difficult for Hodgson. There are three poems in his notebook, all very downbeat. Little more than a week before matriculation – he may have been in Oxford already, still at home, or somewhere else – he was struggling with unrequited love. At least, he wrote a poem on the subject with the Latin title *Qaulis Noster Amor* [What sort of love is ours], which traces the course of a relationship from intense loathing, through silent infatuation to a mutual realisation – then a falling out:

> *So here am I with wounded heart,*
> *And sad insatiate longing.*
> *And every fibre meant for joy,*
> *Remorse and grief are thronging.*
> *I know not of your heart – perchance,*
> *You have some tiny token,*
> *Of this poor moth who sought the flame,*
> *And lies so burned & broken.*
> *I still recall the eyes of blue*
> *Which hurled the glance that maddened;*
> *Do you recall the eyes of brown*
> *Now mischievous now saddened?*

At this point the muse seemed to leave him. The last four lines are clumsier than the rest, but they ask the question implied by the title: is it all over? Is it still worth hoping?

A poem written in the first person may not reflect the writer's own experience. A good writer should be able to enter the head of another person, and it may be that he was still just playing with the idea of love. But the brown eyes and the mischief do sound like him, and the notebook poems seem to follow a recognisable pattern of adolescent love, particularly in a society where the sexes were so carefully segregated. He admires from a distance; the least sign of attention fills him with delight. The poems build into a consistent narrative of growing up. An untitled poem written a few weeks later suggests that if this was a real relationship he was struggling with, he had come reluctantly to the conclusion that it was over:

> *A moment of madness a life of sorrow;*
> *Pleasure today & grief tomorrow,*
> *Joy for a day & grief ever after;*
> *A life of tears for a moment's laughter;*
> *And I sit alone & my heart is breaking,*
> *And you are alone and your heart is aching;*
> *We have held our jewel & cast it by,*
> *So the tear of remorse has dimmed our eye;*
> *The flower we loved is slain by frost,*
> *The star we worshipped in cloud is lost;*
> *In our heart Joy's palace is taken by Pain,*
> *To relinquish it never oh never again!*

The third poem of the Michaelmas term, written at the end of October and sandwiched between these two, takes the form of a conversation between himself and a 'voice from the void'. He is restless and crying out for answers: the question posed repeatedly through the poem is 'Why'. He wants to know what use he can make of his life. This may have had something to do with the Rev Bell's approach and the reminder, implied or explicit, that his father was longing for him to enter the church. If the prospect of love was all over, was this the way forward?

> *The Voice was silent, and, in bitter pain,*
> *I said aloud, "Oh, make the riddle plain!"*
> *The low Voice answered, "Make yourself a slave*
> *Who labours all for others, if you save*
> *One single soul, you have not lived in vain."*

This resolve is drawn from his Christian upbringing. The terms he uses are over dramatic, but he was only eighteen and at that age emotions run high. Curiously, the poem finds an echo both in Bell's reminiscences and in Smith's. George Bell had taken his watching brief over Noel Hodgson very seriously. 'I remember being particularly struck by his friendships,' he wrote.

> *'There were not a few men of his own year whose tastes and abilities were of a kind to match his own, and easily and naturally enough he made friends with them. With them he talked and walked and read and did a thousand happy things. And yet the man to whom his virtue most went out was a man, from the ordinary point of view, totally unlike him, morally inclined to be a weakling, rather dull and with no particular taste for literature or knowledge of the classics or interest in philosophy. Like Hodgson, he could play a good game of rugby, but that was the only obvious link. Yet not deliberately, or of set purpose, but instinctively, Hodgson adopted him, gave him most of his company and, though I do not think they ever had much in common, became his prop.'*

Smith made it sound less judgemental, but he had still noticed the same tendency: '*nobody needed his sympathy and help, and failed to get them. His strength was the support of many less happily endowed than himself, and his sacrifice of time and patience, despite the natural hastiness with any weakness of disposition, was generous.*'[7]

So the desire to help others was real. The sacrificial gloom of the October poem was mercifully short-lived. In his second term the mood of his writing changes completely, a change ushered in, it seems, by the first appearance of what was to become the dominant theme of his poems – the fells, and the joy of climbing, literally, above life and its problems. On 3 January 1912, his nineteenth birthday, he wrote:

> *When the great sun brings on his splendid wings*
> *The breath of the newborn day,*
> *It's good to feel beneath your heel*
> *The spring of an untrod way.*
> *The clouds race by in a cream-flecked sky,*
> *Your forehead feels the breeze;*
> *There's life up there in the good fine air*
> *And strength to the feeble knees*
> *And the lungs are strong and the stride is long*
> *And the heart is light and free,*
> *And the fowl are near and the great red deer*
> *To be your company.*

Then come with me where the fells sweep free
From here to heaven's rim;
Where the good green sod is the altar of God
There we will worship him.

A few weeks later he returned to the subject of falling in love, but in a much more humorous mood, asking himself why we do it if it causes so much anguish, and concluding that the pleasure outweighs the pain: *'Yet never the passion passes, never the wonder dies;/ Still earth has no such glory as that of a lover's eyes.'* It becomes clear from all the poems written around this time that love to him was a thing of the emotions and the imagination. An ideal, excited by the smallest gesture – a glance, a touch, at most a kiss. He drew a very clear distinction between this romantic love and sex – 'lust' – which to him was only dark and disturbing. This was his upbringing speaking and it was very typical of his day. At nineteen and not long out of boarding school, he still had a long way to go in terms of experience. An undated poem in the same section of the notebook expresses his disappointment in discovering that a male friend, one he looks up to – idolises, even – has *'proved to be common clay'*. He feels he should avoid him in future, *'Never to see the once dear face again'*, for fear of finding *'what is both common & unclean'*. But at a later date someone has added in pencil the Biblical reference, *'Call thou nothing common or unclean'*. The hand is awkward and strays across two lines, as if it was written in difficult conditions, but the writing could be his own.

There is no clue to the friend's identity or to what prompted the change of heart. Friendship at Oxford tended to revolve around clubs, the hub of the university's social life. Oxford had clubs for dining, drinking, reading, acting, debating, politics, foreign languages: almost anything in which a few men took an interest. There was even a short-lived club for experimenting with hashish. There were clubs that drew members from across the colleges and clubs that were particular to one; small clubs and large ones; clubs that had existed for decades and others that were a thing of the moment. Looking on with an outsider's eye, Prince Obolensky believed that the English needed so many clubs to give them an excuse to meet, overcoming their natural reserve.

No record survives of Hodgson's club memberships except the negative reference from his friend Smith: *'We never belonged to the same clubs'*. But his interests are clear. Literature, history, drama and debate. *'He had a keen eye for the actual: philosophy wearied him but science and social ethics interested him deeply. . . . his circle of acquaintance had nothing to do with politics'* – that was Smith.[8] And it is possible to recapture something of the atmosphere Hodgson would have known through the activities and interests of his friends and the clubs that existed in his time. There was a dramatic society at Christ Church, for example, and that would have appealed to him. Serge Obolensky remembered joining and having a walk-on part as a friar, swathed in a hooded cloak. At Worcester College Nowell Oxland belonged to two literary societies. The first, the Philistines, was an established group within the college, which discussed papers on literary subjects. He joined on 1 June 1912 and was active in meetings until his final term two years later.

More detailed information survives on his membership of the smaller Lovelace Club. They met at two or three week intervals in the room of one of the members; Oxland attended for the first time as a visitor on Sunday, 8 June 1913. The Bursar, the Rev F. J. Lys, was giving a paper that evening on 'The Future of Poetry', and this may have drawn Oxland in. Lys was very sympathetic to him, perhaps because he knew about the difficult circumstances surrounding Oxland's university entrance. In the summer of 1912 Lys offered the College's help when Oxland, who was having to pay his own way, encountered financial problems. *'The grant made me by the College is very welcome and will be of considerable assistance,'* Oxland told him.[9]

At the end of that meeting, following Lys's paper, Nowell Oxland was elected a member. The next meeting was not until the Michaelmas Term, when Oxland presented a paper himself on the essayist Thomas de Quincy, in characteristic style. He opened by announcing that de Quincy's work covered too wide a range of subjects for one paper, so he intended to *'consider him only as an opium-eater'*. Then he proceeded to explore the effects of de Quincy's discovery of opium as an aid to inspiration. This provoked an unusually lively discussion of the morality of opium use. Some were disturbed that Oxland had not condemned it, others compared it to the port members drank at meetings – one said that *'he himself scintillated less brilliantly when sober'*. Nowell Oxland remained silent until the end, when he *'replied to the best of his ability'*.[10]

This gives a vivid picture of an Oxford club from the inside; a blend of genuine scholarship enjoyed for its own sake, understated humour and good manners. From Oxland it was a very confident performance for a new member. Once again, there is that sense that he liked to provoke – to outrage, even – and this is borne out in the minutes of later meetings. He quotes a joke from *Punch*, he insists that the theatre exists only to entertain, not to educate. When someone expresses a strong view, he comes out with the opposite.[11] There is a spark of devilment in his comments and his choice of subjects that his friend would have appreciated; the Lovelace Club minutes illustrate precisely the kind of setting in which Noel Hodgson would have been thoroughly at home.

Similar clubs existed around the colleges. At Corpus Christi two men who would share the last, crowded years of Hodgson's life as fellow officers of the 9th Devons were drawing to the end of their time at university. John Upcott and his friend Harold Rayner were members of the Owlets, their college's dramatic society. In 1912 Upcott became successively secretary and then president. Both men also belonged to the Pelican Essay Club, which would probably have been similar to the Lovelace Club, but with papers covering a wider range of subjects. This time it was Rayner who held both offices in turn. He was also a keen sportsman, leading his college in both rowing and rugby, and in this context he might easily have encountered Hodgson and Oxland. Both played rugby for their colleges; both rose to captain their teams.

Hodgson's sporting activities are easier to track. First rugby: both Smith and Bell recall how well he played, and there are photographs of him in the college team in 1911-12, and in an away match with Downing College Cambridge. In both cases the Christ Church men wear white shirts with the college badge. There is also a hockey team photo from 1913-14. The random collection of clothing they wear and some curious chalk graffiti of hockey players on the wall behind them suggest that hockey might not have been taken quite as seriously as rugby. But Hodgson enjoyed being active whatever the game. *'He was at his best, I thought, on the early summer mornings,'* (this is Smith again), *'when he and several more of us would go to Long Bridges and bathe, scaling the iron palings at the bottom of Christ Church meadows en route in order to seize and make away with the House punt from the barge, or even some other college punt. A good trespass or a roguish theft appealed to him vastly. On those mornings whoever of the party chose to stay in bed, it was not Bill.'*

So, rugby, hockey, swimming, the odd undergraduate prank. Cricket too, in season. *'Dingle and Hodgson are the only O.D.s who play cricket up here. The others divide their leisure time between tennis and the river. . . . Most of us are on the point of departure for Aldershot for a fortnight's training with the O.T.C.'* And that was something else Noel Hodgson joined: the university branch of the Officers' Training Corps. It was always on the cards that he would join, given the way he had written about the need to prepare for war. The Agadir Crisis, which built up during his last term at school, created another spike in international tension, deepening the divisions between France, Britain, and Germany. This was still a hot topic for discussion when he went up to Christ Church in the autumn. In a lengthy address to the university's Canning Club early in 1912, Gilbert Talbot reflected on the fallout: *'It is impossible for anybody who soberly considers the present relations between England and Germany, who is genuinely anxious for peace. . . to feel other than an intense anxiety.'* Gilbert urged that war was threatening but not inevitable; that something might still be salvaged by treading carefully in international relations while working for a friendlier feeling between the two countries.[13] But Hodgson wanted to know what to do if hopes like these proved fruitless. He wanted to be ready.

He was home after the OTC summer camp of 1912 in time for something much happier. On Tuesday, 30 July, Stella was finally married to Bernard Tower after an engagement lasting over two years. Henry performed the wedding service himself; his brother-in-law Sir Pelham Warren stood in for him to give the bride away. The next day, Penelope wrote to her newly-married daughter:

'The last of the guests have left, Father and Hal have gone to see them off. Bill went with the first party, so I have a quiet moment to write to you, but I don't know where to begin there is so much. First your dear little letter last night was given by Bill & I put it under my pillow (how romantic) . . . How well everything went off, people could not say enough in praise of the bride & the whole thing. . . . Dinner was not lively though there was champagne & we all retired to bed early. Bill was an angel & everybody was very nice & I took malted milk & put feet in hot water & was very good. I just don't think you are married, but staying away for a little spree. . . . Hal & Father have just returned with a sheaf of papers, the town is placarded with "pretty wedding in Berwick." '[14]

'Bill went with the first party'. His notebook tells us where. On 4 August, five days after the wedding, he was on Hadrian's Wall, heading for Cumberland. He wrote a poem that day, which he called 'Valeria Victrix':

Over the fells to the eastward, over the fells to the west
Where the curlews swing in the heaven & the red grouse have their home
On by the yellow cornland, river & wooded crest
Down to the eastern foreshore, down to the western foam,
Like a band of thin grey iron, girding Northumbria's breast
Ripples the legions' pathway, the Rampart of Rome.

Only a ribbon of stonework high as a tall man's chest
Only a couple of ditches and a path where the shy sheep pass
Where the conies bask in the sunshine & the wheatear weaves his nest
Splashed with green-grey lichens, fringed with the waving grass.

Here in the dusk of winter rolled once the tide of war
Rolled with the whisper of arrows & the rattle of shield on targe,
Rolled with the Pictish slogan & the Legion's surge-loud roar
And the grim hill-side was shaken by the swell of the Roman charge.

Here on the stone ran reeking the blood of the black bull slain,
Here on the deep-worn pavement did the warwise veteran kneel,
Offering his prayer to Mithras, sunk on the dim red main,
While the silent wall re-echoed to the dint of the sentry's heel.

Vested in pride of purple, harnessed in steel & gold
Lonely, supreme, unbending, the great Proconsul strode,
Before him the hostile moorlands, swelling in fold on fold,
Behind him the Roman legion, building the Roman road.

With hearts deep-sick with longing for the sights & sounds of home
Where in Italy's mellow sunlight the boats on the Tiber ride,
Here the men of the Twentieth roystered & fought & died
And their ashes unsung, unhonoured have fattened our English loam.
But the long grey ripple of stonework thwarting the bare hillside
Is the grandest epitaph graven for the warrior sons of Rome.

The next poem, undated, is clearly inspired by the same scenes and it offers his take on Kipling's 'A Song to Mithras' from *Puck of Pook's Hill*, using the same metre and rhythm but making the thought his own. He called it 'The Roman's Prayer':

Mithras, the sunny Arno, my home, is far away;
I am weary & worn, O Mithras, with the burden of the day,
And I must watch the wall tonight amid the winter snow
And be the Empire's warder against the Empire's foe.
Make me a worthy Roman, true to my Roman name
That through no fault of mine tonight I bring my legion shame.
Give me the verve & power that come of the battle won
Give me the strength of spirit that comes of the hard thing done.

He would have known sections of the wall very well. At school, the Rev Budworth took senior boys walking there at times; Hodgson himself appears in photos in the headmaster's album taken on an outing in 1910. With the importance given to Roman history and language in the boys' education, the Roman footprint in the landscape around them was a godsend for their teachers, providing a tangible link with an otherwise remote past. Hodgson was fascinated by it all and he was not the only one. In Nowell Oxland's poem 'Ilicet' he is out on the Maiden Way at night, trying to conjure up visions of the past. He falls asleep, without realising, and sees a ghostly legion marching towards him. Noticing their troubled faces, he wonders out loud if they have the same feelings they did in life: *'Small hope had I to win reply/ But a pale centurion spoke/ "We war with shame for the Roman name/ Though our hearts be well-nigh broke".'*[15]

These lines are so close to Noel Hodgson's that the two of them might have been together when the poems were written. They might have been together. In fact, they probably were. The Maiden Way is the old Roman road running south across the fells from Hadrian's Wall to Kirkby Thore, to the east of Penrith, and it passes not far from the Oxland's home in Alston. It was a landscape he had been exploring from boyhood, and by 1912 he and Hodgson were certainly sharing their climbing expeditions. When next we find Noel Hodgson he was in Cumberland. The poem which follows 'The Roman's Prayer' in his notebook,

'From my room on Thirlmere', describes moonrise over the lake, and the distant, brooding presence of Helvellyn.

There are many parallels between the poems Hodgson and Oxland wrote. Both had a talent for comic verse. Oxland liked parody. He sometimes slipped verses of his own into the poet's work in his Lovelace Club papers; in his collection of poems there is a description of the food in a Putney boarding house (he spent part of his enforced gap year in Putney) written in the style of Swinburne. *'Cold mutton that claims without reason/ Mint sauce, and the title of "lamb",'* and so on. Hodgson borrowed the format of Harry Graham's *Ruthless Rhymes* to pen a few of his own:

> *I was whacking a full-pitch*
> *'Twould have been a six with ease*
> *When there came a sudden hitch*
> *Short-leg died of heart disease,*
> *And the horrid shock I got*
> *Absolutely spoilt my shot.*

> *Smith is absolutely broke,*
> *I hear his bank went smash last night,*
> *Some people treat it as a joke*
> *I fail to see it in that light*
> *I lent him ninepence yesterday*
> *And now I doubt if he will pay.*

Summer Olympics were held in 1912, and enthusiasm for all things sporting swept Britain. In his most successful – and cheeky – piece of comic verse, 'The Olympic Ideal in Durham College', Hodgson imagines the Dean and Chapter of Durham Cathedral, august gentlemen all, casting off their cassocks to hold games of their own:

> *When Canon Bedford May essayed to whisk us*
> *Back to the spacious days of mythic Greece,*
> *When people threw their javelin or their discus*
> *And otherwise endangered public peace,*
> *We all approved the folly:*
> *'A quaint conceit' we cried 'so classical & jolly.'*

> *And now we fairly revel in the moil,*
> *– The ancient Greeks themselves could not be keener,*
> *Bathe before brekker, and anoint with oil,*
> *And take a morning spin in the arena.*

> *E'en Handley bares his thews*
> *And round the college flash the twinkling feet of Hughes.*
>
> *See Cruikshanks there, how daintily he trips,*
> *His well-crooked limbs arrayed in shorts & zephyr*
> *And Watkins too, how busily he skips*
> *As light and playful as a festive heifer;*
> *And lo the nimble shins*
> *Of Culley, running hundreds for his sins.*
>
> *Now Dolphin gambols up & down the stakes*
> *And Knowling dons the Cestus (alias 'gloves')*
> *While Cooper strains his voice until it breaks*
> *Singing the tale of Nixon & his loves.*
> *The Dean whips off his hose*
> *And prances round the cloisters on his toes.*

He was enjoying himself in Oxford now, but the university, the city and the surrounding countryside never touched his poems. Still he wrote about Durham. Not so Oxland. Oxford and the landscape round about did inspire him. He wrote about students working in the Radcliffe Camera, one girl in particular, *'Pale, with a name and college/ I'd like to know, (but how?)/ She sits absorbing knowledge/ With calm, contracted brow.'*[16] But on one subject the two spoke as one: *'Give us the North – and keep your level shires –/ The high, wet North, lit by a gleam of spring.'* It would be hard to tell which of them wrote those lines.[17]

   With autumn came a return to Oxford and their separate colleges, to prepare for Classical Moderations, the first test of their academic careers. The exams would be held in the spring. It may not have been 'done' for an undergraduate to display how much he worked, but the absence of poems in Hodgson's notebook suggests that he was working hard. *'He had an extraordinarily cool mind, his tutor told me,'* George Bell remembered:

> *'He would not say very much in a private hour, but he would take in whatever was heard and ponder it, literally weigh it in his mind; then, after turning it over, he would make it his own and produce not the same matter, but the matter worked over and even illuminated by a thoroughly fresh and independent mind. There was a clearness, a sense of logic and consistency and grasp, and a marshalling of his facts, which promised great things.'*[18]

Bell never taught Hodgson, but another of the Students, John Murray, did, and he painted a similar picture in a letter to Henry:

'None of my pupils have given me such an impression of spaciousness and coolness of mind, and of perfect control and poise, along with such vivid fresh power under his control. There he would sit – the quietest of a roomful taking in men and things, the brown eyes searching and roaming – scarcely felt by some there and well known to very few. Unless one knew him, one would not know him at all.'[19]

His reward was a first class in Moderations, awarded in April 1913. The published list which appeared in *The Times* on 8 April showed his friend John Nind Smith with a second; 'Tolkien, J.R.R.' of Exeter College is in the same group. Oxland's name is further down, with a third. It was a poor result for him: the Rev Lys, writing a memorial notice later for the *Oxford Magazine*, commented *'His place in the moderations list did not give the measure of his abilities, which were considerable.'* Perhaps the fact that he had not focused on Greek at school told against him – that, or his commitment to various rugby clubs. In any case, following this result he changed course to read history. For them all, the first hurdle was over and a new stage begun, leading to Finals and the future.

Chapter 6

'Time Stands Waiting'
April 1913 – August 1914

The months stretched ahead unpressured and inviting, with Final Honour Schools not due to take place until the summer of 1915. A few days after Easter someone was staying with the Hodgsons at the vicarage; someone Noel trusted enough to give them his notebook to read. His poetry was not shared with everyone. George Bell, for example, had no idea that he wrote at all. *'A great many men have their secrets at Oxford, and this was Hodgson's. . . I remember feeling a little surprised when I first heard that Hodgson wrote poetry.'*[1] The guest sat up through the night reading the book, then responded in kind, with a poem in a minute copper-plate script on the vicarage headed notepaper:

> **The Vicarage, Berwick on Tweed**
> **4. IV. 13**
>
> *I have read in your book of verses*
> *As the night treads on her way,*
> *Till my light is burning dim*
> *And far on the distant rim*
> *Gleams faintly the hand of Day.*
>
> *I have read in your book of verses,*
> *But my pen can scarce write clear*
> *The thoughts which they cause to stir in my heart,*
> *Or the memories they bring near.*
>
> *Some sing of the days that have passed away*
> *And some of the days to come,*
> *Till they mingle the sob of the wailing pipes*
> *With the cheer of the rolling drum;*
> *And some sing of the present*
> *– of all these sound most far*
> *For the future is what we choose to think,*
> *And the past is a cup we need no more drink,*

> *But at present we stand on a dizzy brink*
> *And at once must make or mar:-*
> *Yet through all shines unceasingly*
> *The light of a single star.*

The poem is signed 'N.N', which points to one person. 'Nestor Neleides' was Noel Hodgson's nickname for Robert Parr, who had left Durham in the summer of 1912 for Magdalen, joining the Oxford circle of Durham boys. Nestor, the elderly King of Pylos in Homer's *Iliad*, is talkative and noted for giving advice. This was an extraordinarily prescient nickname for Robert Parr, but the unfolding of that lay decades in the future. If Noel was looking for advice when he handed over the notebook, it was because he had plans. He was not content to go on dabbling with poetry and prose for fun. He was serious about writing and he wanted publication.

The notebook shows a steady progress in the way he wrote. It became less orderly as the years passed and he abandoned the index. Sometimes with the later poems he made alterations or added a verse in the margin, and after June 1913 he no longer dated work except to add a date of publication. By 1912 he had moved away from the Latin and Greek verse translations which amused him at first. He wrote more of his own in English, occasionally using work by established writers as his model – Kipling, for example, in 'The Roman's Prayer' and a later, longer poem which takes its metre and inspiration from 'The Glory of the Garden'. Oscar Wilde was another poet he looked to, and G.K. Chesterton, using their poems as an art student might use a classic painting, to learn their techniques as he developed his own. He tended to use 'poetic' diction, with deliberately archaic words and sentence structure, but in him this was not a sign that he lacked originality. He just loved playing with language. He used a kind of linguistic mock-Tudor in everyday speech too, when he was not being serious. In the family it lived on long after his death: *'as Bill would say, "these be but toys"'*. [2]

His first success in the quest for publication seems to have been with a poem written that same month, April 1913. 'The Hills' appeared in *The Spectator*, his father's favourite magazine, on 23 August – how proud Henry would have been. 'The Hills' was published under Noel's own name, though it seems to have been around this time that he started to use the pen name Edward Melbourne. A typescript survives of a short story that was clearly prepared for submission to a publisher. *Out of the Sea*, by Edward Melbourne, (c/o W. Noel Hodgson, The Vicarage, Berwick on Tweed, 2,000 words), is undated, but cannot be later than January 1914 because it uses the vicarage address. In style and content it is not much earlier: 1913 seems likely.

Out of the Sea belongs to his life in Berwick, to the coast and the east winds, and the exposed bleakness of the town in winter. The story opens with its narrator standing with a friend, the coastguard, on a breakwater looking out to sea. *'It was a November evening, with an East wind blowing chilly from the sea and rising and falling in an unhappy moan.'* The coastguard begins to talk about the sea as a malign force; *'"It is wicked," he said, almost angrily. "I'm not fooling. Live by it and on it as long as I have and you'll know it is. Why, it makes men wicked to live on it; how many stories are there of murder and lust among seamen, horrors of cannibalism and things worse – " he broke off suddenly'.* He is thinking of something in his past but refuses to say what, and they part. Three nights later the narrator calls on him and finds him on edge; he has been ordered out to look for poachers at sea and there is no one available to go with him; the narrator offers himself.

They set out in a pinnace, rowing until they reach a place where the coastguard says they must anchor. While they wait the wind rises, and the coastguard becomes increasingly withdrawn and irrational, muttering about the evil of the sea and the wandering souls of dead men. *'The darkness was round us like the walls of a room, and never in my life have I felt so completely alone or so completely helpless. All thought of the object of our voyage had vanished and the horror of my position filled my brain. By degrees the ground-swell was getting heavier, and the wind stronger, so that the eerie sighing was continually about us.'*

The tension builds to a climax in which the pinnace lurches and something begins to climb aboard. It fills the narrator with revulsion and terror, but the coastguard, suddenly himself again, says, *'I'm coming',* and dives into the sea; *'The poachers picked me up, half senseless with fright. Tracy was never seen again.'* But as to whether Noel submitted the story, no clue remains.

Trinity, the Oxford summer term, passed peacefully. Noel was in different rooms, on Tom Quad, room 4, staircase 2, diagonally opposite the Deanery. He also acquired a new tutor in Gilbert Murray, Regius Professor of Greek, a liberal humanist and one of the foremost classical scholars of the day. He had time to write poetry too, mostly about his beloved hills but with the occasional stab of pained introspection – like this, tucked at the bottom of a page in June 1913, the last piece to have a date of writing:

> *Honour was cast behind you,*
> *Manhood forgotten – Why?*
> *I saw a cheek that dimpled*
> *And a winking eye.*

The Oxford letter to the school magazine summed up the early summer:

'This term has been very uneventful as far as O.D.s have been immediately concerned. We believe that some of our number were sent back to their Colleges by the Proctors during the recent train strike, but

none of them figured in the Vice-Chancellor's Court for questioning the paternal jurisdiction of the City Police. . . . We had an excellent camp this Summer at Mytchett in the Aldershot Command. We did a lot of hard work and gained a decisive victory over the Cambridge O.T.C. on the only occasion when we were opposed to them.'

After the OTC camp came the vacation, the last untroubled summer of the pre-war world. July found Noel fell walking in Cumberland with Nowell Oxland and James Tombs. A postcard to his mother, sent on the morning of 12 July, tells her they have climbed Helvellyn and arrived safely at Coniston the previous night, and are about to set out over the Old Man of Coniston. After this, he used the backs of several other postcards to scribble a rough holiday diary. First, on 'Ascent and summit of Scawfell Pikes':

'Monday July 14 1913. This peak – known familiarly as Scaw-piece – we ascended from Rossthwaite. The ascent was enlivened by the sight of two men bathing in Sty-head Tarn, and by a narrow escape of J.D.T. who politely stepping aside for a descending lady omitted to remark a neighbouring precipice. Our comment was that his escape relieved us of the necessity of carrying his body down. This cynicism was ill received.'

They continued to the summit where they found an elderly woman and four men in cycling costume sitting on the cairn, drinking tea from Thermos flasks. Nowell Oxland didn't approve of this: *'N.O. much exercised, especially at their posing for a photo.'* But the view was fine – clear to Snowdon and the Isle of Man – and they watched a waterplane flying over Lake Windermere.

Moving on to another card, 'Scawfell and Mickledore', he described their descent *'by Tongue Ghyll to Wastdale Head & not continuing over the Mickledore to Scawfell itself. The journey employed in a discussion of Rawnsley's epitaph on the victims of the Scawfell disaster.'* This was a fatal accident that happened ten years earlier, when a roped party of four young climbers fell to their deaths attempting a new route up Scafell Pinnacle. The disaster, the first of its kind in Britain, had been widely reported, so it was natural that they would remember it when passing close to the site. As for Rawnsley, Canon Hardwicke Rawnsley's name would have been hard to miss when travelling in Cumberland. A founder member of the National Trust and an Honorary Canon of Carlisle Cathedral (with Noel's uncle William, Rector of Distington), Rawnsley was a towering presence in the life of the Lake District. He appears in Noel's wartime letters too, and plays a part in the unravelling of Nowell Oxland's story.

The three friends had tea in the hotel at Wasdale Head, where talk of death and epitaphs gave way to amazement – and amusement – at the amount of liquid James Tombs was able to put away. The others calculated that by 6pm he had drunk two pints of water and one of shandy, seven cups of tea and some whisky. By then they were in the hills again, taking advantage of the remaining hours of daylight to climb the Black Sail Pass, heading for Buttermere. While in Wasdale Head they saw the tiny church where three victims of the 1903 accident were buried, the verse engraved on their headstone enshrining the sudden immensity of death:

> *'ONE MOMENT STOOD THEY AS THE ANGELS STAND*
> *HIGH IN THE STAINLESS EMINENCE OF AIR*
> *THE NEXT, THEY WERE NOT, TO THEIR FATHERLAND*
> *TRANSLATED UNAWARE.'* [3]

No one watching the three young men climbing back into the hills that summer evening, talking, laughing, would have guessed that in just three years they too would be dead, snatched from life as suddenly as the three climbers buried nearby. Noel Hodgson had been climbing in the fells before and he would again, but this holiday in 1913 was very special to him. It was on his mind in the last few months of his life, the memory sharpened by his awareness that his two friends had already fallen victim to the war.

But in 1913 the three climbed Black Sail in peace and *'into the head of Ennerdale & then over Scarfe Gap into the Buttermere Valley. In the top of the pass three buzzards were seen fighting for possession of a rock-pigeon. Along the road to Buttermere we tramped at a good few miles an hour to the tune of an amoebic rendering of Lewis Carroll's celebrated verses 'An old man sitting on a gate', 'Jabberwocky etc.'*

They took rooms at the Buttermere Hotel, had supper, and *'J.D.T. continued the liquid process with 2 pints of shandy.'* Then they went out again, in search of the Scale Force waterfall, *'but in the darkness got astray in the mist and haar of the low land between the two lakes, and failed to discover anything. Three servants passed us and caused us great fear, for we thought them to be ghosts of Mary of Buttermere & two friends. When they had passed us we remembered that we wanted to be...'* and there the diary ends. After the long day they had had and all that climbing, it would seem reasonable to guess that they wanted to be in bed: in fact, they sat by the lake talking until late into the night. The next day they parted company.

But the vacation was not over. Noel's postcard album places him on the Norfolk Broads in September. *'Two wet days, but plenty of wind,'* he tells his mother on Wednesday, 3 September, from Potter Heigham; *'today fine again, but cold, wind still holding. I am a mosquito-bite entirely and swollen to a preposterous size. . . Much love Bill. . . Don't tear this up or send it to Uncle Pelham or anything.'* The next day a card to his father from Acle: *'thanks for copies of pome. Just run onto a hidden snag and put in for repairs. On to Yarmouth to-night, windy and sunny, very jolly.'* Given the date, the 'pome' was probably the published version of 'The Hills'. The following Monday he was at Oulton Broad, *'don't expect until you see me,'* and by Thursday had returned to Wroxham, his starting point; *'Salaams to Hal if he has come. Thanks for parcel.'* He was with someone but does not say who. The album contains a number of other postcards of the Broads and the churches in the area, but no more writing.

The time had come to return to Oxford and a new academic year. To Greats and rugby: he was made captain of the Christ Church team in the autumn of 1913, as Nowell Oxland was at Worcester. Robert Parr was playing rugby for his college too, and was a keen member of the OUDS, the University Dramatic Society. *'Parr has been playing in the O.U.D.S. The other O.D.s have been working.'*[4] But Noel had made good use of the summer. In between Cumberland and the Broads, his notebook suggests he had also been climbing nearer home, in the Cheviots, which straddle the border between Scotland and England a few miles south of Berwick. 'On Cheviot' was written that summer and later published in the *Oxford Magazine*:

> *I know a stream that tumbles down*
> *Among the purple heather,*
> *With waters of a russet brown*
> *Like an ancient friars gown,*
> *To a little hidden spot*
> *Sheltered from hard weather,*
> *Where the vagrant winds come not*
> *But the lazy sun lies hot.*
>
> *And there I make my pilgrimage*
> *When the summer days are born,*
> *To sleep upon the yielding lawn*
> *That lies along the waterside;*
> *And turn the unreflecting page*
> *And gaze upon the prospect wide*
> *That old Northumbria like a scroll*
> *Of hill and valley doth outroll.*
>
> *The air is fresh and dry as wine*
> *And from the distant glen below*
> *Steals up the perfume of the pine*
> *Sweet as the thoughts of long ago.*
> *There I bid farewell to sorrow,*
> *Care is spirited away*
> *Past the thresholds of the day;*
> *For today at least is mine*
> *And the sun sinks before tomorrow.*

The remaining poems in the notebook all seem to date from the summer of 1913, perhaps running into autumn. Most celebrate the hills and sky, sunset, dawn and wind. A handful speak of something more personal. There are contrasting views of love: from *'What are the ways of women,/What is the lure of love,/ To the open road before me/ and the open sky above?'* to *'For threescore years or more/ My life is meted me/ Yet I would freely give all for/ One day with thee'* in the next poem. Then 'Regret', one of the few notebook pieces Henry would later choose for a posthumous edition of his son's work:

> *Mine – & I would not take it;*
> *Waiting – I passed it by;*
> *The blossom has withered & fallen*
> *And I but wait to die.*
>
> *Only a word was needed;*
> *Pride left the word unsaid;*
> *Life lay there for the lifting,*
> *Pride turned away his head.*
>
> *Mine – & I would not take it,*
> *Waiting – I passed it by.*
> *The night is near and in secret*
> *We're lonely, my Pride & I.*

But the poem that best sums up his summer is probably the last in the notebook, 'Wander-lust':

> *I've followed the road for good and ill*
> *While hurrying years went by*
> *I have wandered & wondered & sought & seen,*
> *And all that my heart has learnt has been*
> *That ever the road runs over the hill*
> *And under the edge of the sky.*
>
> *I love to see the world's fair*
> *The side shows by the way*
> *And ever as I travel*
> *The breezes laugh and say –*
> *"Come with me, oh come with me*
> *The road is winding still!*
> *There's more to see, the world to see*
> *Over the hill!"*[5]

On 3 January 1914 Noel Hodgson turned twenty-one. An adult. And though he would not have known it yet, his family was poised for a decisive break from the familiar world of his childhood. The previous August an Act had been passed in Parliament enabling the creation of three new bishoprics in the Church of England: Sheffield, Chelmsford, St Edmundsbury and Ipswich. Various well-known clergymen were tipped as likely candidates but no one thought of the modest incumbent of the most northerly parish in England. No one, that is, except the people choosing the new bishops. *'Darling child, Are you astonished? Are you pleased?'* This was Penelope, writing to Stella on 5 February. Since her marriage Stella had been living in Worcester, where Bernard Tower had a teaching post in the King's School and was a minor canon in the Cathedral. By the time the letter arrived the news was in all the papers: Henry was the new Bishop of St Edmundsbury and Ipswich.

The offer had been made to him in January, but deciding came hard. He was happy among his working men, in the town that had been his life for over sixteen years. He also had to contend with the memory of his father, who turned his back on 'better' appointments to stay where he thought he was needed. *'The dear A.D.* [short for Archdeacon, the family's nickname for Henry] *has had an awful time making up his mind, but it seemed really the right thing to do, he was not allowed to tell anyone but the few friends he consulted.'* And once his decision was made the pace of change became overwhelming: *'It has been a dreadful shock to him on reaching home just now to find a telegram from the archbishop today, the consecration must be on the 24th. It is cruel, the people here will hardly realise he is going before he is gone. . . . dear Dad, you will think of him much won't you, you know how hard things will be for him leaving & all the anxiety of the new place.'* The Hodgsons had only a few weeks to organise the move, and there was no certainty that the new house in Ipswich would even be ready for them.

But though she was sorry to leave friends and appalled by the speed of it, Penelope was not as torn by the move as her husband. In fact, she and Stella had attempted some gentle string-pulling behind the scenes, through Dr Edgar Jacob, Bishop of St Albans. He was closely involved with the creation of the new sees and in 1897, as Bishop of Newcastle, he had been responsible for Henry's appointment in Berwick. *'Don't mention to the A.D. that you ever wrote to St Albans,'* Penelope added as an afterthought, *'though it is not certain he ever had anything to do with, he says he mentioned Dad's name to P.M. as one who would make a good Bishop but that is all.'*[6]

The consecration took place in St Paul's Cathedral on Shrove Tuesday, 24 February, in a three-hour service attended by official representatives of the towns concerned and, it was said, of every parish in England; by countless clergy and by friends and relatives of the new bishops. The Hodgsons too, except Arthur, who was still in Canada, and Hal, Assistant Commissioner in

Sierra Leone since 1911. Afterwards, in the interval between the consecration and the enthronement, Henry and Penelope went back to Berwick to say a proper goodbye and wind up their affairs in the town. They were greeted with a remarkable demonstration of affection:

> *'Great enthusiasm was shown last night when Bishop Hodgson returned to Berwick for a ten days' stay prior to taking up his duties in his newly created diocese. . . . The railway station was crowded when the 9.20 train arrived last night and the Bishop was given the heartiest of welcomes.*
>
> *'The horse was taken from the carriage which was waiting to convey the Bishop and Mrs Hodgson to the Vicarage, and the carriage was pulled down the street by the cheering crowd. At the Vicarage the Bishop addressed the people from the steps, thanking them for their hearty and unexpected welcome.'*[7]

The days that followed were full of meetings and presentations. Henry preached twice in the church on Sunday to packed congregations, but the parish's gifts to him and Penelope were not ready. They were presented at a reception at the end of April. In one of her rare speeches, Penelope teased Berwick with the unspoken truth, much to everyone's amusement:

> *'I do not say we have loved you all the time or the town either. . . . It was rather a habit of the Bishop's and mine, when people annoyed us and said unpleasant things about us, to say to each other before we leave Berwick we will say what we think and speak our minds. (Laughter.) That was always a great comfort to us. (Laughter.) The day has come before we go and we do not want to say anything unpleasant, in fact our feelings are those of great sorrow for going, in fact, we love you all.'*[8]

So the move was made, and when Noel went home for the Easter vacation in April 1914, home was 'Parklands' in Ipswich, the Bishop's house. A photograph of the family taken that Easter, or perhaps in the summer, shows Henry holding Rory, the family dog, on his lap, Penelope turning away from the camera towards him, Noel standing to one side, hands in pockets and Stella and Bernard Tower behind. Henry made Bernard Tower his chaplain during the year and the younger couple moved to Ipswich too.

Noel spent part of April walking in the Malvern hills. He was still actively pursuing publication for his work, and it seemed not to matter to him who published so long as someone did. In December 1913 he had a poem accepted by *The Nation*. His friend John Nind Smith said he was indifferent to politics and this confirms it, for while *The Spectator* was a Conservative magazine, *The Nation* had a strong Labour bias. In the notebook the *Nation* poem has no title:

The golden hour of noon begins,
The sun unchallenged holds the sky
And like a living sapphire spins
The arrow of the dragon-fly.

The song and chatter of the brook
The fairy organ of the bee –
Pan could not find a fairer nook
In all the glades of Arcady.

Where are the gods of tree & stream,
The Hamadryads, milky-hued,
The elusive Naiads, like a dream
Who fled, and eager gods pursued?

Here where the roses intertwine
The Zephyr learned Aurora's wiles,
And echoes of the parle divine
Went floating down the forest aisles.

The winds still wander in the trees
The poplar sways his graceful head;
No laughter rings along the breeze –
The merry gods of Greece are dead.

He had taken to showing poems to John Murray at Christ Church for possible inclusion in the *Oxford Magazine*, which Murray edited. *'Dear Bishop,'* (this was Murray writing to Henry in 1919), *'I came upon the enclosed some days since in my rooms in Christ Church and I am sending them to you as I think you would wish to have them. I expect your son showed them to me with a view to printing them as I sometimes did his pieces in the Oxford Magazine. . . But I cannot remember that I did print them.'* He gives no clue to what they were. After the notebook ends in 1913, the surviving manuscripts of Noel's work are few and random. There must once have been a later fair copy book or collection of loose manuscripts, but no trace of it remains and it becomes harder to say what was written and when. It is clear, though, that some time in 1914, June at the latest, Noel Hodgson made the most important literary and publishing contact of his life.

On Thursday, 11 June 1914, his poem 'Labuntur Anni' appeared in the weekly paper, *The New Witness* under the pen-name Edward Melbourne. 'Labuntur Anni' [The years glide by] is a quotation from Horace. Horace's poem laments the swift passage of time and the inevitability of old age and death.

Hodgson's celebrates, and with a light touch waves goodbye to, the imaginative freedom of childhood:[10]

> *O land of youth! Where over dale and hill*
> *Adventure's silver trumpet call was borne*
> *By every breeze that heralded the dawn –*
> *Thy vagrant breezes are forever still,*
> *And stilled the silver summons of thy horn.*

The New Witness was a campaigning newspaper started in 1911 by Hilaire Belloc and Cecil Chesterton (younger brother of G.K. Chesterton) as *Eye Witness*. The following year Cecil Chesterton took it over and renamed it. The paper aimed to expose corruption in political parties and promote the freedom of the individual, and it boasted some of the leading writers of the day among its contributors – George Bernard Shaw, H.G. Wells, Arthur Ransome, Edith Nesbit. Sometimes Cecil Chesterton's eagerness to expose corruption led to trouble. In 1913 he was prosecuted for libel: prosecuted, found guilty, but given only a nominal fine. *The New Witness* survived. How Noel Hodgson found his way to it is a mystery, but 'Labuntur Anni' was the beginning of a long association. Soon he was a regular contributor, and *The New Witness* was not simply taking what he offered, it was actively encouraging him to write more, through a contact named Miss Hedley.

Meanwhile the summer term went its leisurely way. On 15 May Robert Parr turned twenty. Hodgson gave him a newly-published anthology of recent poems, *A Cluster of Grapes*. It included work by G.K. Chesterton, Frances Cornford, John Galsworthy, Thomas Hardy, Alice Meynell and others, and he inscribed it to 'Nestor Neleides' (teller of tales)'.

It was an exceptional summer. The weather was fine and the Durham boys played tennis, *'though only Oxland was accredited skilful enough to play for his college, Hodgson and Caeser assisted their colleges at cricket, and all were frequently seen on the river, but not rowing.'*[11] For those who were there, Oxford seemed to have a special aura:

> *'They called it "the Golden Summer" afterwards, that last summer before our world came to an end. Were the king-cups really more golden in the water meadows that year; the lilacs and the laburnum and the may more brilliant? Was it through a rarer air that the young men walked in the evenings coming up from the river with the sun in their eyes?'*[12]

With the term's end in early June, OTC members left directly for camp and the sun still shone.

'It is very difficult to discover what the O.D.s have been doing lately. At present they are in camp, where they are usually too sleepy or sunstruck to remember doing anything as far back as yesterday even. You may be quite sure they have done their full share of some amazingly hard work, and equally hard grumbling in the last fortnight.'[13]

The Prince of Wales was at camp with them for a week. Harold Rayner from Corpus Christi was there; so was another future 9th Devon, Alan Hinshelwood of Hertford College. He had a series of photographs of himself and his friends fooling about for the camera in a bizarre mixture of clothes: striped blazers and white shorts, sunhats, caps, uniform breeches and puttees, drinking, laughing, singing; around them the rows of white bell tents and piles of equipment that would become familiar in the months to come. Noel would have done his share of messing about with friends too; otherwise he seemed in a reflective mood. It comes out in his poem 'Glimpse – O.T.C. Camp, June 1914':

> *I saw you fooling often in the tents*
> *With fair dishevelled hair and laughing lips,*
> *As who had never known the taste of tears*
> *Or the world's sorrow. Then on march one night,*
> *Halted beneath the stars I heard the sound*
> *Of talk and laughter, and glanced back to see*
> *It you were there. But you stood far apart*
> *And silent, bowed upon your rifle butt,*
> *And gazed into the night as one who sees.*
> *I marked the drooping lips and fathomless eyes*
> *And knew you brooded on immortal things.'*

News of the Sarajevo assassinations broke as the camp neared its end, but it would have seemed very remote. In July Noel was climbing again, this time around Aviemore in the Cairngorms. The postcard album is his witness, with cards of Loch Avon and Loch Eunach, the precipices of the Garrachorry and the Falls of Dee, Loch an Eilein, the Lurcher's Crag and the pass to Braemar, the mountain Ben Macdhui. He is unlikely to have been alone, but there is nothing to say who was with him. His poem 'Visions' appeared in *The New Witness* on 9 July, born of the long summer nights in the hills:

> *When in the blue dusk of a summer night*
> *I watch God's largesse of His silver stars*
> *Sometimes, it seems, the adamantine bars*
> *Fall from the tall gates of the Infinite;*
> *And Time stands waiting. Then I seem to hear,*

> *As one that listens from a lonely height*
> *To waters breaking on an unknown sea,*
> *The strong pulse of the world-heart throbbing near;*
> *The mists roll back, and for a space stand clear*
> *The great white windows of eternity.*

The distant sounds from Central Europe were more uncomfortable. From unqualified sympathy for the Emperor of Austria over the loss of his heir, comment in the national press was turning towards hope that his government, which saw the hand of Serbia in the assassinations, would be moderate in its response. In the next issue of *The New Witness*, on 16 July, Cecil Chesterton's editorial, 'The Call to Arms' mentioned the crisis and uncertainty about how it would develop before going on to discuss – in purely hypothetical terms – a nation's willingness to fight as the ultimate test, the proof that its people still valued justice above their own comfort. As yet there was no general feeling that the Serbian crisis might escalate beyond a local conflict. Chesterton was pre-empting it and his was just one voice, at a time when others were vehemently opposed to the idea of war. And as war in Europe looked increasingly likely, many were against British involvement. For others the crisis was all very far away, and would surely blow over as other crises had done.

By late July, around the time the armies started moving, Noel Hodgson was heading south from Scotland and he paused somewhere where the imprint of Rome was still visible on the ground – probably around Hadrian's Wall. He was aware of what was happening in the Balkans and, surrounded by the open landscapes he loved so much, his mind turned over the meaning of war and its ultimate ending. With the clarity of vision so often remarked on – the perspective from the mountain tops that was woven into his being – he thought of Virgil's *Aeneid* and the lines spoken by Panthus, priest of Apollo, on the fall of Troy, *'The final day and the hour which we cannot avoid has come upon our Trojan land. We Trojans are no more: Troy is no more.'*[14] He cannot have known how appropriate these lines were to the weeks leading up to the Great War: with a century of hindsight, they leap from the page. For him, they were no more than an anxious foreshadowing. He took the idea and the landscape round him, his own feelings on the crisis, and shaped them into a poem he called 'Roma Fuit' [Rome is no more]. It appeared in *The New Witness* on 6 August, two days after Britain's entry into the war:

> *The mellow sunshine lies upon the grass,*
> *And peace and restfulness so deeply brood,*
> *That you might think this place had been asleep*
> *Through all the years; the slowly moving sheep*

Set up a gentle cropping as they pass,
Drowsily woven with the solitude.

Yet here of old men's restless spirit stirred
The deeps of war; the crash of shield on targe
Filled all the hills, and drowning all was heard
The swelling thunder of a Roman charge.
And now the play is ended, and they lie
Where sheep are feeding and the curlews cry.

The hero lies no softer than the craven –
Roman and Pict, they share the common bed;
Like men they battled over life's high seas,
And now laid sleeping in the windless haven,
Sheltered from sound of storm, they take their ease,
And share the great alliance of the dead.

The great alliance of the dead. That was where he thought it would end. Whatever happened in the immediate future, a day would come when none of it mattered. Old enemies would lie together, the earth would cover them, and life move on. For the summer of 1914 it was a remarkable poem.

His next port of call seems to have been St Aidan's Vicarage at New Herrington, to the north-east of Durham, where Robert Parr's father was vicar. Parr's younger sister Dorothy remembered him staying with her family around that time, and conversations that were all about the crisis. As an OTC member, she said, Noel knew that he would be called up if Britain entered the war. She believed he had left by Sunday, 2 August, the day the Germans invaded Luxembourg and demanded free passage across Belgium; passage which the King of the Belgians refused, seeing it as a violation of his country's neutrality. Dorothy Parr recalled sitting with her brother in the garden that day, and his frustration that the war was coming so close and Britain's position was still uncertain.

This was a frustration many shared, leading on the one hand to demonstrations against the war and demands for neutrality, on the other to a growing fear that the government would stand by and do nothing. But behind the scenes, things were moving. That same day, 2 August, the adjutant of the Oxford OTC received instructions to contact past and present members of the corps immediately, asking if they would be willing to apply for a commission in the event of war. If yes, they were to report to Oxford for interview. No one had made arrangements to deal with an influx of volunteers. Being vacation and a Bank Holiday, the adjutant turned to Dean Strong of Christ Church, then Vice Chancellor of the University, for advice. Strong formed an ad hoc interviewing board with himself as president, to interview OTC members. Before war had even been declared the volunteers began to arrive in Oxford. At 11pm – midnight by German time – on 4 August, Britain's ultimatum to Germany to withdraw its troops from Belgium had expired, and Britain and Germany were officially at war.

Noel had probably gone home to Ipswich from New Herrington and received the OTC letter there. By Sunday, 9 August, he was in Oxford: he had a medical that day and was passed fit: the fact and date were noted on the application form he filled in when he was interviewed by Dean Strong on the Monday. He gave his OTC rank as 'Lance Sergeant', but there was some confusion on the question of *'Regiment or Corps for which recommended'*. First someone wrote 'Northumberland Fusiliers'. That was afterwards crossed out in favour of 'Devonshire Regiment, 6th Battalion', in Noel's own writing, but written with a different pen from the one he used to fill in the form. Dean Strong attested to his moral character and suitability, signed and dated the application. And then – nothing. Nothing to do but wait for a letter from the War Office confirming his commission and posting him to a regiment. There was no saying how long that would take. Months, perhaps.

Waiting was hard. So was the uncertainty. The image of his generation skipping off to the recruiting offices with a naïve grin and a music hall song on their lips, sure it would all be over by Christmas, is so deeply ingrained that other possible reactions to the war are rarely considered. Noel Hodgson volunteered within the first week of the war. The OTC 'call up' was not binding in the way later conscription would be; he chose to go. But to see this as an example of the fabled lemming-like eagerness for war would be a complete misreading of him. His writing shows that he made the choice knowing what it would, and could, entail. If he was in a hurry, it was anxiety and not patriotic fervour speaking, to get on with the thing and get it over. And in this he was surely not alone.

It was the invasion of Belgium that tipped the balance. In the summer of 1914 few were privy to what went on behind the scenes in the seats of power in Vienna, Berlin, St Petersburg, Paris, or London; no one had access to them all. Ordinary people had to react to the rapidly developing crisis as they saw it. And what they saw, Noel Hodgson and countless others, was a small country being invaded by a far more powerful neighbour – a small country whose neutrality Britain (and Germany) were bound by treaty to defend. This made Britain's entry into the war a matter of honour. It changed minds. Once Belgians began to die it became increasingly hard to look on.

And beyond the desire to help them, there was a practical question. If Britain stood back and let Belgium fall, France too, was there not a real threat to Britain in the longer term, once Germany controlled the Channel ports? In the summer of 1914 few would have had the confidence to say that there was not. So

Belgium's interests and Britain's merged. The war had come too close to home. But however right, however necessary the thing may have seemed, that did not make it easy. *The New Witness* of 6 August, which carried Noel Hodgson's 'Roma Fuit', opened with Cecil Chesterton's editorial, 'Why we fight'. Chesterton mixed relief that the country's position had been decided with a profound apprehension:

> *'Stern as is the struggle ahead of us, dreadful as are the possibilities which defeat would involve, it is something to have done with the sickening fear that hung over us all last week – the fear that we were going to see England lose her honour.'*

This was the setting that produced Noel Hodgson's two poems of August 1914. 'The New Spirit', his response to the declaration of war and the end of the sickening uncertainty, was first published in *The Saturday Review*:

> *When England of the quiet heart*
> *Flung back the covenant of shame*
> *A dignity of high resolve*
> *Upon her councils came.*
>
> *Freedom's old flag for long laid by*
> *Unfurled its tattered folds once more:*
> *And rank on rank with steady eyes*
> *Her sons went out to war.*
>
> *Unbroken in these quiet fields*
> *A Sabbath calm dwells in the air;*
> *And men along the shady road*
> *Go quietly to prayer.*
>
> *Vial of wrath has burst the seal,*
> *Thrones fall and dominations cease.*
> *The silent face of England wears*
> *The dignity of peace.*

The second poem, 'England to Her Sons', may not have been published in his lifetime. It appeared in the posthumous edition of his work with the date August 1914 and was afterwards reprinted in regional newspapers. It dispels once and for all any idea that he was happy or excited about the war, or that he expected anything but profound sorrow to come of it. He casts England as a mother, watching the young men volunteer and accepting that they will go, praising their best qualities, and predicting what lies ahead: *'Loss and failure, pain and death'.*

All they have, she says, is belief that they are doing the right thing, and hope. All she asks is *'a little space to weep'* for them:

> *Sons of mine, I hear you thrilling*
> *To the trumpet call of war;*
> *Gird you then, I give you freely*
> *As I gave your sires before,*
> *All the noblest of the children I in love and anguish bore.*
>
> *Free in service, wise in justice,*
> *Fearing but dishonour's breath;*
> *Steeled to suffer uncomplaining*
> *Loss and failure, pain and death;*
> *Strong in faith that sees the issue and in hope that triumpheth.*
>
> *Go, and may the God of battles*
> *You in His good guidance keep:*
> *And if He in wisdom giveth*
> *Unto His beloved sleep,*
> *I accept it nothing asking, save a little space to weep.*

'England to her Sons' was born in the atmosphere of Oxford on those August days, with a steady flow of past and present students arriving to volunteer. The city was buzzing with nervous energy and Hodgson may not have stayed very long. With so much on his mind, there was only one place he wanted to be. The Lake District. *'How the Lakes delighted him,'* George Bell remembered, *'he felt for them as a lover or a child. I have heard him speak about them as a lover, not ecstatically, but with the controlled passion of one with whom they were things too deep for speech'.*[15] He needed them now; needed the space to think, the view from the mountain tops and the wind in his face, to enjoy what was left of the freedom he had just signed away. He might have waited a week at most; Nowell Oxland, not an OTC member, was interviewed in Oxford for a temporary commission in the regular army on 17 August. They probably went north together.

The fells were as they had always been; that was their strength. Hodgson visited Braithwaite and Bassenthwaite Lake, Bowfell and his favourite summit of all, Great Gable, then Scafell Pike and Styhead Tarn, Sprinkling Tarn; Saddleback, Scale Hill Hotel, Grisdale Tarn and the Honister Pass. It was as if he wanted to sum up a whole lifetime of visits in a few days. He probably did. On 22 August he began what he called his 'Farewell Walk', starting from Rosthwaite and climbing over the Styhead Pass to Wasdale Head, where he spent two nights in the Row Head Inn. He explored the Screes on the shore of

Wastwater; visited again the tiny church at Wasdale Head and climbed towards Scafell. He left the way he came, starting early and veering off at the top of the Styhead pass to climb to the summit of Great Gable. Then the descent.

On 26 August, Nowell Oxland's commission came through and with it his orders to join the 6th Battalion of the Border Regiment.

Hodgson seems to have been thrown by this. He had volunteered a week earlier than Oxland and had still heard nothing. Also, having had time to draw breath, he seems to have regretted the way he made his application. His friend had requested a commission in the Borders, the local regiment for Cumberland. The confusion on his own form suggests that he had not even considered a regiment before applying. Now he did, and knew what he wanted. On 9 September he had a second army medical at Carlisle Castle, the headquarters of the Border Regiment. The form, still in his War Office file, notes that the medical was part of an application to join the regular army. The only possible explanation is that he was making a second application – a last-ditch attempt to join Oxland in the Borders. He was too late. Before anything could come of it his first commission came through. On 16 September Second Lieutenant W.N. Hodgson joined the 9th (Service) Battalion, The Devonshire Regiment, at Aldershot.

Chapter 7

'The Work of Men', September 1914 – July 1915

The battalion was little more than a week old when Hodgson joined it. Britain had entered the war with a Regular army that was tiny in comparison with the forces it faced: 250,000 men, with enough Territorials and Reservists to swell the figure to almost three times the size, against around 3,800,000 on the German side. And though Britain was part of an alliance, the psychological and practical impact of these figures could not be ignored. Within the first few days the newly-appointed Secretary of State for War, Lord Kitchener, had secured Parliamentary approval for a massive increase in the size of the Regular army: 500,000 volunteers to serve for three years or the duration of the war, whichever was longer.

The 9th Devons were part of this 'New Army', distinguished by the word 'Service' in their name: the 9th (Service) Battalion, The Devonshire Regiment. The formation of the battalion was ordered on 7 September and four officers and six NCOs of the regiment's first service battalion, the 8th Devons, were loaned to set things in motion. By evening they had 500 recruits on their hands. One of the officers, Bryan Freeland, set out from Exeter with a draft of 100 men and by the time he reached Aldershot had 126; he never knew where the extras came from. And the official drafts were mostly Welsh or from Birmingham: only a small handful were truly 'Devons'. They arrived without uniforms, equipment, NCOs to organise them, even papers to say who they were, and the scratch staff had to cope as best they could. Until the end of the month they did not even have proper office stationery. They sent telegrams to two retired warrant officers, pleading for help: Sergeant Major Grubb – a formidable figure in the early days of the 9th Battalion – replied that he would join them, but only as regimental sergeant major, his old position. No one argued.

Over the next few days newly commissioned officers began to report to Rushmoor Camp; Noel must have been one of the first. Alan Hinshelwood's letter from the War Office is dated 21 September, so he would have been a few days behind. Officers had to provide their own uniform and kit, including a revolver and sword, and were given an allowance of around £50. According to the Regimental History, most of the early arrivals turned up without uniforms and had to be sent away again; if they had received the same letter as Alan

Hinshelwood this was no wonder. The letter instructs him to report to Aldershot *'at once'*, adding *'You should draw your outfit allowance from your Army Agents or Paymaster.'* For a newcomer this was easily misunderstood. But in the early months everyone was learning on their feet.

Those who did arrive fully equipped were thrown into the job straight away. John Upcott joined the battalion on 24 September, and the next day told his mother:

'I arrived here without trouble about half past three yesterday & was instantly turned on to drill a squad. I was also told to improvise a lecture to the company to be delivered the same evening, but this was counter-ordered later on. A fearfully protracted mess dinner followed, after which I turned in as I was feeling tired. I was glad that I had brought the blankets, as I had to sleep on the floor; I seemed to sleep there as well as I should have anywhere else, though I had no mattress. We were up at half past five & did a couple of hours' company drill before breakfast; I succeeded in manoeuvring my platoon more or less in the desired direction. Then in the morning the whole battalion marched off to the Queens Parade Ground to be inspected by the King & Kitchener. I had rather a good view of both of them, as my platoon was the leading one in the company. The King looked very bored, but Kitchener seemed genial. In the afternoon I went into the town & bought a bed, which will turn out in time for tonight I hope . . .

I am commanding No.10 platoon in C Company. I have about 50 men & 2 sergeants. Luckily I have got a capital Company officer, a special reservist, who knows something about the job. The battalion is in camp about a mile out of Aldershot, not far from the aviation sheds. It contains a colonel, major, adjutant & some ten subalterns; we have no captains at all yet. I am very sorry to say that very few of the men are Devonians; the 8th & 10th Battalions were recruited in Devon, but these men come mostly from Wales, London, Birmingham. On the other hand a good many officers, I think the majority, come from Devon. Capt. Tracey's son is here; another fellow (don't know his name) instantly asked me whether I came from Cullompton.

(I continue after dinner) The colonel's name is Davies, a white haired old dog, who used to be in the 1st Batt. The men are a very cheery lot & seem very contented; I went round to look . . . this morning & they all said that they were very satisfied; (all except one, who said that the meat was tough; this was nonsense; I ate some to see & told him so). They are mostly young & practically all clean shaved; a lot of them speak with a jolly Welsh accent. Very few have got uniform & none have got rifles; we shall be getting them soon, as the 8th Batt are practically fully equipped.

Their drill isn't at all bad, & they are some two months in front of their proper drill, though of course all the rifle exercises will have to be taught them. Yesterday we paid the whole company; when I say 'we' I should say my company officer did; my share was limited in counting out heaps of money into 10/- piles. There are plenty of blankets; the greatest want is boots; many have theirs tied up with string. By the way, now that I have untied my blankets, I think I will keep them for a bit anyway; it is pretty cold at nights. But I will keep them clean.

Tomorrow I am taking a platoon for church parade; my company have no regular parades tomorrow or Monday as they have just been inoculated. I have also got to drop in on the King tomorrow & write my name in his visitor's book; all officers have to.

Well, it is getting late & I think I shall turn in. My camp bed has now arrived.'

The relentless pace of this new life would have distracted Noel Hodgson from any regret he still felt over the missed opportunity to go to war with Nowell Oxland, or frustration at the need to go to war at all. A poem he wrote in the summer appeared in *The New Witness* on 10 September, shortly before he joined the battalion. 'The Hungry Heart' is testament to his restlessness, with regrets both for the past and for the future he had set aside:

> *Oh hungry heart of man, insatiable*
> *As the great sea and restless as the wind;*
> *What is it you would have, oh hungry heart?*
> *'Our youth!' you cry, 'give us our youth again,*
> *The days of gold.'*
> *Your youth? And what was youth?*
> *Some buildings of grey stone, and a broad field*
> *With trees about it, laughter, friends and health.*
> *What more than that?*
> *'It is to come!' you cry, 'The thing we seek.'*
> *What is to come to you*
> *Save what has come and gone? More friends,*
> *More love, more knowledge? Are you silent?*
> *What would you have, oh hungry heart of man?*

Nowell Oxland was far away now, training in Grantham with the 6th Battalion of the Border Regiment. Robert Parr was even further, or soon would be. He was turned down by the army because his eyesight was not up to standard. But not for nothing was that generation taught to be resourceful and self-reliant. Finding the British Army's door closed to him, Robert Parr took himself off to the Serbian Embassy in London, and calmly talked his way into the Serbian Army – the first step in a long career in the diplomatic service. When Hodgson wrote 'The Hungry Heart', he seemed to be feeling that more friends were unlikely to come his way – that it was unreasonable even to want them. He was wrong. The battalion was not very different from school and university. The officers' mess was steadily filling with men whose backgrounds were very similar to his own. They spoke the same language, and his even temper and unexpected streak of devilment had always won friends for him before and would do so again.

Alan Hinshelwood was probably his first friend in the Devons. They were both in D Company and there are several photographs of them together. Hinshelwood had been to Berkhamstead School before Oxford and his father was a Fine Art dealer and – curious profession, this – Artist's Colourman to Queen Alexandra. The younger Hinshelwood could draw well and he gained a reputation in the battalion for being a very smart dresser; the others called him 'Nobby'. He was also noted for eating anything that was not squirreled away. The other D Company subalterns were Bertram Glossop ('Flossie'), of Repton School and the Royal Agricultural College at Cirencester – another clergyman's son – and Mervyn Davies ('the Bart'). A Barrister of the Inner Temple on the outbreak of war, Davies was Australian by birth and Jewish. But his family had moved to England when he was a child, and a public school and Oxford education had probably blurred any sense of otherness.

John Upcott had left Corpus Christi in 1912 to teach at the Royal Naval College at Osborne. Then came a year's leave in France to study the language: according to his records at Corpus Christi he took a course at the University of Grenoble. He also fell in love with Renée Motte, the daughter of his host family. He proposed to her in the summer of 1914; she accepted but her father would not allow them to marry because of the deepening crisis. All men had their own reasons for volunteering to fight, and John Upcott was disarmingly frank about his, writing in his diary in the spring of 1916: *'Personally I know I did not make any sacrifice in coming out, I joined up because I wanted to add war to my experience; if I had been given the choice about coming out a second time, I am convinced I shouldn't have come — but I had to.'*[1] When he wrote to tell his parents about his engagement he also told them he was coming home to volunteer. If he could not get back he would join the Foreign Legion.

Upcott had two ready-made friends in the battalion. John Chantrey Elliot Inchbald, 'Jack', or 'Inchy', was a few years behind him at Winchester School and matriculated at New College, Oxford in 1913. He volunteered from his school's OTC camp in September. Harold Rayner, Upcott's friend from Corpus Christi, was late in volunteering as the outbreak of war caught him travelling the world. Rayner applied for a commission in Oxford on 3 December, requesting either the 9th Devons, *'or failing that, Royal Sussex'*. There would be no failing. The 9th Devons' Commanding Officer, Colonel Davies, saw to that by writing to the War Office on 14 December, *'I have the honour to request that Mr Harold Leslie Rayner, of 7 Oriel Street, Oxford, who submitted an application for a temporary commission on the 3rd inst, via Oxford O.T.C., and applied for this Battalion, may be so posted, please.'*[2] The War Office duly obliged.

Colonel Thomas A.H. Davies had taken command of the battalion on 20 September. A veteran of the regiment called out of retirement, in photographs taken while the battalion was in training he looks like a man in his seventies: in fact, he was fifty-seven. His officers called him 'Uncle Tom'. He had an impressive service record, having joined the regiment in 1876 – before most of them were even born. A veteran of campaigns in Afghanistan, Burma and South Africa, a holder of the Distinguished Service Order and a Companion of the Order of the Bath in the Military Division, his years in the army had given him a network of contacts which he used to find good officers for the 9th Devons. Harold Rayner was not the only man head-hunted by him. The service records of several of the battalion's other officers show that they were men Colonel Davies knew or had recommended.

On the application form of Noel Hodgson's company commander, Ralph Whitney Mockridge, Davies noted, *'He is so much older than the general run of 2nd Lts and will I am sure soon fit himself for this position* [Captain]. *I have known him for two years.'*[3] Three weeks earlier, Mockridge had applied for a commission in the Naval Brigade, but the 9th Devons claimed him. He proved to be one of the battalion's more colourful characters. Born in Chicago of a Canadian father and an American mother, Ralph Mockridge was British in name, but far more cosmopolitan than the normal run of British officers. His father, Whitney Mockridge, was a well-known concert tenor and his mother the accompanist; professional engagements took them round the world. Ralph's first school was Colet Court in London. From there he moved to the Höhere Privatschule Hansa-Gildemeister, an exclusive (and expensive) private school in Hanover. Then back to New York and Columbia University: the 1908 Yearbook, listing the 'awards' for the students of Ralph's year voted by their fellows – 'Biggest Fusser', 'Best Dressed' and so on (a tradition in American colleges) – names him as one of the three 'Most Lady-like'. That might have raised eyebrows in the mess if the others had known!

From New York, Ralph Mockridge went back to London and worked for a photographic company. Then he spent two years as a private tutor in Montreux. He must have had an excellent command of languages, and his parents' music rubbed off on him too. In the years leading up to the war he had at least four songs published; the battalion christened him 'the Ragtime Cat' – 'Mog' for short.

Another of Colonel Davies's chosen men was Duncan Lenox Martin, one of the two who stood with Noel Hodgson that last morning watching the bombardment of Mametz, and, with him, one of the best-known names in the 9th Battalion. For the last forty years Martin has featured in almost every popular account of the Somme. Tour groups visited his grave, yet he remains an enigmatic figure. He was a week older than Ralph Mockridge, born in Algiers in May 1886. In 1891 his father Thomas Martin described himself as an ostrich farmer in the Cape Colony, though at that time the family was living in Hailsham in Sussex. The children, Dorothy and Duncan, were five and four years old then, and had a German governess. The only other record of Martin's education is at fifteen years old when he was a boarder in a tiny private establishment, the Channel View School in Walton in Gordano in Somerset. His parents appear to have separated; his father was in north London while his mother was living in Crowborough in Sussex as head of her own household, with her daughter and three servants.[4] In August 1903 she was issued with a passport to take Dorothy and Duncan to Germany. Passports were not a legal requirement then and most people travelled without them; there is nothing to say why Anne Martin applied, or where in Germany she and her children were going, or for how long.[5]

After that Duncan Martin disappears from the written record until the outbreak of war. According to his application for a commission, he had not been to university and had not served in the Home, Indian or Colonial Offices. He had no OTC training, had not been to the Royal Military College or passed an Army entrance exam, yet his character witnesses were two high-ranking officers: Colonel Davies, who attested to knowing him for four years adding, *'Can strongly recommend, very active, very good French & German'*, and a retired lieutenant colonel of the Royal Artillery, whose address Martin gave as 'present address for correspondence'. Later he crossed this out in favour of an address in Folkestone, citing a solicitor in Kent instead of a permanent address. But the grant of probate on his will describes him as *'of St. Ives, Cornwall'*. Francis Gresson, headmaster of a preparatory school in Crowborough (and a county cricketer) testified to his having a good standard of education. And though the form was completed at the regimental depot in Exeter on 9 September, still very early in the war, a note was added in red ink, *'This gentleman explains his late application by his difficulty in returning home from France where he was when war broke out'*.

The form gives no clue to Martin's pre-war occupation. He is variously said by other sources to have been an artist, a maths teacher, or, intriguingly, a secret service man. This last comes from an eyewitness account of his death by a private soldier in the battalion.[6] There is nothing to corroborate it or, for that matter, to contradict it, but Martin's whole story is a patchwork of the unexplained. Even his battalion nickname, 'Iscariot'. It stands out in sharp contrast to 'Inchy' and 'Nobby', 'Flossie' and 'Mog'. It might suggest he was unpopular, given its association with the betrayal of Christ; in fact, the others both liked and respected him. In France he became a dominant figure in the battalion, twice mentioned in despatches and assuming command of the whole battalion on more than one occasion. There was something larger than life about Martin. *'The only souvenir I can think of sending you would be one of Iscariot's duds';* John Upcott tells his sister Gwen early in 1916, *'a dud is a shell that doesn't burst & Iscariot has a large collection of them at his house. But 1) they weigh about half a ton, because the Germans never fire anything smaller than a 6 inch at Iscariot & 2) they might go off at any time. This is why Iscariot likes them & why you probably wouldn't.'*

In the autumn of 1914, though, all that was a long way off. Early in October the battalion left Aldershot for the National Rifle Association grounds at Bisley, where they would spend two months training on Pirbright Common. More drafts of men from Exeter were bringing the battalion up to strength, though few of them were Devon men. They had been issued with uniforms at last, but only in 'Kitchener blue'. With so many new soldiers to equip at once khaki cloth was in short supply, and dark blue uniforms a common sight. While the Devons were at Bisley, an enterprising local photographer printed postcards of men and officers beside their distinctive white bell tents. Hodgson posed for one wearing full uniform from the waist up, sword hilt proudly on view, with ordinary trousers and shoes. It seems to have been a joke; he sent the card to his mother on 25 October with the message, *'Excusez s'il vous plait les pantalons avec les armes'* (Please excuse trousers with weapons). On another card, with Alan Hinshelwood, his uniform is complete.

He had a little pocket book with him which he used during training. It would have fitted the top pocket of his tunic, and has a few pencilled lists of officers and men, and what looks like an attempt to decode a message: *'DCOY SCOUT ANMSWER/ ING HAVE INTERCEPTED/ YOUR MESSAGE NO NEED TO RETIRE ENEMY BEING ATTACKED IN FLANK HOLD ON AS LONG AS POSSIBLE.'* But in spare moments he turned the book upside down and drafted poems, and unlike the pre-war notebook, here he was working things out, striking through lines, adding ideas or a pleasing word when it came to him, all in a miniscule pencil script. Boyhood and its fragility was still on his mind. The book contains drafts of the two similar poems, 'Fragment' and 'To a Boy' which his father later chose for *Verse and Prose in Peace and War*, his posthumous book of Noel's work, dating 'To a Boy' to October 1914. Neither is the same as the book version, so perhaps there were also fair copies. The draft of 'To a Boy' runs:

> *Oh arrow-straight & slender*
> *With grey eyes unafraid*
> *You see the roses splendour*
> *And care not that they fade*
> *Youth in its flush & flower*

> *Has a heart of living flame;*
> *That conquers the world in an hour*
> *And lives and dies in a game.*
>
> *Could youth but always weave us*
> *His magic round our ways,*
> *And Time the thievish leave us*
> *The boy's heart all our days.*

In the book the last verse, like the first, is addressed to the imaginary boy. In the draft, though, it is clear that Noel is really thinking of himself and his companions. Several pages are taken up with drafts of the long poem on the same theme, 'The Call', also included in *Verse and Prose*, which begins, *'Ah! We have dwelt in Arcady long time,'* and ends:

> *And white roads vanishing beneath the sky*
> *Called for our feet, and there were countless things*
> *That we must see and do, while blood was high*
> *And time still hovered on reluctant wings.*
>
> *And these were good; yet in our hearts we knew*
> *These were not all, – that still through toil and pains*
> *Deeds of a purer lustre given to few,*
> *Made for the perfect glory that remains.*
>
> *And when the summons in our ears was shrill*
> *Unshaken in our trust we rose, and then*
> *Flung but a backward glance, and carefree still*
> *Went strongly forth to do the work of men.*

He made several attempts at this, crossing out lines and adding new ones, changing words, squeezing extra verses into any available space; even recasting the whole thing in a completely different verse form. One version is addressed to Robert Parr:

> *Nestor, we dwelt awhile in Arcady's*
> *Enchanted hollows, where the golden mists*
> *Of love and laughter and immortal youth*
> *Were round our ways. . .*

But the most touching poem in the pocket book is a perfect little quatrain in the style of the *Rubaiyat* which seems to have come spontaneously, needing no correction, and which encapsulates the sadness he was feeling for himself, his schoolfriends, and his new friends in the battalion, for the change that was coming over all their lives:

> *The glorious passion of the rose shall die*
> *And all our youth go from us as a sigh,*
> *The silver cord is loosed, the golden bowl*
> *Lies broken & its draught long spilt & dry.*

He already had good reason to feel apprehensive. By October Durham School was counting its first casualties, and the pain of war had touched his own family. His Distington cousins, George and Charles, joined the Regular Army before the war. Charles, his own age all but a week, joined straight from Westminster School in 1910, and was commissioned in the Northumberland Fusiliers. Among the first soldiers of the British Expeditionary Force to land in France in August, Charles Hodgson lasted only a few weeks at the Front. He was invalided home during the Retreat from Mons and served out the rest of the war on the Staff.

Worse was to come: George, the elder brother, read for the Law Tripos at Cambridge as an OTC member. Military subjects were part of his course and he became a second lieutenant in the 2nd Battalion of the Border Regiment in September 1911; his degree was awarded the following year. George was a real charmer; good-looking, impulsive, and idle with the idleness of the very gifted, who know precisely how much effort is needed to achieve a result. He shared Noel's passion for acting and dramatic reading. He was funny too. The Cambridge Letters in *The Grantite Review*, the journal of his old House at Westminster School, celebrated him in 1909 as, *'the inimitable Hodgson, who is, of course, as charming as ever. The time that he saves from adorning his person is given to pacing Jesus Lane with a slow and solemn gait'*. From the moneyed side of the family, George was able to enjoy *'a luxurious and aristocratic life'* at Cambridge. *'He occasionally goes beagling; more often he has made us leap for our lives as he flashes past in the 40 h.p. motor in which he scours the country.'*[7]

George landed at Zeebrugge with his battalion on 6 October. They moved up by stages to Ypres, where battle was already underway. After more than two weeks of fighting, on the night of 31 October, they took up positions at Klein Zillebeke. Heavy shelling on their trenches was followed by an enemy attack in strength on the night of 2 November. The battalion came close to being encircled and struggled to hold the line for three hours before reinforcements reached them. George Hodgson was severely wounded during the night. His part in the fighting earned a mention in despatches, but he did not live to see it. He died of his wounds on 6 November in No 13 General Hospital at Boulogne.

In the family the shock was profound. So much life and potential reduced to the few personal possessions the Army returned; a silver cigarette case, a gun metal cigarette case, a leather letter-wallet, a safety pin, a locket and – oddly touching, this – a farthing. Even in 1914 a farthing (one quarter of an old penny) did not buy very much. It was found with the safety pin in one of the cigarette cases; perhaps he carried them for luck. His mother petitioned the War Office twice for the return of his sword, binoculars, wristwatch and revolver, but there is nothing to say that she ever received them. She mentioned that her youngest son, still at school, had written to ask for some war work in England and had received no reply. [8]

The poem entitled 'To a Friend Killed in Action' that appears in *Verse and Prose*, '*I saw you richly gifted, filled with fire/ And splendid hopes to run your course of days;/ With strength and beauty to command desire,/ And love and laughter to delight your ways,*' dated November 1914, was almost certainly meant for George. A lot of the titles in the book were added by Henry, and the only other casualty at that time with a traceable link to Noel was Cyril Hosking, a King's Scholar of Durham turned pilot in the Royal Flying Corps, who was shot down in Belgium on 26 October. But in either case, the poem was a sign of the war becoming personal, the casualty lists weaving their way into the fabric of his own life.

At the end of November the camp at Bisley became uncomfortably cold and wet. The battalion moved back to Aldershot, to Tournay Barracks. They spent the next three months on the New Army musketry course, having at last been issued with real service rifles, a hundred of them, which the whole battalion had to share. On 24 February the 9th Devons left Aldershot by train for Haslemere in Surrey. There they found comfortable billets and as winter gave way to spring, their training continued. They were based at Haslemere for over a month. Photographs show them drilling in the streets; their orderly room in a building called 'The Corner House', opposite the hardware shop; a sentry on guard outside what appears to be a church hall, while the everyday life of the town carries on around them.

April came and with it orders to prepare for a move, this time to Salisbury Plain. What followed was an epic, to be remembered every time the battalion made a long march, or they were moved around the countryside with no idea where they were going. On 6 April, in heavy rain, the trek began. They reached as far as Alton in Hampshire where they spent the night. C Company was the envy of all, being billeted in the brewery; the next day, '*A very beery Coy. marched to Winchester. Lovely day. Beer all absorbed and 9 platoon (Welsh) full of song after Four Marks Hill!*' [9] This is from the diary of Bryan Freeland, John Upcott's '*capital Company officer*'. Two of the four original officers had stayed on: Freeland and Captain Nation of A Company. Bryan Freeland's younger brother Rowan – Hodgson's other companion in the last hours before the Somme – had enlisted as a private in the Public Schools Battalion in August and was commissioned in the 9th Devons in September. Known as 'Babe', in the early months of 1915 he was one of four nineteen-year-old second lieutenants, the youngest subalterns in the battalion.

On 8 April the 9th were ordered to leave Winchester and march back to Alton. They remained in Alton the next day, then received orders to march – not to Salisbury Plain, as expected, but to Bordon Camp, half way back to Haslemere again. They had spent four days marching to a place they could have reached in a few hours. After a similarly roundabout march on the Somme in January 1916, Noel Hodgson told John Upcott, then back in England recovering from a wound:

> *'We were all deeply gratified by your welcome letter, which arrived safely and found us in the pink as it left you at present. In point of actual fact we had just completed the Alton-Winchester stunt over again. "Ninth Battalion Devonshire regiment will move from X to Y (25 kilometres)." Ninth Battalion Devonshire regiment moves. "Ninth Battalion Devonshire regiment will move from Y to X at once (25 kilometres)." Ninth Batt Devonshire regiment moves. Quite home-like.'*[10]

Guadalupe Barracks at Bordon, nominally the married quarters, would be home to them until they were ordered overseas, and their time was taken up with specialist training in bombing, trench warfare and night operations, with mock battles on the common and inter-company cricket matches. They were fully equipped with real service rifles at last, for the final musketry course, and those still in blue uniforms were issued with khaki. There was time to go on leave. Jack Inchbald celebrated his 21st birthday at home in Devon on 3 May; *'I've no desire whatever to return to Bordon & the military atmosphere'*, he told his father. *'We leave here today about 1.30. I don't suppose I shall reach my destination till two in the morning . . . Still my rest has been absolutely enjoyable from start to finish.'*[11]

Noel Hodgson wrote a clutch of poems that spring. In 'Splendide Fallax' ('Gloriously Deceptive'), he pictures two lovers about to be parted by war:

> *It was the time of snowdrops,*
> *They wandered thro' the lawn;*
> *Her eyes were like the ocean,*
> *His hair was like the corn;*
> *And she saw nought besides him;*
> *But he that duty guides him,*
> *And love must be foresworn.*

> *It is the time of roses*
> *And she goes by forlorn,*
> *Nor feels the summer splendour,*
> *Not feels the breath of morn.*
> *The trees are green above her,*
> *But no more comes her lover,*
> *And hark! they mow the corn.*

The image in that last line is chilling in its understated simplicity. *'His hair was like the corn... And hark! they mow the corn.'* The poem has been taken as evidence that Hodgson had a girlfriend, but it seems far more likely that he was describing a common situation; many of the Devons would have had wives or girlfriends. If there had been someone in his life, she would surely have been mentioned at some point. His focus seemed to be on Durham still. From nostalgia for a time that could never return he was moving towards a different understanding, in which the continued existence of the School and the way of life it represented became a source of strength. He expresses this in 'Durham', written in May 1915, also in another 1915 poem, 'Ave Mater – Atque Vale' (Hail, Mother, and Farewell), part of which survives in manuscript on a scrap of paper. It appears to have been written during a leave visit to the school:

> *Last night dream-hearted in the Abbey's spell*
> *We stood to sing old Simeon's passing hymn,*
> *When sudden splendour of the sunset fell*
> *Full on my eyes, and passed and left all dim –*
> *At once a summons and a deep farewell.*
>
> *I am content – our life is but a trust*
> *From the great hand of God, and if I keep*
> *The immortal treasure clean of mortal rust*
> *Against His claim, 'tis well, and let me sleep*
> *Among the not dishonourable dust.*[12]

The poems leave no doubt that he was apprehensive. In some ways this must have been the worst time, with the idea of overseas service hanging over them and no actual experience of what it would be like, imagination could run wild. But poems were also the way he processed the fear. Outwardly he was cheerful, dependable and up for anything. The Hodgson the battalion knew is more apparent in a letter he sent at this time to Robert Parr, who was already in Serbia:

Bordon Camp
17. 5. 15

'Dear Nestor;
This will be the longest letter you have ever received from me, the reason being not any radical alteration in my attitude to letter writing as a whole, but the lively hope that you will have only one more letter sent from here. The mists are dispelling and there appears —

Fisher is already somewhere in France – in the R.E. with headquarters in a cathedral town as nameless as Odysseus; Todd is well and happy. Callinan, Robinson, & Herbert Stewart have found the answer to the questions that still perplex you & I. [All three were dead; killed in the Second Battle of Ypres.]

I don't know whether you will ever get your parcels; a series were sent to Mrs. P, but she has thrown up the idea of going out and has sent them on to somebody else who is connected with Serbian relief. If the war continues a sufficiently long time they may get into your neighbourhood about the time that peace negotiations begin.

I shall be extremely annoyed if the Odyssey does not reach you as I was very near keeping it for myself. Who will write the Epic of the Second Trojan War I wonder; perhaps some friend of ours who is battling now at windy Ilion and Helles' Sea.

These are wonderful times – think of kids like Wardle, and Walker, and Greville Jones fighting for their lives with bayonets. I think Walker will be killed, it seems somehow the only possible denoument to his career; unless 'he himself shall be saved, yet so as by fire.' Were you in the sixth when we did that with Dutton – whom the Gods reward – one summer term, when the air was sleepy among the trees and the mower murmured up and down the playground in the sun? Hei mihi praeteritos referat si Jupiter annos! ['If only Jupiter would restore me those bygone years']. *They say only the very young dare to be retrospective, but I spit in their face who say it. Dunsany has it well in the tale which I enclose.*

The other night some twenty of us became weary of the life of 'an officer & a gentleman', and after mess we cast off our dignity as a rag . . . Captains of sedate presence were flung to and fro like sacks, a subaltern fell through a plate glass window, two armchairs and a table suffered shipwreck, and the door came off its hinges, while silver wristwatches were nothing accounted in the time of the rag. And some twenty officers knew the delights of folly, the gift that is from heaven but dwells with man.

Among my scant possessions is a Bungite Rugger cap, which I prize much; it stands for all that was best, all that was me in the days that are done. For pride in one's achievements – it was my first footer cap; for

*honourable rivalry; for friendship – so many times I wore it 'after call-
over'. They wear them when going down town now, bless their hearts.*

*On Sunday I went round Wellington with an old Wellingtonian who
did not know when his school was founded nor by whom, nor could he
find his way there without assistance. It's a mad world, my masters.*

*Well, have I written enough, and shall I go now to sew pads in the
shoulders of my tunic to keep the equipment braces from galling?
Goodnight then old man,*

yours always, Michael'[13]

Michael? The signature is unexplained and probably beyond explanation, but
the handwriting is unquestionably his. This letter was found with another, also
signed 'Michael' and written from the Somme in May 1916, and a third, written
to Parr by Penelope Hodgson after her son's death. All three were folded into
an envelope pasted in the back of the copy of *A Cluster of Grapes* that Noel
gave Robert Parr for his birthday in May 1914. Presumably 'Michael' was Parr's
nickname for him. But among his fellow officers, Noel Hodgson was always
and only 'Smiler'. *'Always to me my "Smiler"'*. That was how Frank Worrall
of B Company, the old Wellingtonian who knew nothing about his school,
summed him up when the news came of his death. Worrall was another of the
battalion's characters and a good friend to Noel Hodgson. *'So you have met our
Worry,'* John Upcott wrote to his uncle in the spring of 1916, after their first
battle, *'I christened him that way soon after he joined. He is rather a dear, isn't
he? Also he taught me all that I know about cross country riding. You mustn't
believe all he says, He is quite mad like all his family & consequently it took
three bullets & a broken leg to stop him.'[14]*

In April Nowell Oxland's battalion had moved to Frensham in Surrey, about
six miles from where the Devons were; he and Hodgson could easily have met
in the months that followed. The 6th Borders left England at the end of June,
not for France or Belgium as they might have expected, but on a much longer
journey. They embarked from Liverpool on the transport ship *Empress of Britain*
for the Mediterranean, heading for Gallipoli. For the 9th Devons, time began to
drag. After ten months the battalion was still in training and there was no sign
of their moving on. Just three days before the order came, John Upcott was
acting adjutant; a sheet of battalion orders among his papers still has instructions
about men going on leave, and plans for a mock attack that was to involve the
whole battalion. The day after it was due to start, 17 July, the 9th were ordered
to prepare for overseas service. Twenty surplus officers were sent to the 11th
Battalion at Wareham in Dorset, among them Rowan Freeland. Bryan Freeland
believed Rowan was too young to go overseas, but others of his age went. It
may just have been a matter of numbers.

For the rest, the order meant an onslaught of last-minute preparations and a last chance to see friends and family if it could be managed. John Upcott gave his sister a letter to be sent to his fiancée in France if he was killed. Jack Inchbald wrote to his father on 18 July:

> *'I couldn't do anything more than tell you we were under marching orders, this afternoon, as not only was I speaking from the Orderly room, as I think you realised, but also I had to hang as the adjutant was waiting for the telephone. But I wanted just to let you know we were off in a day or two.*
>
> *Last night our colonel had a telegram from the War Office telling him to wire them as soon as we were ready for embarkation. This we should be by about Wednesday & I take it we may move any day after that & probably will clear out by the end of the week, though of course its just possible we may even now have to stand by for some days.*
>
> *I have written to tell mother. I don't know whether she will want to come up again. You might write her & come to some arrangement . . . We shall be very busy indeed & probably unable to get away from Bordon. The men are all confined to Barracks from tomorrow morning . . . . You must try & see me before we go.'*[15]

Mobilisation stores were drawn and ammunition handed out. On 20 July Noel Hodgson wrote his will. This was something many younger single men did not do. His cousin George had not, and perhaps that was the point. It was no longer possible to pretend that death could not happen, and Noel was intent on handling the business as lightly as he could, yet making sure that it was done. He shared the feeling that comes very strongly through Vera Brittain's wartime writing, that his own generation would cope with whatever was to come; it was their parents, left at home, who would need support and protection. On 26 July, the last day before they left, he wrote to Stella, who was on holiday in Cumberland:

> *'Dear Star*
> *'En état de partir I write to wish you many happy returns of the 30th* [her wedding anniversary], *and to enclose a small something at which you must not sniff; also an envelope with a will leaving everything to Dad, and a paper of small bequests for him to attend to if necessary.*
>
> *Don't have any qualms about the little gift; it is in order that you may be able to visit the Gable and explain that being unable to make the pilgrimage myself I am sending excellent representatives. For this purpose you will drive in the car to Rossthwaite or even Seathwaite & leave it there, continuing over the Sty-head to the Row Head Inn at Wastwater – not the Wastwater Hotel – a distance of about five miles. Here you will stay two nights in order to see the Screes and the Church,*

and to walk up Tongue Ghyll a little way and look at the Scawfell crags. On your return journey you will start early, if fine, and reach the top of Sty Head (not quite as far as the tarn) by midday at latest. Then on your left you will see a gully which runs up to the col between Great & Green Gables, and is traversed by a ghyll and a rough track. Climb this gully (say 400-500 feet) and on arriving at the col you will observe a path leading over some broken rock on your left, which affords a rough but perfectly straightforward ascent to the top of the Gable. Descend by the same route. Do not attempt in a mist. The climb is shorter than to Scawfell Pikes and gives a better view.

You will not, probably, regard this advice at all, but in any case it gives much pleasure to write of these things. Many thanks for your nice letter, old girl, and don't worry at all about

Your loving brother, Bill'

The tone is altogether different from his earlier letter to Robert Parr. In that he is striking an attitude; the flippant, consciously arch use of language sets a protective barrier between him and the emotion in the things he writes about. He is laughing at himself. The letter to Stella is simpler and his real feelings come through. Describing his 'Farewell Walk' of August 1914 went straight to the heart of who he was and what mattered to him. He must have written to his parents before leaving too, though no letter survives. But Henry knew he was going, and that night had a nightmare which woke the whole household. It was unlike him to display so much emotion.

For Noel the next day began with a breakfast served soon after midnight. Then the battalion paraded in the dark: at 1.45am on 27 July, the 9th Devons marched off by company to Bordon Station, entraining there for Southampton. Most would sleep on the way. They arrived four hours later and spent the whole day confined to the docks, kicking their heels in the dock sheds or sleeping still, waiting. They left in stages: first the transport section, then A and B Companies. At 4pm, with the rest of C and D, Noel Hodgson embarked on board their transport, an Isle of Man paddle steamer, and after several more hours in waiting in harbour, set sail for France.

Chapter 8

'Interminable Land', July – September 1915

The Channel crossing was rough and not without danger. The boats waited for the approach of darkness and set out with an escort of two destroyers: even so, a party of soldiers had to remain on deck to watch for submarines. John Upcott was in charge and found it, *'an awful job, as it was blowing hard & the sea was coming over the forward part of the upper deck, where my party was stationed. We had a fairly wet time of it, until 11 o'clock when the captain of the ship told me we shouldn't be much use & sent us away. He wasn't far wrong as most of my men were too sick to see a submarine, much less shoot at it.'* Sea-sickness was rife on board, and Noel Hodgson one of its victims. *'So I went below,'* Upcott continued, *'& secured Smiler's berth, Smiler being sea-sick, very fortunately or I should have slept on the floor. I had a very comfortable night & never felt sea-sick. The boat was a fast one & we got in at about 3 a.m, though we did not disembark until 7.'*[1] Bryan Freeland thought they disembarked at 5am; in either case, thirteen hours on board or fifteen, it must have been a huge relief to set foot on dry land, especially for those who were still feeling fragile.

From the docks at Le Havre it was a five mile march to No 5 Rest Camp, and the horses found it hard to keep their footing on the cobbled streets. The camp, *'a jolly place, right up on the cliffs overlooking the sea'*, was the first destination for many newly-arrived battalions. The streets of Le Havre were full of soldiers and Upcott thought it seemed almost as English as it was French. In July there was no hardship in sleeping under canvas, and the 9th Devons' introduction to France was no more alarming than a foreign holiday. Once everyone was settled into camp the senior officers and company commanders busied themselves with administration – one of their first tasks was to draw French money from the Field Cashier to pay the men. Everyone else relaxed. Groups of officers went into the town in search of lunch, and several had friends or relatives stationed roundabout whom they hoped to meet. Arthur Hodgson was there somewhere. He returned from Canada on the outbreak of war and secured a commission in the Army Service Corps.

The men were allowed into town too, and next day most of the battalion could be found on the beach. Noel sent his sister a postcard: *'You may be able to see the Gable, but you haven't got the sunshine we have here, so there are compensations everywhere. Very comfortable at present under canvas and hoping to see Arthur before we go. How does the Giaconda go? Bill'*

The 'Giaconda', otherwise 'Monna Lisa' was a car the Towers were using during their holiday: it intrigued Noel and he referred to it often, cars still being a novelty in ordinary families. He said no more about Arthur so may not have managed to see him. On the afternoon of 30 July the battalion left camp and marched to the station. They entrained at 7pm, men packed into cattle trucks, officers sharing a single compartment, and headed north. It was hot on the train and the journey lasted through the night and all the next day: 'we were rather crowded & didn't sleep much,' John Upcott wrote. *'However everybody was cheerful & I rather enjoyed the journey. We stopped at Abbeville & got tea & a shave. Here we formed one of five trains, all one behind the other on the same metals.'*

Journey's end was Wizernes, south-west of St Omer and not far from the Belgian border. The officers of A and C Companies found themselves billeted in a stable with a cobbled floor and straw for bedding. Bryan Freeland was rather taken aback by this, judging by the two exclamation marks he gave it in his diary, but John Upcott was happy:

> *'As for bedding give me clean straw & plenty of it. This morning I had a most magnificent bathe in the mill-pond – plenty of deep green water where one can get a splendid swim. I am writing this sitting on some stone steps leading down to the water. It is a lovely place this, with a beautiful house & garden, at present peopled with Belgian refugees, the owner, an artillery subaltern, being a prisoner of war in Germany. How long we shall be here, nobody knows.'*

He suspected there were rats and spiders in the straw, but had slept too well to notice or to care.

The stable was attached to a paper mill, its whitewashed buildings and paved courtyards reminding him of his grandparents' house in Devon. At first the most pressing thing on his mind was the need to find food for the company mess and to arrange meals with the cooks. These early days were long and hot and there was time for everyone to look around and adjust to their new surroundings. One day John Upcott, Jack Inchbald and Duncan Martin, toured the paper mill to see how paper was made. *'So far everything has been a pic-nic & I think everybody has enjoyed themselves. The hard times are coming.'*[2]

D Company's billets would have been similar, based in and around a local farm, business or empty house. On 2 August Noel snatched a few moments to send Stella another postcard; he must have know how anxious she would be. *'Your letter received; very good to hear you're having a good time, so am I, and am tremendously fit. Seen no fun yet. Send me some Keswick toffee some time for auld lang syne.'*

Wizernes was within sound of the guns but too far behind the fighting lines to be dangerous, and the local people were friendly: *'The French are very cheerful,'* John Upcott remarked, *'& if they are tired of war, they never show it. They show very little emotion & hardly ever shout or wag flags. We were hardly ever cheered coming up, but lots of people came up to shake hands as we passed.'* There was some concern about German aircraft flying over but no one seemed to take it very seriously. Through the long summer days, while the rest of the battalion was kept busy with parades, route marches and field training, one platoon was always deputed to man an anti-aircraft gun. This was a popular duty, and one idyllic morning it fell to Hodgson and his platoon. He told Stella:

'Dear Star
I don't think I do envy you so very much just at present, though you are in the land of Heart's Desire; I am lying on my back on a heap of corn shucks in the sun, watching a stout Frenchman mow his oats, after an excellent breakfast and with a pipe of excellent tobacco between my teeth. You see I happen to be in charge of an anti-aircraft gun, the chances of whose being needed are remote, but I have to be on the spot, so it amounts to a soft day with the remote chance of a little excitement. It is a very pleasant if not desperately thrilling countryside to look on as you know, this Northern France. Anyway I wouldn't be elsewhere for thousands, as Nelson remarked on an historic occasion.

I think of you – striding over the fells, with your skirts kilted to the knee, to the fearful admiration of your old man; and devouring wet bleaberries with splendid abandon. You must write and tell me all about the ascent of the Gable, and the Screes, and how you found Sty-head and Scawfell Pinnacle.

My lads – Welshmen – are helping the farmer's son and daughter stack the corn, they talking Welsh the others French, neither understanding the other, and both perfectly contented. You would not like this spot because of the spiders, large ones, size of a five bob bit, with lank hirsuite legs, unprepossessing creatures but affectionate and harmless. I ought to make up a leeway in correspondence today so for the present accept all good wishes
from Bill'.[3]

While his Welshmen enjoyed helping on the farm, some men from C Company almost drowned swimming in the river. But the weather was about to break and the holiday atmosphere to end. It rained the next day and was humid and damp. On the morning of Saturday, 7 August, the battalion left Wizernes, heading in gentle stages towards the front line. An officer's business was the care of his men, and John Upcott marched behind his company, watching for those who were finding it hard, and even taking over their duties when they reached their destination. They spent the night in Mollinghem, *'a straggling village of ugly houses, dusty and dirty,'* which had already seen twenty-eight of its former inhabitants killed in the war. Next afternoon they moved on again, through Robecq to Calonne-sur-la-Lys. The heat had returned, and marching took its toll:

> *'Our route lay along the banks of a very long dull straight canal. Here we passed the Scots Guards, whom we are to relieve. Their piper & brass band cheered the men up a bit. But they made heavy weather of this short march, especially of the last five miles, which we did without a halt. At Robecque [Robecq] we passed our brigadier - Trefusis. After that we had the devil's own job to keep the column closed up; we passed the 2nd Gordons in an awful mess; our men seemed done up.'*[4]

At Robecq the 9th Devons became part of 20 Brigade, 7th Division. It was a source of pride to them, and to their sister battalion the 8th Devons, that both were joining a Regular Army Division which had already distinguished itself in the fighting. Also that they were replacing two Guards' battalions: to them that seemed a great honour, though John Upcott did wonder whether 20 Brigade would feel the same about it. For Noel Hodgson there was a personal element, because his cousin George's battalion, the 2nd Borders, was one of the units of 20 Brigade whom the Devons would now fight alongside. Battalion Headquarters was established at Calonne, with A and B Companies billeted there, C and D about a mile away, in the orchard and fields of a farm on the road to Robecq. The officers of D Company made bivouac tents in a field and posed for photos beside them, with Mervyn Davies and Bertram Glossop's tent labelled 'Claridges'.

Preparation for the front line now began in earnest. The Devons were inspected by their new Divisional Commander, Major-General Capper, who told them he hoped they would live up to the men they were replacing, promised them a gentle introduction to the trenches, and solemnly shook hands with each officer in turn. The Brigade Major, Charles Calveley Foss, who had won the Victoria Cross that spring in the Battle of Neuve Chapelle, lectured them on trench warfare. In the days that followed there were lectures and demonstrations on trench warfare, wiring and sniping, gas and bombs, by officers and NCOs coming directly out of the line to pass on their experience. On 14 August gas helmets were issued. For the Devons' officers it was a case of learning something one day and passing it on the next, as John Upcott found:

> *'I have been instructing in the use of all sort and kinds of bombs from a very slender pedestal of knowledge. In fact what I learn from the bombing officer one evening, that I teach the men next morning. They*

are fearsome looking things, but one gets used to their looks & I take very good care not to let anyone blow me up. Rayner has been walking about in asphyxiating gas this afternoon, doing smoke-helmet drill. We are all specialists now; he runs the gas; wire is my line though just now I am rather absorbed in bombs.'5

He thought that Charles Cecil Thompson, the youngest officer in the battalion, was going to be made battalion bombing officer. In fact, Noel Hodgson got the job. The date is never given, but writing to Stella on 12 August, he did mention an explosives course which might have been the reason, or perhaps the result, of his being chosen:

'Dear Star
The Keswick toffee arrived safely and without any complications among the postal authorities, and was eaten in a remarkably short space of time. I am glad to learn you appreciate my correspondence, and I will continue it if you send me out some thin paper and a packet of envelopes, as I am running out of them. By the time they arrive I may have some news to tell you; at present things are pretty stagnant. If you were to use pictures of the Gable etc as your medium of communication with me I should appreciate it. By the way I am accumulating some English postal orders, having been turned into a bureau de change by my men, as there is no post office at hand. These I purpose to forward to you, to be spent on worthy Cumbrian travel or any other object you will; they may arrive, or again they may be pinched on the way by knaves, but that must be chanced. They are no use here.
At the moment I am engaged on a course of instruction in explosives which is rather interesting and a little exciting at times. The only excitement I get, except the faint thrill when one sees an aeroplane being shelled.
Well, so long old thing, don't forget your affect. brother, Bill'

He sounds in his element and would have enjoyed the activity and the increased sense of purpose now the fighting was so close. The road running past the farm where his company and John Upcott's were living saw a steady stream of traffic passing to and from Brigade HQ. *'Every other moment something goes by in a cloud of dust, motor ambulances, staff-cars, buses, strings of mules & an occasional platoon of foot.'6* But the constant shifting around of men and equipment carried its own danger: spies, or the possibility that there might be spies around, unnoticed in the general bustle. The battalion had already had an incident at Wizernes, which culminated in the arrest of an elderly man on two walking sticks, and the adjutant's frustrated attempts to interrogate him, neither speaking a word of the other's language. *'Next to bathing, spy straffering is the most popular amusement,'* John Upcott told his uncle, *'it is quite harmless, especially for the spy.'* [7] Closer to the Front, there were stories of disguised Germans operating in the area. The Devons played their part in manning guard posts along the La Bassée Canal, and in each post there were descriptions of wanted men – four Germans in a Canadian staff car; a six-foot German dressed as a colonel in the Royal Engineers, and so on. Much to everyone's amazement, this six-foot German was real; Bryan Freeland happened to be at Brigade HQ the day he was brought in.

The battalion spent a week at Calonne, during which the first two companies left to be introduced to the trench lines. On 17 August the rest set off on the march again, following them along roads made muddy and slippery by heavy thunderstorms the day before. Bryan Freeland's horse, Ginger, slipped into a ditch and had to be rescued with slings improvised from his men's puttees. They spent the night at Le Paradis, the site of an infamous massacre of British troops in 1940, but then just a straggling hamlet in open, flat farmland. Next morning they marched out again, heading for Locon and billets close to the La Bassée Canal.

Stella had been keeping Noel supplied with letters, postcards, toffee, and gifts for Private Jones, his servant. Still in the Lakes, on 17 August she sent a card of the Doctor's Chimney, Gable Crags, with the message,

> *'Very many thanks for your last. We are going into Keswick this afternoon & will get & send you the writing paper. Hope that by now you have had the other parcel. We have just been up the gorge between Causey Pike & Barrow. Very lovely. Fear these cards are not much good but Stair P.O can do no better! Will try elsewhere. Much love & prenez garde de vous même* [take care of yourself].*'*

He carried the cards in his writing case when on the move; in billets and bivouac tents they were fixed above his bed, where other men hung pin-ups. On 18 August, newly arrived at Locon and in playful mood, he wrote:

> *'Dear Star*
> *I got your letter of the 14th, written from Dalton, yesterday, and the very charming snapshot along with it, for both of which many thanks. Why do not your sex adopt that style of dress for all outdoor pursuits, it is extraordinarily becoming. The toffee and the book arrived two or three days ago in safety; the former I had read before, but it is well worth reading twice or even three times, and the toffee was quite delightful. You will see that I am enclosing one of the batches of stray postal orders which come into my hands from time to time; they are perfectly useless to me, so I send them on to you to help defray Monna Lisa's petrol bill or*

*repairs account, two this week, and you might just mention if you get 'em
safely or if the Censor scoffs them en route.*

*I wish I could tell you where I am but it is imposs; perhaps if you
recollect the affair of Ajib Prince of Tartary, and the opening remark of
the two strangers, that may afford you some clue. More than this hint I
dare not give.*

*The noble Miss Hughes sent me a plum cake the other day, enclosed
in a single sheet of paper; of course it arrived in pieces like the sand of
the seashore in multitude; I wish she would send me a Bun Loaf, my heart
yearneth for a Bun Loaf, Well, la – la*

    Bill'

They were close enough to the Front now to see star shells at night and their
preparation for the trenches intensified. In a stubble field beside the canal the
battalion practised making various types of wire entanglements and throwing
live bombs. On Thursday, 19 August, Brigadier General Trefusis, commander
of 20 Brigade, watched them at work and, as Bryan Freeland noticed, *'Kitchener
of Khartoum, CIGS, prowled round.'*[8]

The next day A Company came out of the trenches and Jack Inchbald briefed
C Company on their experiences. They were to go in on the Saturday for 48
hours; after that it would be D Company's turn. On 22 August Noel wrote to
Stella:

'Dear Star

*Many thanks for the paper – this is it – and book – very good too – and
toffee; also much gratitude on the part of Jones – though he thinks that
"A.G. Shag" and a packet of cigarette papers come in handier. He is an
invaluable man.*

*Don't send me anything more please, as I have huge stores now and
am near a village where we can purchase most things. As many letters
as you like and P.C.s of the Lakes.*

*Here's another P.O. for you (5/-) Keep it for yourself as it's no good
to me; we live very cheaply at present. I hope this letter catches you at
Wastwater; not a bad pub there – by Jove I'd give something for a pint
of good beer at this moment – go up Tongue Ghyll its very easy & the
cairns show the way onto the Pikes. Love to you & Toby* [Bernard Tower],
& I hope his arm gets better soon; never trust a doctor!

    Bill

*PS. Thanks for P.C. of Great End & the Gable; they hang over my
bed – or rather blankets.'*

He and his fellow officers would probably have been briefed by someone from

B Company before setting out on the evening of 24 August, to relieve C Company in trenches near Richebourg-l'Avoué. These had been the scene of heavy fighting in the spring. The company went by road at first, roads which became increasingly crowded with transport, ration parties and reliefs as they drew nearer the point where their guides were waiting, one per platoon. Then past a cluster of ruined houses and across open ground, plunging down into a brick-paved entry to a maze of trenches, and so to the front line:

> 'The trenches run through old cornfields, now covered by dry weedy seed-oats. Just in front is a big ruined farm. The trenches themselves are enormous, deep, with high breastworks of sandbags. All night the Germans send up those greenish star shells, which light up everything like a great electric flare. There is a continual bickering of rifle fire going on all night; every now & then a machine gun joins in & occasionally a shell comes over. Both sides have every man out on the parapets digging like rabbits; you can hear the German picks & shovels going away opposite you. You can walk about all along by your own trenches even on a moonlight night like this; when a flare comes along, you stand still & try to look like a tree. Every now & then a sniper has a shot at you, but he never seems to hit anything, though you can hear the bullet come by. As dawn comes up, both sides get their working parties, patrols & listening posts back into the trenches under cover. Then comes "Stand to Arms", a horrible business, when one is cold & tired & hungry. Afterwards rifle inspection, trench inspection & breakfast'.[9]

That was how it began. C Company divided into working parties immediately and set to strengthening the parapet, and D Company's experience was probably much the same. John Upcott also asked to go out with a small patrol, because he knew he would hate it and wanted to get it over with; it was the sort of thing Noel is likely to have done. While D Company learned the routines of trench life the other three companies, back in billets at Locon, were being briefed about the trench lines the battalion was to hold in its own right, to the south of where they had been and closer to Festubert, in an area where the ground water was too close to the surface to permit deep digging; the line was protected with breastworks of sandbags. C Company went in on the night of 26 August: D would have left the Richebourg trenches the next night; the next, 28 August, they relieved C Company in the first line at Festubert. Upcott said:

> 'We had a great bother getting out owing to the inability of the men to pass messages. Freeland had the head of the coy waiting to enter communication trench. It was my job to close up the rear & to let him know when all were ready to move. Message after message failed to

reach him, even in writing. Meanwhile there was a large board hung on the wall of the trench above me saying, "This section of the trench is liable to heavy enfilade". I suppose we waited there ½ hour before a message got through.'

His company moved into the reserve line, where it was comparatively safe and from where he was able to capture an extraordinary view of their surroundings:

'Just below us lies the deserted village of Festubert; its streets choked with fallen brick & masonry & its church blown half to pieces, still lifting its white ruined arches against the blue August noon. Just by us an old road runs through the trenches, pitted with shell holes & overgrown with weeds now, for the Germans snipe down it & make it unsafe for use. Nibby & I have spent all the afternoon on walking up the old German line which runs just in front of us here. A more desolate place you could hardly imagine; it is all blown to pieces; what remains is just a ditch full of flapping black sandbags, charred rifles, old overcoats, uniforms and equipment.'

Meanwhile, in the front line Noel wrote to Stella on 29 August, giving her a first real glimpse into the world he now inhabited:

'Dear Star
Today is Sunday – Hal always said you could tell Sunday anywhere by the feel of the day. It's not true at all. Up here the shells come over, the snipers lurk in their ambushes, the corpses stink, the men grumble, and the world goes on just as usual. It's not a desperately exciting game, and very far from dignified; there's no doubt that a dead man loses all vestige of dignity and acquires a very lamentable odour. I sit in a dug-out, 12x8x6 feet, where six officers have their being, on the hardest seat imaginable, in a constrained position and no light. We don't get much pay but we do see life. The really interesting work begins at dusk and continues till about three in the morning, when the space between the trenches abounds with men carrying bombs, rifle grenades and flares, men sniping, men patrolling; while we all climb out in front and improve our parapets and wire, what time the stray bullets sigh about our heads and between our legs, but remarkably few ever hit anything. The first time I got outside just as I emerged from our sap a bullet whined over and buried itself in the earth just in front of my foot, that cheered me up a lot of course. Soon after I went outside our wire to post some men, and an officer of the party I was relieving said he had observed something, in a shell hole in front, which might be a sniper. 'Let's have a look' said I, and with drawn pistols we advanced cunningly. Over the edge of the hole was a white blob; 'it's

not alive' and we went right up to it. It was a Highlander, without any legs, regarding the moon from a supine position. As we [were] *returning we met our M.O. who had a Bosch helmet in his hand with a completely clean skull in it.*

Your P.C of the Gable for which much thanks made me long for the untainted air of my own country. Send another if you have it.

Love from Bill

Your letter from Row Head has just rolled in, and given me great pleasure. I have had one parcel with a book since you last wrote, "Romance" sent from Keswick; very nice too. I tell you what I <u>do</u> want, some of Savory and Moore's gelatine medicines in a flat pack for the poche – chlorodyne, cascara, coca, quinine; 'gelatine lamels' one calls them. Did you get a letter from me at Row Head? Bill.'

'Your P.C of the Gable . . . made me long for the untainted air of my own country.' That says it all, and she would have understood. He was describing experiences that no amount of training could have prepared them for. They coped by assuming an air of detachment and by a shared streak of gallows humour. Remarks that would have been callous at home became a survival mechanism at the Front. He also coped, privately, by hoarding souvenirs of the places he really wanted to be. Before the letter could have reached her, Stella had found and sent a different postcard of Great Gable, *'Here is another aspect of an old friend. . . . Cairns has been commanded to send a 'bun loaf'. I hope it arrives safely. Toujours & oh! be careful. Thine, S.M.T.'*[10]

But some horrors could penetrate even the strongest defences. The Devons came out of the trenches on the night of 30/31 August and returned to Locon. It was probably there that Noel was scanning a casualty list when he found Nowell Oxland's name. Oxland's battalion had reached Mudros on 18 July and landed at Cape Helles two days later. Withdrawn to Imbros at the end of the month, they then took part in the large-scale landing at Suvla Bay on 6 August. Oxland was killed three days later in an attack on the Turkish lines. At first the information reaching England about him was confused; even the date of his death was uncertain. But he was dead, and for Noel Hodgson it hurt most of all to think of him caught out of time in a landscape so alien and so very far from home.

In the days that followed the Devons were constantly on the move. First, on 1 September they marched 12 miles back along the La Bassée Canal to Guarbecque, to the accompaniment of the divisional band. They rested the next morning, and word among the officers was that a major attack was being prepared and they would be moved further north to be part of it. But their next move was south and east to Bellerive. Interminable travelling. *'It is always the same thing;'* (this was John Upcott): *'long winding roads with green ditches &*

*poplars on either side & at the end of the day a white square built farm round
a courtyard with a midden heap in the middle. The men go into the lofts & barns
& we have the house, except sometimes when there isn't room & we separate &
go into the cottages round about. It is quite good fun & I enjoy the marches
though one feels rather like a snail with these immense packs on our backs.'*
Next morning heavy rain fell, and they rested. *'One gives up trying to guess
where we shall be the following day. We are moving somewhere this afternoon.'*

'Somewhere' turned out to be La Bourse, reached late at night on 4
September after marching through Béthune. La Bourse was crowded with
soldiers from two divisions; the officers managed with some difficulty to find
billets for the men, then piled together into a single loft. Someone persuaded
the local baker to produce a meal of bacon and eggs, and they were just settling
down when orders came to move again at short notice; the transport section
would remain at La Bourse and would have charge of all the battalion's packs.
The battalion, meanwhile, marched to Noyelles, a half-ruined village close to
the lines.

For Noel Hodgson this constant marching had been a stimulus to thought.
When the body is active the mind can wander, and his mind was focused on
Nowell Oxland. The thought found expression in verse. In the version in *Verse
and Prose*, the poem 'Reverie' has a subtitle, 'Written on route march, August
1915'. Noel did date some of his war poems this way, but with this one the
month seems too early. He sent the first three verses to Stella on 20 September
titled 'Fragment', minus the final verse and with 'to be continued' scrawled in
the margin. Perhaps it was the initial idea that came to him in August; that his
subject is Nowell Oxland is apparent from the first verse. There were no
Cumbrians in the 9th Devons:

> *At home they see on Skiddaw*
> *The royal purple lie,*
> *And Autumn up in Newlands*
> *Arrayed in russet, die,*
> *Or under burning woodland*
> *The still lake's gramarye.*
> *And far off, grim and sable*
> *The menace of the Gable*
> *Life up his stark aloofness*
> *Against the evening sky.*
>
> *At vesper-time in Durham*
> *The level evening falls,*
> *Upon the shadowy river*
> *That slides by ancient walls*

Where out of crannied towers
The mellow belfry calls.
And there sleep brings forgetting
And morning no regretting,
And love is laughter-wedded
To health in happy halls.

In France – are blood & blisters
And thirst as harsh as sand,
Interminable travelling
An interminable land,
And stench & filth & sickness
And hate by hardship fanned;
The home of desolation
Wherein a desperate nation
Struggles to unloose murder's
Inexorable hand.

This from the original manuscript. The final verse, added later, runs,

Above the graves of heroes
The wooden crosses grow,
That shall no more see Durham
Nor any place they know,
Where fell tops face the morning
And great winds blow;
Who loving as none other
The land that is their mother,
Unfalteringly renounced her
Because they loved her so.

The Devons remained at Noyelles until 8 September, taking working parties into the trenches each night. It was cold and wet, they came back caked with mud, and no one had a change of clothes because their kit had been left at La Bourse. *'This is the saddest country you ever saw,'* Jack Inchbald told his father. *'Naturally flat & dull it is too dismal for words now that every town & village has been shelled to blazes. In some places there's hardly a stone standing. Churches, houses, trees are all knocked to bits. The House we are sleeping in has several shell holes through it. However we have found an estaminet which is inhabited by some quite genial females, who dispense delicious coffee to us & have all sorts of groceries in stock. They seem quite indifferent to their misfortunes.'* [11]

John Upcott found himself sleeping in a cowshed, *'& a pretty poor cowshed at that, for it has half its roof off & contains a large number of rats. However it doesn't really matter, because I never get to bed till 4 a.m. & at that hour a man will sleep on a midden heap every bit as well as on a feather bed. We have nothing but overcoats to sleep in. The trick is to take your boots & tunic off; stuff your feet into the sleeves of your overcoat & put your tunic over your head; that gives the maximum amount of heat.'*[12]

And Noel told Stella:

'We have been having a very stiff time lately, not dangerous but extremely strenuous. We go up every night about 6.30 to various localities in the front line on fatigues, helping to dig and build new parapets, fill sandbags etc; and return home any time between 2 and 4 in the morning. We get a certain amount of rest during the day, but one never gets the chance of a decent period of sleep somehow. Coming back in the morning I have actually fallen asleep while walking, and on getting in after putting down a cup of tea or cocoa we lie down on the floor on some straw if we can get it and sleep till about 8 or half past in the morning. Jones is absolutely invaluable to me in these days, getting me straw to lie on and waterproof sheets to cover me, and raising hot water for shaving purposes in the most unfavourable circumstances. Our only grumble at present is that they moved us here at half an hour's notice, and let us bring no valise with us, so we have been for five or six days in what we stand up in, quite unnecessary as we could easily have them fetched up if it was permitted. I haven't got lousy yet though thank Heaven. That is the ultimate indignity of all. Hinshelwood got 'em our last tour in the trenches, to the vast delight of myself and Jones. We expect to be on the trek again soon.'

The physical discomfort was compounded for him by further bad news. The casualty list of Saturday, 4 September, included more friends. George Kenneth Hampton, another King's Scholar of School House, killed at Gallipoli; James Dingle, Durham and Oxford, killed at Gallipoli. Historians now dismiss the 'lost generation' of the Great War as a myth and statistically they are right. Far more men survived the war overall than were killed. But perhaps the idea was never really about statistics. For him, reading the relentless lists of familiar names, it is easy to see why it *felt* as if his generation was being consumed by the war. The deepest pain, though, was for Nowell Oxland. A letter had come from Stella with a very special souvenir of his favourite place; moss from the top of Great Gable. In other circumstances he would have treasured it as a physical link to home. He used it now to make a symbolic funeral pyre for his friend:

'Thanks very much for the moss from the Gable, which I burned at evening in memory of Oxland who died in the Dardanelles a fortnight ago, and was my great companion in my hill climbs. I shall miss him much; also three more school pals who were in Saturday's list.'

He wrote that on 6 September but did not post it. Two days later the battalion was once again on the move, to Verquin first, then, next day, through Béthune to Gonnehem. He continued the letter in the early morning at Verquin:

'We are now in the middle of a trek, and after sleeping out in a field under a splendid autumn night, I have woken up to one of the mornings that make up for anything. Slightly misty with a bright sun shining through the mist, and a freshness in the air speaking of Autumn – a morning like the frost on a jug of iced champagne. I have had a good breakfast and altogether

"The world is none so bad
And I myself a sterling lad."

Only I feel not quite so well when I think of those pals of mine who went out in Gallipoli.

There's no doubt there are good moments in this soldiering. Last night as I lay in my blanket, I could see the whole Heavens, from the Great to the Little Bear, above my head, and in the dusk around were little spots of light where men were bivouacked, and now and then a few words of a song from some unseen lips. Or again once as we marched home about midnight we passed a shed where some gunners lived. Inside was a small fire lit, burning with a deep red glow, by which sat a man playing softly on a whistle pipe, and beside him three more leaning forward toward the fire, which lit up their strong faces vividly. All behind was darkness, stars & the tops of trees. It was a Salvator Rosa picture pure and simple.

Well, I must be getting ready for the trek now, so for the present au revoir, and much love from Bill'

The quotation – 'The world is none so bad . . .' – is from A.E. Housman's *A Shropshire Lad*, a favourite with poetically-minded officers in the trenches. Reading matter was all-important. John Upcott read Spenser's *The Faerie Queen* as an antidote to war and petitioned his family for volumes of Dickens. Stella was sending Noel books regularly, and the lasting effect of Nowell Oxland's death was to re-energise the writer in him, not just in poetry but prose too, to capture his experiences and pass them on. The first stirrings are there in this letter. He and Nowell Oxland had shared the ambition to write; Oxland's death must have made him realise how brief his own time might be and his writing took on a new urgency. He began to experiment with prose accounts of life at the Front, which he hoped might be saleable, and feared might not be. A letter he sent to Stella from Gonnehem one Sunday, probably 12 September, is curiously diffident, at once shying away from the idea of publication, yet at the same time promising to send her two articles which she might be able to sell:

> *'Many thanks for your long letter, and the delightful pictures which reduced me to a state of maudlin sentiment, until I thought of Rawnsley and pulled myself together.*
>
> *Many thanks for the books and toffee which arrived yesterday. Please don't send me any more things just yet; I feel a hopeless mendicant.*
>
> *I don't think I would publish my perpetrations yet; the times are too hardy for such delicate plants.*
>
> *The Gioconda seems to be the goods. I look forward to the time when with an attractive limp and my left arm in a sling I am driven by you round about the neighbourhood.*
>
> *I bought some Boots solid meth out with me and have a couple of tins still; in about a fortnight though I could do with some more.*
>
> *I rejoice to hear of the advent of the kitten; don't let it kill Rory.*
>
> *I am going to send you a couple of articles on 'life in our Mess' which may interest you, and might be saleable.*
>
> *Bill'*

He sent them on 20 September, with the incomplete version of 'Reverie'. The first article, 'Company Mess: In billets', is set in the early evening when the day's duties are over and the officers gather. They are D Company to the life: the second-in-command 'Lance Captain', whose hobby is designing new weapons; 'the Bart', *'a budding barrister thirteen months ago'*; the senior subaltern *'of Repton and the Royal Agricultural College'*; 'Nobby', *'a fresher of Hertford, Oxford;'* and 'Smiler', the Grenade Officer, whose post includes half a pound of Keswick toffee – *'Put it where Nobby can't get it, or he'll scoff the lot'* – and a letter from 'Nestor' in Serbia. They talk aimlessly about dinner and the post. Nobby finds the name of a Christ Church man killed in the Dardanelles, and tells Smiler. *'Smiler looks up, "My God, has he really," he looks troubled, "poor devil, he was a good chap." Such is the dead man's epitaph, and Smiler goes on reading; it is so common, one cannot mourn them all.'* Orders come in from brigade – a new type of bomb, which the men are to be trained to use; then a wire saying that these bombs are at present unobtainable; the battalion's next marching orders. The piece ends with dinner, and the Grenade Officer carefully counting out the tinned apricots.

'Company Mess No.2' takes the same group of men, minus the senior subaltern, on an outing, armed with beer and food from the mess box. It is Sunday morning and they have no duties for a few hours and – great joy, this –

there are hills to climb, the first they have seen in weeks. This inspires a piece of spontaneous verse from the Bart, completed by the Grenade Officer; *'It drives an officer insane/ And makes a flatness in his brain/ Flat ground as flat as bad French beer.'*

At the top of the hill they collapse on the grass, save the Bart, who goes blackberry picking. Nobby begins sketching and the Grenade Officer takes out his Field Message Book and starts to write *'verses in praise of stout'*. Slowly, they reminisce or think aloud, looking at the flat land spread out before them.

> *1 'From the Grenade Officer;*
>> *"Why are people such fools as to fight."*
>> *A pause, and then from the Lance-Captain,*
>> *"A year ago – no thirteen months and a bit – I was yachting at Torquay."*
>> *"And I was lying about in a punt at Maidenhead, reading Herodotus."*
>> *"Herodotus," murmured the G.O. in a retrospective voice; "my Lord, I should have had my Greats viva by now and been a B.A. – Greats – Good Lord."'*

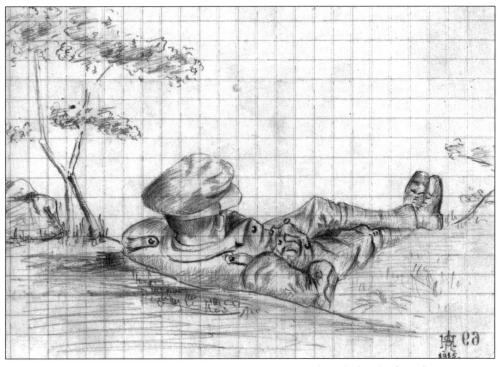

Alan Hinshelwood's drawing of Hodgson, from the outing described in the first 'Company Mess' article, September 1915.

They fall silent for a while, then start to talk about home, and where they would like to be, until they realise the time has come to return – and Nobby's attempts to list the next day's duties are shouted down by the others.

These articles do not seem have sold. Perhaps there was not enough war in them to interest readers at home – the very thing that would have appealed most to him and his companions. But it is striking how closely they mirror his actual experience. The manuscript of the second is dated 19 September, which was indeed a Sunday. The Devons were at Fouquereuil, and an entry in John Upcott's diary for the previous day confirms the existence of the hills: *'There are hills about here, the first we have seen since we left Wizernes.'*[13] He and Rayner also had time off to explore. And the article really is written on pages torn from an army message book. As for Nobby's sketch, he was drawing the Grenade Officer. The real sketch, showing Noel Hodgson lying on his back on a grassy slope and signed 'ASH, September 1915', is still among Hodgson's papers.[14] And the duties the three did not want Nobby to remind them about as they walked back down the hill were the final preparations for their first battle, just a few days away.

Chapter 9

'The Grime of Battle', Loos, September 1915

The Battle of Loos was an offensive the British did not want to fight, over ground the Army would not have chosen. In 1915 Britain was committed to the war, but doubtful of success on the Western Front until the New Army battalions were up to strength, with sufficient stockpiles of munitions and artillery. Lord Kitchener, Secretary of State for War, was particularly opposed to a large-scale attack in France in 1915, despite French demands for a combined summer offensive. Kitchener favoured a more cautious strategy in the west, while putting resources behind the attempt to break through in the Dardanelles. What changed his mind, and the course of Britain's war, was the worsening situation the Allies faced as the summer drew on. In the east, Russia suffered a series of crushing defeats. By May 1915, British representatives in Russia were reporting a general breakdown in morale and with it a feeling of betrayal. The Russians believed they had taken the offensive the previous summer to prevent the fall of Paris. A year on, the absence of a major offensive in the west was leaving them unsupported and increasingly vulnerable. Warsaw fell to the Germans on 5 August: the fear in London and Paris was that Russia might be forced into a separate peace.

The very next day saw the landing at Suvla Bay, followed by the fighting from which so much was hoped and so little achieved. The Dardanelles campaign proved to be a costly failure, and this added to the pressure for a large-scale offensive in the west. Remote as all this may seem from Noel Hodgson and the Devons, trudging along the dusty roads of the Pas de Calais, it was these far-off events which would determine their future.

They could not have known it, but 19 August, the day Bryan Freeland noticed Lord Kitchener 'prowling around' as they trained in the stubble fields by the La Bassée Canal, was decisive. Kitchener was concluding a three-day visit to France to discuss the proposed offensive – the offensive he had been keen to avoid – with the French authorities and his own senior officers. That evening he was to return to London, the planned attack having been agreed. The next day he would lay it before the Cabinet. The 9th (Service) Battalion, The Devonshire Regiment, was just one tiny cog in the whole vast machine, and the Secretary of State is unlikely to have had any particular interest in them. But the New Army battalions were his concern, and as he watched the Devons making their barbed wire entanglements and throwing their bombs, he would surely have been looking for signs of how they would cope in a major battle.

When the Devons joined 20 Brigade the previous week, John Upcott asked himself how the Brigade might feel about taking on two untried volunteer battalions in place of the Grenadiers and the Scots Guards. It was a fair question. After all, the Service battalions were experimental: nothing quite like them had been tried before. And looking through the official records, there are hints of concern about them at brigade level and above. One order sent down from First Army Headquarters in September stresses that all officers must understand that supervising their men's work is their responsibility, even when acting under the direction of the Engineers: *'It has been found that the infantry officers belonging to some of the new formations do not realise.'* Officers, the order states, must understand how to do the tasks allotted to their men. John Upcott and Harold Rayner might have chuckled at this: they often worked alongside the men when it became too boring or too cold to stand by and watch.

Another set of papers concerns the observation that men of the 8th Devons were not wearing their webbing equipment in the trenches. The commanding officer of the 8th Devons explained his reasons and an exchange of messages followed. And John Upcott described an incident in early September, when he was leading his company along the road from Verquin to Béthune. Colonel Davies told him to march the men in single file on either side of the road, *'to avoid aircraft observation'*. He obeyed. On the far side of Béthune he was stopped by no less a person than the Corps Commander, Lieutenant General Gough, demanding to know why the men were in this formation: *'I nearly got it hot & strong from a big general this afternoon,'* Upcott told his sister. *'He was obviously on the lookout for somebody to strafe, & seeing me he opened fire, horse, foot & guns. However I was able to prove complete innocency, when I could get a word in edgewise, & he passed on his way looking for bigger game.'*[1]

These are isolated instances which may not add up to anything much. Similar concerns might have been raised about any incoming battalions. But a stronger indication of unease may be found in the changes made to the 9th Devons in the weeks leading up to the battle. On 11 September Colonel Davies and his second-in-command Major Bedingfield were ordered home because they were considered too old. Major Bedingfield took over command of the Reserve Battalion at Wareham, while 'Uncle Tom' was given a job on an Army Medical Board. *'We shall be sorry to lose Uncle Tom & the Major,'* John Upcott wrote, *'but I wouldn't have either of them killed for anything.'* A Regular officer took command. Major Henry Innes Storey, originally of the 1st Battalion, had played a part in forming the 8th Devons and stayed as one of their senior officers. Now he became commanding officer of the 9th Devons, with one of Colonel Davies's

The Rev Henry Bernard Hodgson and his wife Penelope Maria Warren, Noel Hodgson's parents.

The Hodgson children; (left) Arthur and Hal, in about 1890, (right) Noel and Stella at Thornbury in 1896-7.

The Hodgsons on the steps of the vicarage in Berwick-upon-Tweed: Henry, Hal, Arthur, Stella and Penelope. The fidget in front of his mother, scarcely more than a blur, is Noel, probably taken in about 1900.

The family home for most of Noel Hodgson's life on the defensive wall at Berwick. The photograph above was taken in the doorway, left. In the Hodgsons' time there would have been thirteen guns in the saluting bay by the wall.

Noel and Stella in about 1901.

Stella ('Star') in 1909.

Durham School in the early 1900s; School House is on the left. (Durham School Archives)

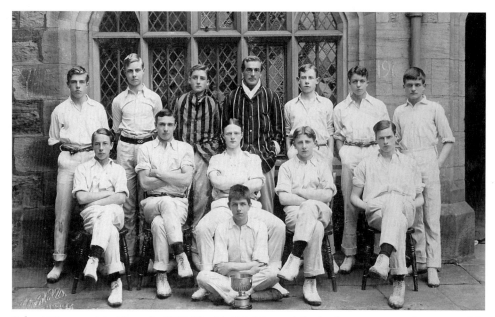

School House cricket team in 1908. Noel is third from right, back row, next to the master, Mr Wilkinson. At least three of the other boys died in the war; Alan Brown (standing, right), died in the crossing of the River Piave in Italy; Francis Adamson (in front of him) was bombing officer of the 2nd Borders, and must have seen Hodgson often. He was killed by a sniper in November 1915. Hugh Dingle (standing left) became a Naval surgeon and died in the Battle of Jutland. (Durham School Archives)

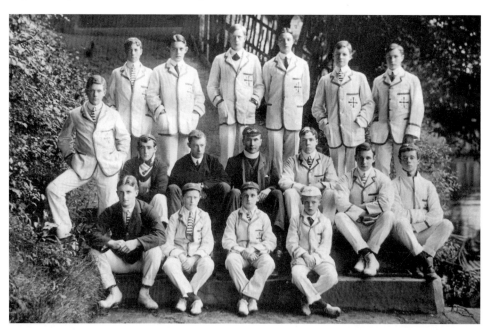

The School Boating Club in 1909, with the First, Second and Third Crews. Nowell Oxland is on the left in front, in the dark blazer. The small boy on the right is Edward Melbourne Martin, who inspired Hodgson's pen-name. Next to him, Max Greville-Jones, is mentioned in one of Hodgson's wartime letters. Five of those shown were killed in the war, a further five wounded at least once. (Durham School Archives)

The Rev Richard Dutton Budworth, the Headmaster, at work extending the playing field.

Noel, 'Bill' Hodgson.

His friends at school and Oxford; (left) Robert Parr and (right) Nowell Oxland (Oxland; Worcester College Archives)

The Christ Church hockey team of 1912 – 13. Hodgson is standing to the right of the doorway. The others are unidentified.

The family outside 'Parklands', the Bishop's house in Ipswich, in 1914. In front, Henry with Rory the dog, Penelope and Noel; behind, Stella and her husband the Rev Henry Bernard Tower, 'Toby'.

Noel Hodgson in the summer of 1914, and a postcard from his holiday diary showing the Black Sail Pass, one of his favourite routes.

So much change in a few months: 'with love Bill, Dec 1914', and (right) one of his pin-ups, Great Gable. The card shows part of his 'Farewell Walk; up the Styhead Pass (bottom of the picture, climbing left to right) and from there to the summit.

(Left) Alan Hinshelwood and Noel Hodgson at Bisley, autumn 1914. (Right) Bryan Freeland, later Captain of 'C' Company, also at Bisley.

Hodgson (left foreground), Hinshelwood and two other officers in camp.

Tennis at Aldershot: Duncan Martin standing, in the light jacket; John Upcott in front with the pipe and dog; George Underhill on the right; Arthur Lewis on the left; the other two are unidentified.

Group of 9th Devon officers at Bordon. Richard Hooper Smyth, 'Chink' is second left; Charles Cecil Thompson fourth left, leaning on Mervyn Davies. On the extreme right, Launcelot Sulyarde Robert Cary – 'little Cary'.

(Left) John Dalgairns Upcott and (right) Frank Clemson Worrall, 'Worry', whom Upcott called 'rather a dear… but quite mad'.

(Left) Upcott on the bicycle, and his Oxford friend Harold Rayner; (right) Duncan Martin.

Mervyn Davies (left) and Geoffrey Tracey, both of whom were killed at Loos.

Rowan 'Babe' Freeland, Bryan Freeland's brother, wearing the white cap band of an officer cadet, and (right) John Chantrey Elliot 'Jack' Inchbald who survived Loos and the Somme, and was killed in an attack on Écoust-St-Mien in April 1917.

Lieutenant Colonel T.A.H. Davies, 'Uncle Tom', leading the 9th Devons on the trek from Alton to Winchester in April 1915.

A rest by the roadside; from the left, Alan Hinshelwood, Noel Hodgson; Mervyn Davies and William Ede 'Pussy' Martin.

Hodgson in training with a Vickers gun. Behind him is Bertram Glossop.

Hodgson and Hinshelwood outside their bivouac tent at the farm on the road to Robecq.

The bombing officer at work. Noel Hodgson in France, probably taken in August 1915, in the weeks leading up to the Battle of Loos.

(Left) Frank Wollocombe, one of the 9th Battalion's diarists, and (right) Cyril Shepard, brother of the illustrator E.H. Shepard. Both were killed on the Somme: Cyril on 1 July 1916 and Frank in September.

Taken in France, before Loos: 'Smiler' Hodgson second right, hand on the shoulder of John Truscott, the transport officer. On his other side, Captain Ralph Whitney Mockridge, then Bertram Glossop. The other man is unidentified.

(Left) Harold 'Nibby' Rayner and (right) Duncan 'Iscariot' Martin, two of the original 9th Devon officers, both killed with Hodgson on 1 July 1916.

The Devonshire Cemetery as it was at the end of the war. The photograph belonged to the Hodgsons and may date from Henry and Penelope's visit in 1920. The board on the right says 'Devonshire Cemetery'; the crosses marking the burial plots were dark wood and are hard to make out; in other photographs the white cross can be seen to identify the two Devon battalions and the date 1 July 1916.

Taken in the mid-1920s, this vividly illustrates how exposed the Devons were as they moved across the slope of the hill. Hidden from the camera, the copse bank drops steeply down to the track, the road and the railway line. On the ground visible beyond the bushes were the German positions to the right which caused many early casualties. The apparent trench line in the foreground is intriguing, but hard to relate to 1916 maps.

chosen men, Major Anderson, as his second-in-command. A week later the formidable Regimental Sergeant Major Grubb was sent home, and the officers stood him a dinner before he left. The Adjutant, Lieutenant William Ede 'Pussy' Martin, (no relation to Duncan) was assigned to a platoon in C Company, while that platoon's officer Frederick John Allen, a former bank clerk who had served at the Front as a private in 1914 before gaining his commission, became signalling officer. A new Adjutant, Lieutenant Philip Brindley, was borrowed from the 1st Battalion, The Royal Warwickshire Regiment.[2]

It was a lot for the battalion to take in. *'We have a young Brigadier,'* Jack Inchbald explained to his father, *'& evidently our old colonel & major were considered too old. So they've both gone home on leave. It's rather depressing – we are now commanded by a young & vigorous major . . . who has come to us from our 8th Battalion & who I think will run us very well. It was rather a wrench to lose our beloved colonel but I'm bound to say he let things go a bit slack & this is undoubtedly a young man's war.'*[3] But Harold Rayner saw it rather differently, commenting when the battle was over, *'The men wished that Colonel Davies could have seen how well we did. They feel they were his battalion.'*[4]

Noel Hodgson was preoccupied with his writing and his bombers. On 30 August, a few weeks after he became bombing officer, ten men passed their bombing test and were awarded a grenade badge. A later Brigade Order stipulated that the battalion was to have six grenade sections, fully equipped with bags to carry grenades – ten in each – and two men in each section were to be designated carriers. The sections were to be ready for inspection by 11 September, and their training and equipping was his responsibility. In the first 'Company Mess' article, written around this time, he gives a vivid picture of the Grenade Officer's life, on the receiving end of a daily stream of contradictory and conflicting Brigade Orders. *'The Grenade Officer scans the pink sheets and uplifts his voice in a masterly denunciation of persons unknown.'*

The battle was a fortnight away. Time was ticking by and the days drawing in. *'The summer I think is over,'* Jack Inchbald wrote from Fouquereuil, *'although the weather is still lovely & it's hot enough by day. But there's an autumn nip in the air in the evenings & early mornings. . . .We are close to a railway siding here where a lot of shunting whistling & other rows go on. You've no idea how homely such irritating sounds can be!'*[5] Small homely things meant a lot. Earlier, in the farm on the road to Calonne, John Upcott had made a friend of the farmer's little daughter, Eugenie, seven years old, *'very ugly but a great coquette. I am trying to decoy her with chocolate, but she generally pretends to be shy'*. He was delighted when she ran out and kissed him as the battalion marched away. At Fouquereuil it was the little boys who amused him. *'They always attend the mounting of the guard & have learnt even the words of command. So that when our guard mounts, a second guard of little French boys always mounts beside it.*'[6]

As the others prepared for the battle, John Upcott expected to be held in reserve while Bryan Freeland led C Company. He was wrong. At Gonnehem Bryan Freeland was asked if he was interested in a transfer to the Royal Engineers. He said yes. He was horrified when the order came to join 173 Tunnelling Company on 23 September – two days before the battle. He tried to persuade somebody – anybody – to postpone it, but his appeals met with no sympathy. The officer commanding 173 Tunnelling Company told him *'I must join at once and said that if my name was on a bullet it would be one intended for a Sapper!'* And that was that. Bryan Freeland was transferred and John Upcott took his place.

During the day on 23 September the Devons rested. At 7pm they paraded as a thunderstorm broke, and they marched through torrential rain to Verquin, the sudden, sharp bursts of lightning a grim forewarning of what was to come. They arrived just over three hours later. After breakfast the next morning, Major Storey called the officers to Battalion HQ to go over their orders for the attack. *'I sat with Tracey in the window, where it was difficult to hear because of the traffic passing constantly over the cobbled streets below'* – this was John Upcott – *'We are to be in support of the Gordons & 8th Devons. . . . The final objective is unlimited, but we are to make for Pontavendin Bridge if we get through.'* The rest of the morning was given over to kit inspections and the testing of smoke helmets. In the afternoon Hodgson marched his bombers to Sailly Labourse to draw grenades from brigade stores. Then there was nothing to do but wait:

> *'We had our last supper together in the back room of a little shop at the end of the street. A parcel had just arrived from home & we did our best to finish it; especially the salted almonds which mother had sent. Many of the men asked for a service. It was too late, poor chaps; there were plenty going before. The R.C.s had one in the village church. All the time we were having supper, a 15-inch howitzer was making the whole crazy little house rock.'*[7]

At 10pm the battalion left Verquin, Noel Hodgson at the back in D Company with his Welsh-speaking platoon and his bombing sections. John Upcott, ahead of him with C Company, and riding now that he commanded them, captured the scene in his diary:

> *'There was a full moon; the guns had stopped & the open fields looked glorious in the moonlight as we followed the tracks across the stubble; once a gun limber at full gallop nearly rode into the column at right angles, but I rode out of the line & stopped it. My sensations were such as I had never felt before – a curious detached feeling combined with a*

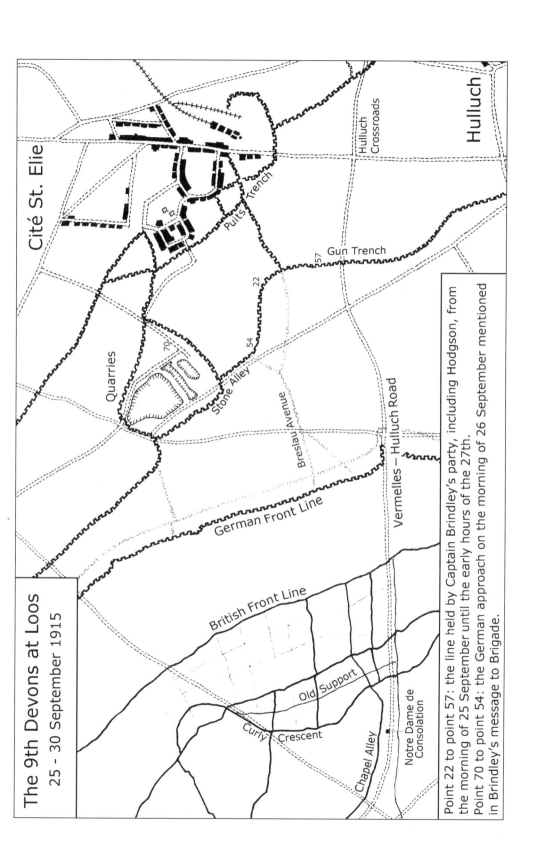

The 9th Devons at Loos
25 - 30 September 1915

Cité St. Elie

Hulluch

Hulluch Crossroads

Quarries

Puits Trench

Gun Trench

57

22

54

70

Stone Alley

Breslau Avenue

Vermelles – Hulluch Road

German Front Line

British Front Line

Old Support

Curly Crescent

Chapel Alley

Notre Dame de Consolation

Point 22 to point 57: the line held by Captain Brindley's party, including Hodgson, from the morning of 25 September until the early hours of the 27th. Point 70 to point 54: the German approach on the morning of 26 September mentioned in Brindley's message to Brigade.

great peace of mind – as someone put it "as though we were all on the brink of the next world." I used the T[homas] à Kempis Prayer, I remember, as I rode. "Defend & keep the souls of thy servants among so many perils of this corruptible life & Thy grace going with us, direct us to the country of everlasting clearness." And yet I was sure that my time had not come. At Noyelles the column halted & I dismounted & sent my horse back by my groom, giving him my greatcoat & spurs.'

Now the companies moved off one by one along the Vermelles Road at fifteen-minute intervals, walking in single file through the ruins of Vermelles. Major Storey watched them pass before going forward himself. Being at the back, in support of the other battalions, the 9th Devons took up positions in trenches just beyond the railway line to the east of Vermelles, some distance from the front line. By 2am they were all in place. The final timings for the attack were received at 20 Brigade HQ at 3.40am, and messages were sent round the various units.

Six British divisions were to lead the advance on a 6 mile/10km front, from Givenchy in the north to the little town of Grenay, near Lens in the south; at the time it was the largest land battle ever fought by the British Army. In June General Sir Douglas Haig, Commander of First Army, had prepared a report on the suitability of the ground for an attack and he was discouraging. On this open, flat land any movement could be seen for miles. The smallest elevation gave an advantage; only in trenches could men advance relatively safely – from bullets, at least – but on the chalky soil new trench digging was impossible to conceal. There were isolated houses, mining villages, pit heads and slag heaps to contend with; and most concerning of all, the fact that Britain did not have anything like the reserves of artillery shells the Army would need. To make up for this it was decided to use gas, which the Germans had used at Ypres in April, hence the training and the gas helmets. As gas too was in short supply, smoke bombs and smoke candles would be used as well to screen the advancing troops. For 20 Brigade, in the centre of the battlefield to the left of the Vermelles – Hulluch Road, the task was to advance across two lines of German trenches to the villages of Hulluch and Cité St Elie, and if possible beyond. No final objective was set.

At 5.50am an intensive bombardment began. *'What one chiefly noticed was not the noise but the steady swish of the shells passing by hundreds over head.'*[8] This provoked German shelling in reply, which caused some casualties among the men waiting in the forward trenches. Then gas and smoke were released along the British line. At 6.25am, five minutes before the attack began, the rear companies of the 9th Devons, C and D, began to move forward along the trenches leading to the front line. As they reached A and B, so they too began to move. That was at about 6.30am, when the first wave of the attack emerged from the front line. There, in front, the scene was chaotic. The rear companies of the 8th Devons advanced too quickly, leading to crowding at the prepared gaps in the wire – creating an easy target for rifles and machine guns in the enemy trenches. There was also gas in the air, the wind being too light to carry it away. A private in the 8th Battalion described the scene for a local paper:

'When we got over the parapet we were met with terrible rifle and shell fire, gas and barbed wire. The enemy seemed to know what we were going to do. My orders were to stick with the second in command, Major Carden. He also had an orderly, Pte. Batt. . . . I regret to say Major Carden and Batt got killed near the wire, just past the gas. It was terrible at that point; I am sorry to say scores got killed just here.'[9]

They did. The 8th Battalion lost all but three of its officers at this point, killed or wounded.

What this meant to the 9th Devons, trying to make their way forward, was that as they drew nearer the Front the trenches became increasingly choked with wounded from the battalions that had already gone over. There were other hazards too. C Company was held up for an agonising 15 minutes when their machine guns became entangled with the telephone wires. The decision to give up on the congested trenches altogether and move forward in the open seems to have been made piecemeal. Noel Hodgson and the rest of D Company climbed out of Chapel Alley at the chapel of Notre Dame de Consolation, close to the Hulluch Road, at 7.45am. John Upcott saw Alan Hinshelwood moving in the open and climbed onto the parapet of his own communication trench to get some idea of what was happening. He could see right across the battlefield to the village of Cité St Elie, far off behind the German lines, where shadowy figures were moving; who they were he could not tell. It was Major Storey who told him to take C Company out of the trench and across open ground.

There was no alternative if they were to go forward, but leaving the trenches exposed them to rifle and machine-gun fire. Geoffrey Tracey, the machine-gun officer, was killed as he climbed out of the trench; his sergeant was awarded the Military Medal for taking his place and getting the machine guns up. Tracey was nineteen, just a month short of his twentieth birthday. Major Storey was hit in the right shoulder a few minutes after John Upcott spoke to him. The bullet severed an artery and he would have died if Lieutenant Brindley had not been able to bind up the wound and staunch the bleeding. The second-in-command, Major Anderson, also had a narrow escape. One hazard of advancing overground from the rear was the need to cross the forward trenches before reaching no man's land. John Upcott saw the major attempt to jump a trench and fall in. He helped him out, then they must have been hit at almost the same moment. The major was shot in the chest, the bullet passing from left to right and grazing his lung, but narrowly missing his heart:

> *'I collapsed like a shot rabbit, completely winded, & thought all my ribs were broken by a piece of shell. After a time Smyth came & relieved me of my pack & gave me 1st aid in a most splendid manner & put me on my back where I lay panting from 8.45am to 5pm or later. Some stray men picked me up & brought me along to an Ambulance motor some 1½ miles & I eventually got to 2nd Red Cross Hospl, Rouen.'[10]*

Upcott had just returned to his men when:

> *'I felt a terrific blow to the shoulder & dropped on my hands & knees. The men thinking it was a signal dropped also. I waved the advance & they went on again. I could see nothing wrong with my shoulder, though my arm & hand were very stiff & numb. Getting up I ran forward & got in front of the line again. M[artin] saw my shoulder & told me I was wounded. Looking down I saw my tunic was covered with blood. Then we separated, he going down the line to the left, while I led the right forward. I remember wishing my wound had been worse, for enfilade fire was sweeping us from the flank & I saw that few of us would get through. The suspense of waiting for one's quietus is under such circumstances almost unbearable.'*

A stretcher bearer in one of the trenches signalled to him to have his wound dressed. He jumped down and was just being attended to when a shell hit the next bay of the trench, exploding an unused gas canister. Gas began to fill the trench; with only one hand useable, John Upcott was not able to put his mask on quickly enough. He took in sufficient gas to make him feel very ill, and a passing chaplain set him on the way back towards Vermelles, and safety.

All this before they even reached the front line. From about 100 yards back, Harold Rayner watched Captain Muntz and Frank Worrall of B Company cross the low ridge that marked the Front under heavy shelling, trying to encourage their men. They passed out of sight; when he reached the place himself with his platoon they were nowhere to be seen. They saw him, though, or at least, Frank Worrall did:

> *'I saw Rayner with a small crowd as he passed the 2nd G[erman] trenches but was too weak to cheer him on loud enough to be heard. I got my leg smashed up there. The other two [wounds] didn't worry me much except I bled a lot and my right arm is still a bit stiff. Yes the lads were grand. . . . I have heard from about 24 of my wounded and my killed were few.'*

John Pocock, also of B Company, had shrapnel in both legs and an arm broken by a bullet. 'Pussy' Martin came across him on the journey back to hospital, and learned from him *'that Worrall got one in each leg below the knees. Poor old Muntz got one in the mouth & had his top lip split & some teeth carried away.'*[11]

'Pussy' was injured himself. He told John Upcott:

'I got a bullet through my leg. I have only a hazy recollection of it getting me, but it must have been during one of our halts, as the bullet entered the top of my left calf, travelled down the bone & came out about a foot lower down. It gave me some hell. After a time I thought it advisable to get back to our trenches . . . I got there eventually, picking up a bullet through my left knee on the way.'

Signalling officer Frederick Allen was shot in the stomach and lay out on the battlefield until evening. He died in the Casualty Clearing Station at Lapugnoy. In D Company, Captain Mockridge was wounded in the thigh, Alan Hinshelwood's arm was broken by a rifle bullet and Bertram Glossop was shot in the leg. His last sighting of the survivors, Noel Hodgson and Mervyn, 'the Bart' Davics, still leading D Company and the bombers forward, was passed on in 'Pussy' Martin's letter:

'I got the latest report from him to the effect that Mervyn with an evil leer on his face and his bandy legs twinkling in and out among the bullets was still going strong. Smiler with his bombers was doing great execution against a M.G. [machine gun] in the Breslau redoubt. When last seen Rayner was rushing along at the head of his men somewhere by the German first line, waving a pistol and shouting wildly!'

Hodgson and his bombers had been called away to the left to help deal with a strongpoint in the German line, where they and bombers from the 2nd Borders took 150 prisoners. Rayner saw the prisoners being taken towards the British lines and felt an uncharacteristic surge of anger, knowing that these were the men who had caused so many casualties in the battalion. He attended to a few of the wounded men close to him, made sure they had water bottles, and pointed them in the direction of the nearest Advanced Dressing Station. Then he paused to take stock. He thought he had about two to three dozen men of C Company with him, and some of B Company. Ahead of him he could see Noel Hodgson and Lieutenant Brindley, who took over, gathering everyone into a German trench the British knew as Stone Alley. Mervyn Davies was there too with survivors of D Company, and Brindley led them into Gun Trench – a series of gun emplacements where eight or nine German guns had been captured by the 8th Devons and the Borders in the first wave of the attack. The bombers rejoined the party. At 10am Hodgson led them in a reconnaissance through a communication trench leading towards Cité St Elie, to see if it was possible to advance further. But at Puits Trench, which encircled the village on the south-western side, they encountered a thicket of uncut barbed wire, so the survivors began to dig in around the captured guns. It may have seemed unnecessary when there were well-dug German trenches nearby, but it was the safest option. German gunners in the rear could range shells accurately on what had been their own trenches but they would avoid hitting the guns. Given a chance, they would recapture those intact.

Only Harold Rayner was no longer part of this group. He had been diverted by a staff captain, who *'appeared from nowhere in front, and told me to make a line straight in front, so I took some fifteen men, and took up a position on the edge of the rank grass.'* They had no trench and no cover except the grass. While things were quiet this did not matter, though it frustrated Rayner that the village looked empty and might have been taken if only reinforcements were at hand. This was a general experience at Loos. Along the battle front, survivors of the first waves watched helplessly while fresh German troops were brought in, strengthening thinly held positions and making their own plight more dangerous. After about an hour, Rayner saw a sudden increase in gunfire from the village in response to an advancing company of the Wiltshire Regiment, most of whom were hit. Somewhere around mid-day shells began to fall too, making his position untenable. So he led his men on a crawl through the grass to the safety of the nearest trench, gathering up discarded ammunition on the way. They found themselves in a different part of Gun Trench full of Wiltshires, who directed them to another group of 9th Devons under Lieutenant Pridham. After the first adrenaline rush of the battle a reaction was setting in. There was a cold drizzle falling, and *'Pridham seemed rather lost and not at all interested in my arrival.'*[12]

During the afternoon they made contact with the adjutant's party under the captured guns. There was also another collection of 9th Devons on the battlefield. About fifty A Company men under Captain Nation and Second Lieutenant Smyth had gone south of the Hulluch road. About mid-day they managed to link up with remnants of the 8th Devons, who were digging in at the crossroads just before Hulluch. According to Atkinson's *The Devonshire Regiment*, Jack Inchbald was with them, but Jack told a very different story. Sent ahead as a 'forward observing officer' in the early hours, he was separated from his own company before the advance began. *' I saw you were hit and I heard you shout 'don't get into the trench – gas!!'* he told John Upcott,

'I saw your chaps were puffed – it was ridiculous to send 'em in with packs wasn't it? – and I saw you and Pussy were done, so I took charge of your fellows and gave 'em a rest. After two or three minutes we went on but lost ourselves. I was told the 9th had gone half right which proved untrue. However I pushed off in that direction and eventually

landed among the 1st —'s in another division. By that time I only had about 20 men with me of all Batts in the Brigade. I spent the next three days with the 1st —'s and had a splendid view of a well known hill . . . as you can imagine the counter attacks of the Huns were an extraordinary sight.'[13]

Meanwhile the digging continued under the captured guns. It was raining steadily, *'the mud slowly mounting from knee to waist and from wrist to shoulder, and on the waterproof sheets flung over prone figures which lie, some ominously still, some terribly unquiet behind the trench.'[14]* Around mid-day Lieutenant Brindley was talking to Mervyn Davies when a shell exploded close by. Brindley was stunned for a few moments. Davies disappeared. Later Noel Hodgson would write to Davies's father, *'We were in a trench during the advance. Throughout the morning he was indefatigable in cheering on his men and his death was due to his leaving cover to see to his men.'[15]* It was a miserable time. Snipers from the village punished every careless move and the shells continued to fall. The light drizzle of early morning had turned to a steady, unremitting downpour. Everyone was soaked, cold and hungry, and out of touch with what was happening beyond their own small patch of the battlefield. In the evening Pridham and Rayner's party joined them. Then Pridham set off with about twenty-five men in search of rations and did not return.

Noel Hodgson left two accounts of his experiences in the German lines: the Battalion War Diary, which is in his handwriting from 21 to 27 September, and a twenty-two page account on odd sheets of paper, written in the third person, as the grenade officer. But it matches Rayner's account and others precisely, and presents an uncompromising picture of the conditions they endured. At one point he finds six men killed in their sleep by a single shell, a shortfall from their own artillery. He sees *'a white hand with a ring on the little finger,'* and, *'thinking of some girl or wife at home, bends down to recover the ring, and finds that the hand ends abruptly at the wrist. There is no sign of the owner about.'* They coped with the horror because they had to and laughed when they could, though it must have been an effort. Irreverence was a great standby. Hodgson described how, late in the evening, the major in command of a regiment further down the captured trenches found his way to them and asked for their commanding officer. He was older than they were and outranked them, and on being told that the adjutant was in command but sleeping, demanded that someone wake him up. He wanted the adjutant's assurance that if there was a counter-attack, the Devons would not retire without warning him first. The adjutant, half asleep, mumbled, *'"We don't retire," . . . Then, in a dreamy voice, "Make sure he isn't a Hun, Smiler." A choking sound escapes the retiring Major.'*

But the risk of counter-attack was real. Around midnight the Germans attacked in strength on both sides of the Hulluch Road. Lieutenant Brindley's party were fortunate in having bombers and two machine guns and they were able to hold their ground. On the right, though, the attack on the Devons at Hulluch crossroads was so fierce that they were driven back into Gun Trench and beyond, mixed up with their attackers. For a moment it looked as if the Germans had broken through. Brindley, Hodgson and Rayner tried to keep their men from seeing the fighting on the road, knowing that if it was a breakthrough, they would be cut off. According to Harold Rayner, some of the defenders on their right did start to break, *'and Chinky* [Smyth] *made them stand fast with the help of the Devons . . . One way and another he stopped the rot and beat off the counter attack.'*[16] Smyth re-took the trench and, with the help of some well-aimed British artillery fire on the road, the counter-attack petered out. *'A few shadowy figures are soon all that is left of the attack, running back to cover. . . . no one can live in that hell of shrapnel.'*[17]

At 12.45am Lieutenant Brindley sent a message to Brigade HQ:

> *'The Germans have just attacked but were driven off without much difficulty though the troops on the right of HULLUCH RD left us in the air. Lieuts HODGSON & RAYNER & about 90 men are with me. Lt PRIDHAM & party of 25 has not returned from drawing rations. We shall want more S.A.A* [small arms ammunition] *& bombs, but cannot spare men to fetch them.'*[18]

Then there was nothing to do but rest, and wonder what the dawn might bring.

Captain Nation had been left for dead at Hulluch crossroads. In fact, he was unconscious. The story told in his company for months after was that he had been bayoneted while in this state, but Major Anderson did not think so. *'Poor N was badly wounded, (thro' the centre of the body, from R to L I believe) and left for dead in a dug out,'* he told John Upcott. *'His wounds were dressed by a German officer & he was not bayoneted but nearly stripped naked while unconscious.'* Nation came to in the early hours of the morning and, finding himself completely alone, managed somehow to crawl back towards Gun Trench, until he was seen by some of the 8th Devons who brought him in. By then he was failing fast. Smyth gave what first aid he could, and two of the company volunteered to carry Nation back to their own lines, using a trench ladder as a stretcher.

Dawn brought the welcome sight of Duncan Martin and the other officers and men who had been held back from the first day's fighting. Pridham was with them too. They joined Brindley, Hodgson and Rayner under the captured guns. Captain Martin assumed command and set about organising the defence of their position. It was not over yet. They were still tired, wet and hungry. They were still in the middle of a battlefield, closer to the enemy than they were to their own side and out of reach of any support the Army could give, save artillery. The Quarries at the end of Stone Alley, yards north of their position, had been lost during the night leaving them completely exposed. At 9.50am Lieutenant Brindley sent another message to Brigade HQ which emphasises their tension and uncertainty:

> 'The enemy are working along from pt 70 to pt 54 [the southern edge of the Quarries leading into Stone Alley] from where they can enfilade our position in GUNPITS 22 – 57. . . It appears as if a flank attack were meditated . . . . Could you please get the artillery to fire on the QUARRY area . . . We are badly handicapped by the lack of a wire to Hdqtrs . . . Capt Martin is now in command. He says that there are about 80 of the 9th Dev on the other side of the HULLUCH Rd but we are not in touch with them . . . Will you please inform me what arrangements have been made about water tonight. . . Our artillery has sent a good many premature bursts into our trench.'

The Germans did not attack. During the morning Duncan Martin was able to establish a reliable line of communication with the Devons south of the Hulluch Road. At mid-day a runner from Brigade HQ brought news of an impending attack on Cité St Elie, but despite a heavy bombardment which lasted all afternoon, no attack came. As darkness fell, another runner warned the Devons to expect relief from the 2nd Royal Scots Fusiliers. Hours passed and nothing happened. It was after midnight when the relief at last arrived and the depleted battalion was able to move back by companies – what was left of them – to the original front line. But they were still in the battle. By 3am they had taken up the positions in Old Support and Curly Crescent – the very positions they had been aiming for on Saturday morning at the start of the battle, when the crush of wounded men in the trench forced them to climb out and advance in the open. Later in the morning saw the return of the Prodigal – Jack Inchbald and his handful of men, after their visit to 1st Division:

> 'I didn't know what on earth had happened to our battalion and when I eventually rejoined them on the Monday morning I was quite relieved to find Prid, Smyth, who did magnificently and saved both Anderson and Nation, Smiler, Brindley & Nibby. We six alone were left after the strafe. Of course Thompson, Iscariot and Findlay came up the next day.'[20]

For the next three days they remained in the line, moving forward to dig trenches or stand to arms when ordered. 'We had stuck in Curly till Thursday in misery,' Harold Rayner wrote, 'being wettish, and the chalk mud awful. The men never complained and were splendid. We got no rations, and despite all, stuck it. The *officers who came through were very popular with the men. I was plastered with mud. My tunic badly torn with wire, my fingers very tender from crawling on the ground, and my beard terrific.* [21] Finally, at 2.30am on 30 September, their relief came and they began the march back through Vermelles and Noyelles towards rest billets in Beuvry, just east of Béthune.

They were still marching at dawn, dirty, dishevelled, exhausted, but alive, and the clean air, the rustling trees and the early bird song had a new clarity and sharpness. Noel Hodgson found a poem forming in his mind – as he often did on the march. What he took from that first experience of battle, apart from the sheer joy of living, was a deepened appreciation of the men around him; a new understanding of the very best that humanity could be, born in the very worst of circumstances:

Back To Rest
(Composed while marching to Rest Camp
after severe fighting at Loos)

A leaping wind from England,
The skies without a stain,
Clean cut against the morning
Slim poplars after rain,
The foolish noise of sparrows
And starlings in a wood –
After the grime of battle
We know that these are good.

Death whining down from Heaven,
Death roaring from the ground,
Death stinking in the nostril,
Death shrill in every sound,
Doubting we charged and conquered –
Hopeless we struck and stood.
Now when the fight is ended
We know that it was good.

We that have seen the strongest
Cry like a beaten child,
The sanest eyes unholy,
The cleanest hands defiled,
We that have known the heart blood
Less than the lees of wine,
We that have seen men broken,
We know man is divine.

Chapter 10

'The Old 9th',
October 1915 – January 1916

The 9th Devons had not suffered so badly at Loos as their sister battalion. But with 15 officers and 461 men dead, wounded or missing it was bad enough. When the survivors were finally taken out of the line, the fighting strength of the battalion was down to 12 officers and 325 men. They had been through a lot in six days on the battlefield, but if they expected a long rest they were disappointed. Arriving in Beuvry early on Friday morning, 30 September, at 2.30 on Saturday afternoon they marched out again to take over a new trench line at Cambrin. A day and a half to draw breath: to wash, sleep, eat and take stock. They reorganised as best they could, with Duncan Martin in acting command and the others doubling up to make sure all jobs were covered. Second Lieutenant Charles Cecil Thompson, who at 19 was not much more than a schoolboy, found himself in charge of a company for ten days – the remnants of one, at least. He loved it, and would look back on these ten days as *'the best "soldiering" I've ever done.'*[1]

To the south, the Battle of Loos carried on for another fortnight, but the 9th Devons would do no more than hold the line at Cambrin, where things were quieter. Even so, in the days they spent there they lost three more men to trench-mortar and sniper fire, two killed, one wounded. Philip Brindley, whose leadership beside the captured guns had won everyone's respect, was recalled by his own regiment on 4 October. Noel Hodgson took over as adjutant until a replacement was appointed. The adjutancy was an administrative post, and on 9 October he wrote to Stella aping the language of his new burden of Army paperwork:

'Dear Star;-
Beg to report situation here normal and myself in excellent health. Your letter has been received and noted this day and action taken accordingly. This for your information and retention please. You will note that I have got the official style already in my correspondence.
Thanks muchly for the large parcel of vests, mufflers etc. and the long letter. I am wondering whether I shall remain adjutant long enough to warrant my purchasing a pair of riding boots; I do hope so, then I shall be happy; in haste. Bill'

Major Robert Milne of the 2nd Devons took over command of the battalion in the Cambrin trenches on 2 October. A week later new drafts of men began to arrive to fill the vacant places. Officers too. The focus was on rebuilding the battalion and it had to be so, but the strongest bonds still existed between the survivors and their dead and wounded friends, whom they missed. In the confusion of battle some were known to have died, some to have been wounded but not how seriously, and of others there was only rumour. It took weeks to find out where everyone was and to re-establish communication; then letters began to circulate between France and the hospitals in England – letters which open an extraordinary window on the life of the battalion in the aftermath of its first battle.

The person who played the greatest part in tracing the wounded and putting them in touch with one another was 'Uncle Tom', Colonel Davies, their original commanding officer. He had brought the 9th Devons together and trained them, and would have led them into battle if the Army had let him; they were still his men, and his job on a travelling Medical Board proved invaluable for tracking them down. John Upcott must have been about the first he found: a week after the battle Davies sent him news of the whereabouts of Major Anderson and Captain Mockridge. The colonel had also been told about Captain Muntz's injuries, but was still looking for him. He found 'Pussy' Martin in the Queen Alexandra Hospital for Officers in London, worrying about John Upcott. *'I have just had a visit from the dear old Colonel,'* Martin wrote, *'I was so pleased to see him & he gave me news as to your whereabouts. I have been trying to find out where you were & what eventually happened to you, ever since I got hit.'*

As individuals were found and reconnected so the same stories recurred. Once injured, each of them had found his own way or had been helped off the battlefield into a bewildering world of strangers, suddenly losing contact with everyone he knew as he was passed back through the system: first to an Advanced Dressing Station, then to Casualty Clearing, Base Hospital or a Hospital Ship, ending up somewhere in England. Often paths crossed and re-crossed, and news was exchanged on the way. *'I saw Sergeant Woodrow come in slightly wounded in the foot,'* Martin continued. *'During my wanderings on a stretcher between Vermelles and Rouen, I saw Pocock at Sailly, who has a shrapnel wound in each thigh & upper right arm broken by a bullet. . . . I saw Storey at Choques with a bullet through an artery in his right shoulder. From him I learnt that Tracey was not killed, only wounded. In the train I saw Major Anderson . . . At Rouen I was in a bed next to Pocock & he told me that Whiteway had been wounded.'*

Inevitably some of the information became confused. Tracey in fact had been first to die and Whiteway was one of the reserves. He did not go into battle until the second day and came out unhurt. But gradually, as the weeks passed, a truer picture emerged and news – sometimes an actual letter – was passed around the hospitals, or between England and those still serving. So Colonel Davies: *'Many thanks for Rayner's very interesting letter, I have taken liberty of sending it to Anderson to read and asked him to return from* [he gives an address]'. Or John Pocock: *'Worrall sent on your letter, and I am writing just a line to say how glad I was to hear you are so well recovered. . . . If Rayner's account is not private I shd like to see it very much.'* Or Jack Inchbald, writing from France: *'Thank you so much for your letter, I was delighted to get it. . . . I knew that you were in touch with us via Nibby. . . . Nibby will have told you which of us got through.'*

That knowledge really mattered, on both sides of the Channel, but once they were reassured about one another the old banter was quick to resurface. When the wounded were hurried back through the system any belongings they were not actually carrying were left behind with the battalion, while anything they lost on the way was probably lost for good. Upcott enquired about his things, and Noel Hodgson, still with his adjutant's hat very firmly in place, replied:

> *'Dear John*
> *Doubtless you cannot help your rather pathetic ignorance on the subject of kits, officers, casualty. By now your valise will have arrived and you will be feeling three or four parts of a tick for having indited such a foolish epistle to me. Your pack you will certainly not see for many years to come, so the sooner you invest in some new glasses the better.*
>
> *News has leaked through that you are in good health & dressing for dinner – precisely the unscrupulous conduct one would have expected from you. . . .*
> *Signature – address*
> *W.N Hodgson*
> *Unit – Devons'* [Normally he would have just signed 'Smiler'.]

In the year they had spent together the battalion had become a family and all ranks were included. During the counter-attack on the Hulluch crossroads one private of C Company was shot accidentally by his own side and wounded in the bombardment: his sergeant major went out under fire to bring him in. John Upcott wrote to Company Sergeant Major Kelland, who was still in France, to ask after Private Price and others, and Kelland replied:

> *'You did see me in the trench after you was wounded, I was Bandaging up Pte Turpitt who had a Bad wound entered his Neck and came out in his Back it was rather a warm time getting up to their first Line. After we had taken the guns it was not so bad. I remember poor Price he seemed to be badly knocked about when I got hold of him. Well Sir a lot of old C Coy went under that day.'*

Price was eventually traced to the 1st Eastern General Hospital in Cambridge, which was run by the staff of Addenbrooke's. Many of its patients were housed in tents and temporary buildings in the grounds of Trinity College. *'Dear Sir,'* he wrote to John Upcott:

> *'Many thanks for your kind & welcome letter, also thanking you for the Xmas gift. . . . I am afraid it will be some time before I am able to rejoin the regiment.*
>
> *I was wounded on the 25th September in the evening in a counter attack. My wounds were very bad. First I got hit in the left hand with a bullet; then in both arms by a shell; after that with a bullet which went right through & smashed my lower jaw. I am going on satisfactorily but shall have to undergo some operations shortly on my left hand and right arm.*
>
> *The treatment here is all open air and is rather cold at nights. There are about 1500 beds here altogether & about 64 in each ward. I am unable to write myself & so am dictating this letter to one of the other patients.'*

John Pocock was in regular contact with members of his No 5 Platoon in B Company for months, sending them letters and parcels while they kept him in touch with the battalion. *'Dear Mr Pocock. . . . I was very pleased to hear from you & I thank you very much for very welcome parcel. I am still with No 5 & the Huns havent got me yet.'* [2] Relatives also took the 9th Devons to heart. When one of Noel Hodgson's aunts found a member of the battalion in the hospital where she worked as a volunteer, she wrote to him at once. He passed the news on:

> *'Do you remember L/Sgt Norman? He is in Murrell Hill Hospital, Carlisle, with a fractured leg which won't mend. I discovered his whereabouts by the fortunate fact that my aunt went there to wash bed-pans or grates, and happened to hear of him. He would like, no doubt, to hear from his late commander.'*

The papers preserved by John Upcott and John Pocock represent a fraction of the whole communication that passed between members of the original battalion. It was part of an officer's duty to care for his men, but the caring *about* them and about one another that the letters demonstrate was genuine and human, born of the extraordinary times that brought them all together and the experiences they shared, good as well as bad. Their families were drawn in too, providing gifts and food parcels for the battalion in France and visiting complete strangers in England, just because they were in or were related to the 9th Devons. There was fellow feeling for the 8th Battalion as well, with particular concern expressed for Second Lieutenant John Bridson, at 18 years old the youngest officer in either battalion. His fate after Loos was a mystery. *'I'm sorry to say nothing at all is known of Bridson,'* Hodgson told 'Pussy' Martin on 27 October. *'He is supposed to have been seen early on in the show lying in No Man's Land, but his body was, as far as we know never found, so either he was buried & not identified or he is missing.'* Nothing more about Bridson was ever discovered.

Pain for the spaces in the ranks and in the mess was always present but understated. There were things they could not afford to dwell on. *'I have had a glowing account of poor Davies from one of his N.C.Os here, who tells me how coolly he behaved & how well he rallied our men and numerous Jocks who had lost their officers,'* John Pocock writes. And Jack Inchbald, usually the bounciest of letter-writers, could not quite hide the strain: *'Poor dear old Mervyn, & Tracey & Allen. One simply can't believe they've gone. And yet one finds it impossible to go into sackcloth and ashes over them. I've had two most pathetic letters from Tracey's fiancée – poor little girl, she's fearfully cut up.'* His letter ends, *'I'm afraid you may find this letter very nearly incoherent but so are the impressions and you asked for them. There are several more or less blanks in my mind. One thing I'll never forget and that is a certain road you wot of. Also the sights on the German wire!'*

The battalion had done well at Loos and they knew it, and their pride in seeing it acknowledged was some consolation. On 1 October, before the survivors left Beuvry, Bryan Freeland lunched with Charles Cecil Thompson and Harold Rayner, the last officers left standing from his former company, and afterwards he told John Upcott, *'The whole place was ringing with praise for the Devons. I saw your 4 guns and the 8th's 5 guns coming down the V*[ermelles] *– B*[éthune] *road on the 27th. I wish I had been with you all. I can tell you I felt proud of the men we had trained John and I bet you were.'*

'Our Brigadier came to our billets and congratulated the Bn on their good work,' Company Sergeant Major Kelland reported, and Jack Inchbald had even better news:

> *'The rest of our Brigade from the General down are delighted with & proud of us, & poor old Capper simply hopping with excitement about us I'm told. Not many regiments get hold of guns in their first engagement. . . . We've just had a Batt parade in which 6 men were presented by the C.O. with cards from the General pending, we hope, subsequent decoration for conspicuous bravery. They were Sgt Stevens MG section; Sgt Brown. Bomber; Cpl. Melhuish Bomber; Pte Bugler C Coy; Pte Moody S-B A coy. I believe Smyth has been recommended for the Military Cross.'*

Smyth had, and so had Noel Hodgson. Both were also mentioned in despatches, with Sergeant Brown and Privates Bugler and Moody. Hodgson was especially proud to see his bombers honoured: *'A little thought would have shown you that the Brown mentioned in despatches was not Brown of 'A' Coy,'* he teased Upcott, *'but – naturally – a grenadier (we don't use the word bomber now – not in the active army) and of D Company.'*

Meanwhile the rebuilding went on. Several of the officers drafted in after Loos were members of the original battalion who had been left behind in England in July. Men like Francis 'Frank' Wollocombe and Arthur Lewis, both Devonshire vicars' sons. Lewis was the younger – eighteen on the outbreak of war – and had signed up for the Royal Fusiliers before gaining his commission in the Devons. Frank Wollocombe took his father's advice and completed his degree at Oxford while training with the OTC. He joined the 9th Battalion in Aldershot on 26 January, but was posted to the 11th Battalion when the 9th went overseas. He received orders for France on 30 September, the day the survivors left the battlefield. The Army gave him less than a day to prepare: he set off for Folkestone the next day and sailed on the evening of 2 October, one of a group of fifteen officers bound either for the 8th or the 9th Battalion. Frank said that seven of them were original 9th Devons, one more from the 11th Battalion was posted to the 9th. They caught up with the battalion on 6 October in the Cambrin trenches: *'I met a lot of old friends among the men though I missed a lot. . . . everyone says the British advance was a washout as it wasn't worth the enormous casualties (the Germans suffered comparatively lightly) and we have lost a lot of ground again'.*[3]

As more new officers and men arrived the battalion was steadily rearranged around them. The letters suggest frustration among the old hands that so many senior positions were given to men newly drafted to France. Those who had come through Loos felt they deserved better – if not for themselves, they felt it for their friends. Command of B and C Companies went to Lieutenants J.W. Palmer and George Underhill, both part of the original battalion but new to France. Harold Rayner, meanwhile, was posted to command a newly-formed trench mortar battery, with no ammunition and a few half-trained men. *'As O.C. 95mm Battery 20th Brigade, I am theoretically some personage,'* he wrote, *'in practice I am no one in particular & as such am left to myself. So I'm O.C. Self &, so far, O.C. soft job.'*

Hodgson made the wry comment:

'The excellent Underhill presides, in a rather anxious-hen fashion, over C Company, ably assisted by Eardley-Wilmot. Nibby, in disgust, has taken an independent command – of a trench mortar battery. He took a four-hours course in one kind of gun & the brigade put him in charge of another sort, which he had never seen before.'

It was for Hodgson in particular that the others were disappointed. When his Military Cross finally appeared in the Honours List in January, Thompson commented, *'I am awfully glad for Smiler, and it is some consolation to no promotion.'* And Rayner, speculating a few weeks later on the promotions that ought to be given out, remarked that *'Smiler . . . seems to miss his destiny – tho he has the M.C. of course.'* If 'Smiler' felt the same way he did not show it. Not for himself, at least. He told 'Pussy' Martin on 27 October:

> *'The battalion is pretty well up to strength again, but it is not the old 9th Devons, either as regards officers or men. A lot of new officers from the 11th, most of them fairly useless, & one or two old friends like Palmer & Underhill & Lewis. Pridham is O.C. D company, and is amazingly full of doubts and complaints. "I say, about this man"— "its all very well , but look here" — "its all the fault of the NCOs etc" – you know how he talks. Its rather a sickening state of things for Inchy & the others who went through the show, and are now 2 Lieuts in charge of platoons under these new hands.'*

Apart from this, and the letters to John Upcott, there are few clues to what Noel Hodgson was thinking and feeling as the immediate experiences of Loos receded into memory. But there is a poem, never published, that exists in a fair copy manuscript among his papers. According to the title it was composed on the march again, sometime during October. It was prompted by death on a battlefield, but not one of the many deaths he had witnessed so recently. His own experience of battle seems to have brought him closer to the death of Nowell Oxland, and in doing so, to have allowed his imagination to escape briefly into the peaceful world they had shared:

> ### In Memory of Nowell Oxland, Killed at Suvla Bay August 9th 1915
>
> *You were a lover of the hills, and had*
> *From them some measure of their Roman strength;*
> *You that are laid in hearing of the sad*
> *Aegean waters, by a whole sea's length*
> *Severed from these: above your nameless bed*
> *The pitiless forehead of an alien sky*
> *For the cool peace and spaciousness that lie*
> *Upon the slopes of your own valley-head.*
>
> *So if in happier times I climb Black Sail*
> *Over the Gable to Bowfell, and drop*
> *By Sticks as evening comes, to Borrowdale*

> *For tea at Rosthwaite, where the coaches stop*
> *Often, my friend, shall I remember you*
> *Taking your long rest on the distant shore,*
> *And say I love my ancient hills the more*
> *Because you wandered here & loved them too.*

Written on the March in France, Oct 1915

In its simplicity and directness, the natural flow of one line into another, 'In Memory of Nowell Oxland' is among Hodgson's best work, and it gives some indication of what he might have achieved if only he had had more time.

The Devons were in the lines at Cambrin or in support until 16 October, always with the noise of the continuing battle further south and the air alive with rumours. Then they withdrew into rest billets near Béthune – a rest which lasted just three days rather than the fortnight they hoped for. On 19 October they were ordered to stand by – spoiling their plans for a concert – and moved by night to different billets, the men singing loudly as they went. The next day they marched on, to take over a particularly unpleasant and muddy trench line at Givenchy, just across the La Bassée Canal.

Here they set about digging, improving the parapets and firesteps. A Brigade Order of October stressed that *'officers must keep their men busy and not allow them to remain in mud and water without doing something to remedy conditions. Officers must continually be thinking – What can be done for the improvement of moans* [sic] *of security and for the comfort of their men?'* They were also to encourage the men to do the work this entailed *'cheerfully and with energy'*.[4] But it was hard to be constantly cheerful in a muddy trench, particularly when unknown horror might be just around the corner. One day Duncan Martin encountered some terrified men, all new to the trenches, whose digging had struck something wet and red under the soil. They were too scared to investigate further. He took a pick from one of them and unearthed a tin of jam. That at least gave them something to laugh at.

The Givenchy trenches even produced an unexpected – and literal – shaggy dog story. A very unusual prisoner was taken by A Company during the early hours of 23 October. It was a wolfhound, *'a fine brute'* from the German trenches opposite; it had crossed no man's land in the dark and Duncan Martin brought it in. Its collar was marked with its name, 'Greif' [Griffin], the name of its handler 'LTN Stennes', and a unit number '6/16'. *'The Boches were calling for it for a long time, but they won't see him again for a bit, I hope,'* Frank Wollocombe said. Greif would have been a working dog: both sides used dogs at the Front for a variety of duties. A Company made a pet of their 'dog prisoner' – Frank took it ratting – but a few days later Captain Martin went on a week's leave and the dog was sent for by Brigade HQ, *'to be examined'*.[5]

The battalion left Givenchy at noon on Sunday, 24 October for billets in and around Essars, to the north of Béthune. They were there a week, drilling, marching, and training, and two important new arrivals joined them. First, on the Monday, a new second-in-command, a Regular, Captain Holsworth of the 2nd Devons. Tuesday brought Second Lieutenant Herbert Hearse, also a Regular and a former sergeant-major, to take over as adjutant. *'We're getting along fine now,'* Hodgson told 'Pussy' Martin, *'Milne the new C.O. is a good chap, & we've got a good 2nd in command from the 2nd battalion. And now a regular adjutant has rolled up from the first battalion.'*[6]

If he minded giving up the adjutancy and the enticing prospect of riding boots he showed no sign of it, and in all likelihood he did not mind. It had been a job someone had to do, but he was too active to be satisfied with paperwork for long. Besides, there were his bombers. They needed training now, with so many new men in the battalion.

But though he liked Major Milne, and does not seem to have minded surrendering the adjutancy, it was in this same letter that Hodgson said the battalion was *'not the old 9th Devons'* and was critical of some of the new officers and men, voicing a blend of discontent and nostalgia among the old hands which the coming of Holsworth and Hearse seemed to intensify. Hodgson's letter was the first to use the phrase 'the old 9th'. As the weeks passed, the idea of 'the old 9th' as a lost ideal took hold and grew. The year the original battalion had spent together training in England and in France had forged bonds between them that would be almost impossible to replicate. Hodgson was the sort who would knuckle down and make the best of things, taking refuge in being as busy as possible. Jack Inchbald too, though in December he told John Upcott, *'you can't think how heart-aching the prospect is sometimes out here under the new regime. Ours is a fine Battalion – but it is not the dear old 9th. Sometimes I get black days and then I find it hard to be even fatuous.'* Lieutenant Truscott, the Transport Officer, told John Pocock *'everything is strange in the battalion',*[7] and to John Upcott he complained, *'The 9th isn't what it was. Officers or men & personally I really am sick to death of it. HQ mess is now all 2nd Devon shop, what with the CO, 2nd in command and Adj all coming from them.'* Truscott had considered the Royal Flying Corps before; now he couldn't wait to transfer. Those who stayed found another motive, as Jack Inchbald wrote, *'we hope to lick the drafts into shape & keep the Battalion going for the sake of all you chaps we have lost and for the truly great name we have won.'*

November was a terrible month, which added to the strain. For the first few days they were in a different part of the Givenchy trenches in heavy rain. These trenches were constantly falling in – Major Milne said they were badly built – and though it was pointless to try to dig and improve them while knee-deep in mud, the men had to attempt it and the officers to encourage them. One night the ration party was lost, another a German mine blew, destroying a sap the Devons were digging for the Engineers. The Germans in the trenches opposite were Saxons and they could be heard at night singing the bawdy anti-Prussian songs the British themselves sang. They also seemed to have an uncanny knowledge of the men they were facing. When the Devons came out of the line, *'The Saxons got up on the parapet and waved and shouted. . . They were calling to some of our men by name this morning.'*[8]

Soon after moving into rest billets Noel Hodgson went home on leave, so he missed the battalion's last stint at Givenchy. His stay in England coincided with a celebration of the battalion's exploits at Loos, when two of the captured guns were presented to the city of Exeter. The guns had been on show in London and were dispatched to Exeter by train. On the morning of 12 November they were escorted in triumphant procession through the streets by men of the 8th and 9th Battalions who fought in the battle, cheered on by flag-waving crowds. John Upcott had returned to duty then and was, in Jack Inchbald's words, *'assistant – acting – deputy – sub-adjutant – aidecamp and bottlewasher-in-general to Lt Col Bedingfield of the Asthmatic Eleventh. For the which may the Lord make us truly thankful.'*

Upcott and Frank Worrall represented the 9th, with eight of the recovering wounded: *'After a good deal of speechifying by the Lord Lieutenant, Mayor, General Commanding, the guns were handed over to the City,'* Upcott told his uncle, *'& we proceeded round the town. . . . I marched at the head of my party just behind the guns; we got rather reduced in going round, as two who had been wounded in the leg, failed to stay the course.'*

Jack Inchbald, back in France after his own recent leave, had seen the guns for the first time in London. When the press accounts reached France he found the pomp – and pomposity – of the occasion irresistible. *'Of my Punch,'* he wrote, Punch being his nickname for John Upcott:

'I have had but isolated, fragmentary and sporadic news during the past three weeks. He was present I believe with our Worry at the Great Occasion, Der Tag, when our two precious popguns were installed with due solemnity and mystic rite in the Township of Exeter. The which Guns I went to see when I was home and I can well understand it if a populace, spoonfed by our paternal Press, and expecting to see some machine that would throw 10 tons of metal from Exeter to Torquay, were in their heart of hearts a trifle disappointed. Still you must have had quite a great day and I can quite imagine that Worry-worry was absolutely in his element "I mean to say, I've got 5 brothers in the army――"'

Hodgson would have shared his amusement. With vivid memories of *'the leering and futile gun muzzles'* dripping rain on himself and his companions as they dug in and prepared to defend themselves on the night of 25/26 September, he knew more about the Loos guns than the cheering crowds in Exeter would ever know, and had probably seen enough of them. He might have gone to watch the procession although there is nothing to say that he did. He was probably happier to be at home and read about it in the papers.

But on the home front the ceremony did mean something, if only as a physical link with the men gone away. Mrs Churchill, the wife of John Upcott's servant who was still in France, wrote to Upcott after seeing them:

> *'I went to Exeter and saw the guns that the 8th and 9th captured a bit of good work to get them for they look so heavy to wheel along. I think myself that the Devons has worked very hard all through this awful war. I only wish they could only get hold of that Kaiser Bill so they could give him Guns. Churchill writes very cheerfull so far but I do miss him so. If ever you come to Sidmouth Sir I hope to have the pleasure of seeing you, it's not a very large place but we have sent away some men lately even married men are gone.'*

Hodgson returned to the battalion on 17 November and found them cleaning off the mud of Givenchy in new billets at Bellerive. They had six days of resting and basic training – days when it seemed that change was in the wind, though no one could be sure what it was. There was talk of a move south to a new area. There were also rumours that they were no longer to be assigned front line trenches, but would be kept in reserve as a working battalion. Then on 21 November Major Milne called his officers together to discuss their next trench lines – at Festubert. The battalion had come full circle. The very first trenches they had held in their own right were at Festubert, only that was in summer. Now those same trenches were underwater, five feet deep in some places. The Devons marched to new billets in and near the ruined village and were sent up on working parties each night. But there was precious little work anyone could do, and the men in the battalion holding the front line were dejected and close to breaking point. Before long they were taken out of the line and two companies of the 9th sent in to take their place.

It was a low point in their experience. As Jack Inchbald told his father:

> *'The last two days were perfectly grisly. Front line: ghastly mud, no communication trenches as they had all fallen in and where I was we were isolated completely by day – just my platoon. By night you could get back over the top and it took any time from 2 to 5 hours to make it back the 500 yards – owing to mud & water. When I tell you we nearly had a man <u>drowned</u> in the mud and we did have several literally exhausted you'll realise dimly what our fellows have to put up with.'*[9]

The old hands distracted themselves by making plans. Jack sent his father a long list of sheet music he wanted from home, so that he could organise concerts for the men over Christmas: the complete musical score of 'Tonight's the night'; 'May I call you Dearie'; 'I want to go back to Michigan'; 'The Foxtrot Ball'; 'Gilbert the Philbert', and so on. And before that, there was a wedding to consider. Frank Worrall was to be married on 11 December, providing the perfect excuse for an 'old 9th' reunion. Alan Hinshelwood was his best man. *'Nobby is I should say the Beau Ideal of a Best Man. Tactful without being efficient. . . . A sartorial dream and altogether quite a suitable foil to the leading Bridesmaid.'* And though the *'Survivors of the Old 9th'* in France could not join in, they intended to make their presence felt with what they thought was an appropriate gift: *'Very topical with plenty of inscriptions about Hulloch and Loos and No8 Platoon, several crests and engravings and all the sort of thing which, an I am not mistaken, will make his soul rejoice. The pièce de resistance is I believe a shell fuse picked up by Smiler boy, and Smyth (now on leave) is entrusted with the mounting and setting and stamping and strafing and so forth.'* Hodgson, Duncan Martin, Rayner, Thompson, Truscott, Smyth, Pridham and Inchbald clubbed together to pay for it.

December brought welcome relief from the Festubert mud. In the barns and outhouses around Busnettes, sheltering from torrential rain that made outdoor work impossible, the Devons cleaned themselves up and repaired damage to uniforms and equipment in readiness for the anticipated move south. At 5am on 7 December they marched to the station at Lillers. By midnight they were finally settled in new billets in Ailly-sur-Somme.

After the waterlogged landscapes of the north, scarred and tormented by months of war, the gentle, rolling downland beside the River Somme, with its open fields and little woods, was a treat for the eyes and the spirit; a reminder, for those who knew it, of the farmland of southern England. The trench lines were some miles east of Saleux near Amiens, where the Devons left the train, and of Ailly, on the bank of the river, but in this part of France even the trenches were quiet. So far, war had made little impression on the countryside. Perhaps that was why the local people seemed less welcoming than their counterparts in the north, at least at first. After considerable difficulty sorting out billets on arrival in Ailly and then in arranging better ones the next day, and problems finding food of any sort, Frank Wollocombe remarked, *'they want a few Germans.'*[10]

The first month on the Somme passed quietly in training and assimilating new drafts of men. It was good to be out of the line, but news that the 9th Devons were to become the Divisional Pioneer Battalion was met with general dismay. The Army needed pioneers. They did the labouring and construction work without which the infantry could not move freely around the countryside. Britain had gone into war in 1914 without any Pioneer formations and had had difficulty at first in finding men to do the labouring. Trench digging, fetching and carrying and similar duties had become part of the infantry's daily life, but to be designated a pioneer battalion was different altogether. As the Devons began training under the Royal Engineers for their new construction jobs – mining, building railways and roads, digging deep dugouts in the chalky ground – Frank Wollocombe probably spoke for many when he said that if this continued he would think of applying for a transfer.

Basic fighting training did continue alongside the labouring. On a typical day the first hour would be given over to drill and discipline, then one company would be held back to work on the rifle range, march, or practise attack formations, while the rest trained under the Engineers. A further reorganisation towards the end of the year saw those men who already had specialist training – the bombers, machine gunners, scouts and signallers – withdrawn from their companies and formed into a new Headquarters Company of 170 men, with Thompson and Whiteway as their officers and Noel Hodgson in command. Officially he was still a second lieutenant; his War Office file suggests that he was promoted in the field on 15 September, but he was not gazetted lieutenant until 4 February 1916. Both the mention in despatches and the *Gazette* announcement of the Military Cross refer to him as 'Temporary Second Lieutenant'. But the new company did go some way towards alleviating the feeling among his friends had that he had missed out on a deserved promotion. *'We now call the Coys I, 11, 111 and 1V,'* Thompson told John Upcott, *'and also we have a H.Q. Coy with "Smiler" in charge, Whiteway & self, so I am very well contented. . . . Smiler sends his love and states that he will write to you.'*

This was only one of the jobs Noel took on as the year drew towards its close. *'Is the Lady Mother well – and Dad?'* he asked Stella. *'I suppose he has done far too much work lately. Myself I hold now the following offices 'Mess President'; O.C. Headquarters Company (170 men); Grenade Officer; Scout Officer; Officer i/c Athletics, so my time is pretty full too.'* The last weeks of December and early January were busy ones for him, organising the Christmas Eve dinner and party for the officers, his own Headquarters Company dinner, and sporting fixtures to keep the battalion occupied and give them something to cheer for.

Over Christmas the new battalion and the 'old 9th' came together and celebrated. There were parties in plenty: one for each company, one for the sergeants, one for the officers, a Christmas dinner for the men, all generously provided for with enough left-overs to last into January. Only beer was a problem: one barrel had been ordered per company but the delivery was short. So the officers drew lots and A and D had their barrels for Christmas while B and C had to wait. But the people of Paignton and Torquay had sent Christmas puddings, and hampers of goodies came from the officers' families: other communities in Devon may have obliged as well. As the day drew near everyone could expect at least two Christmas dinners.

And what a Christmas it was. One to write home about – except that very few loving parents would have been told everything. First came the officers' party on Christmas Eve, which Hodgson organised. About twenty sat down to the meal at 7.30pm *'to the strains of 'any old night is a wonderful night if you're there with a wonderful girl' energetically delivered by Mr George Grossmith on the Grammaphone,'* (this is Jack Inchbald reporting to John Upcott):

> *'The walls of the room were tastefully decorated (2nd Lt RP Whiteway O/C decorations) with Rafael Kirchner's nuder females. Figure to yourself three tables, all about 18 inches wide, at the longest being seated the C/O and all the heavier members of the Battalion, including all those of the old 9th, less Mills. An enormous stove fills the centre of the room and we are packed like the proverbial Sardine. Deft (?) batmen flit (?) among the jovial diners, bearing bread and wine and right good viands. . .*
>
> *So much for the mise-en-scène. We sat down then to the following menu – Huitres d' Hulluch – Potage Festubert – Dandon roti á Boyau 15 – Plum Pudding sauce Givenchy – Harengs au Mâitre des chevaux – Dessert – Café. . . . I found Hulloch oysters well and truly named. Better still perhaps would have been Huitres de Loos for their innate beauties were lost on me. Festubert soup is as thick and clinging as Festubert mud. Why the wretched Turkey should have been named after one of our more deadly communication trenches I don't quite know. But I detect the handiwork of Smiler.'*

After dinner, the games. At first there was an awkwardness in the air:

> *'There was not that feeling of complete accord and unanimous though fatuous benevolence that would have been in order had it been the old 9th of blessed memory. I mean to say one can't hit Eardley-Wilmot on the head with a tambourine, or prod any of the old men or babes from the 11th (who have taken your places) in the tummy with one of those elongated French loaves. Luckily however the old men in question* [in their late twenties and early thirties] *drifted off to the bar, and the babes were mostly drunk and incapable by 10pm. By the way don't think I'm running down our new officers. The majority of them are extremely nice fellows. But there are just one or two . . .'*

The evening soon gathered momentum:

> *'The first coherent attempt at amusement was a performance by B company officers' orchestra. This consists of Cary (conductor-man)*

Adams (castanets) Butland (triangle) Smiler (any instrument he can get hold of) myself (tambourine) and the Grammaphone (tune). The performance unfortunately was spoilt by the heavy humour of Holcroft who, with that coquettish spirit of mischief which suits him so well, insisted on suddenly stopping the gramophone or altering its speed at various parts of the melody. Undeterred by this we put up a very passable fight.'

At ten o'clock, Jack rescued one of the 'babes', *'a most delightful lad from the 11th'*, who was being plied with glasses of neat whisky he was not used to. Jack guided him back to his billet to sleep it off:

'When I returned I found that the rest had thinned out a bit & Smiler had the situation fairly well in hand. The result was some fairly amusing chorus-singing at the piano, where weary Woolacomby put in a good evenings work. The CO had by now departed.

It was at this point that the adjutant (an enormous and very nice fellow, erstwhile Sgt Major of the 1st Batt) took a hand. He had been drinking solemnly but solidly, at a side table. Suddenly he took his place at the piano, bellowed forth 'Hymn no. one-hundred-n-thirty-two The ole ole story!' and proceeded to thump. This he was induced by many tactful encores to keep up for a considerable time chuckling to himself the while, 'any ole nights wunnerful night'! He afterwards rose and had a terrific wrestling bout with little Cary (who having got outside much punch and 2 bottles of port was in merry though incoherent mood). Cary was eventually stretched on the floor where he lay spitting and giggling for some little while. Rising finally he seized the triangle and put it in his pocket. But he was very much intrigued by the fact that he couldn't find the small steel rod used to smite the instrument. So he lurched about the room – looking like nothing on earth with several things tied onto his back – yelling with laughter and shouting 'Whersh other-part-triangle?' Occasionally someone would offer him a piece of chalk or a glass or something. He would gravely and carefully examine it and then shout 'thatsh not other-part-triangle, whersh other-part-triangle?' and so the good work went on.'

Now Duncan Martin, Pridham and Smyth, joined in, emerging from the corner where they had been drinking quietly on their own since dinner, with a bottle of vinegar. The game was to see how many of the others could be persuaded to drink a toast, thinking it was champagne. The sober were in on the joke; seven of the others drank it without even realising. *'But I think the find of the evening was dear old Whiteway. He sat stolidly staring in the face of a rather comely wench who belongs to the place, with calf like admiration in his fatuous eyes.*

Afterwards by the way he was nearly killed through being sick on the level crossing just as a train went by.' At midnight the party broke up and Inchbald, Smyth, Pridham and Hodgson took charge of steering the others back to billets. It took three of them to manage Cary, while *'It was Smiler who took the adjutant home. Unfortunately they met a French tommy in the same state & for some minutes the two of them strafed the Bosch together and rolled up against one another shouting "Camarade!" And so we ate our Christmas dinner!'*

They were young and a long way from home and they needed to throw responsibility aside for a while. The ghosts were never far away. And eleven of them still managed to attend Holy Communion for Christmas morning a few hours later. After that came the next round of Christmas dinners. *'You need have no fear about my having given the men anything beyond the sausages,'* Noel told Stella a few days later. She and their parents had contributed to the feast; with their experience of parish dinners they knew exactly what to send:

> *'The parcel of sweets I eat myself with all imaginable gusto. The case was opened on Christmas Day, and caused immense enthusiasm, the tin trumpets and the cake in particular. When I went round dinners I was greeted with 'For he's a jolly good fellow' played on cornets and lustily sung, and one gentleman in a voice husky with beer and emotion assured me that if ever I wanted a man to follow me into a tight place, 11132 Private Harry Gay was the man in question.*
>
> *We did jolly well too – I personally assisted at the concealment of four turkeys and five plum puddings in forty-five hours.'*[11]

Christmas did the battalion good. Describing his concert of a few days later, Jack Inchbald said, *'it was really quite like old times and great fun. Cary, Thompson, Palmer and myself performed and we unearthed quite a lot of talent among the men. Poor dears it must have been quite a change for them actually to have a bit of real amusement and if you could have heard 'em yell the choruses – well you would have realised the Battalion, like the ship in Kipling's story, has 'found itself'.'*

Chapter 11

'There and Back',
January – April 1916

The last six months of Noel Hodgson's life were his most productive in terms of published work, particularly prose, which he used more and more to communicate his experiences in France. But working out what he wrote and when throws up a number of puzzles. In a brief note to his sister, written on 9 December and postmarked the next day, he writes, *'Here is the last of the series, if anyone ever wants it; Bill.'* This obviously accompanied a manuscript, but which? There is no obvious candidate among his surviving work. The two 'Company Mess' articles which he sent home before Loos were a series of sorts; this may have been a third one, now lost. It would be tempting to guess that it was the account of Loos itself, the last piece to feature Smiler the Grenade Officer. But when an edited version of the Loos account was added to the third edition of *'Verse and Prose in Peace and War'* in the summer of 1917, Henry described it as, *'another sketch from the trenches by my son, which his sister found among his papers lately'*, suggesting that Stella had not seen it before.[1] Henry's decision to give the sketch the title 'Nestoria (2)', placing it in the book after 'Nestoria', which is set in the months after Loos, rather confirms this, indicating that neither he nor Stella understood the sequence of events the sketches describe.

'Nestoria' poses other questions. There is a manuscript, undated and written on odd sheets of paper, which has the title 'Nestoria' in Noel's handwriting. But in another covering note to Stella, dated 8 February, he suggests that this title was not intended for publication:

'Dear Star
Herewith part 1 of another chatty series for the obliging periodicals, entitled After Dinner, Over the Port, Through the Smoke, or anything else you like. Part II to follow in a day or two. How's it all with you at home? Fit and well yes? All very cheery here; love to all, Bill'

This can only refer to the sketch published as 'Nestoria', which opens with a young lieutenant fresh from the leave boat dining with two friends in a London club. None of the other sketches has a similar setting. It also explains the date of 8 February 1916 which Henry gave to 'Nestoria'. Most of the precise dates in the book are dates of publication, but 'Nestoria' does not appear to have been published before. It was certainly not a *New Witness* piece.

'Nestoria' also marks a change of style. The two 'Company Mess' articles and the account of Loos are factual and can be verified from other sources. Names were omitted; that was all. 'Nestoria' is woven around Noel's own experience but he seems to have used that experience as the setting for a story. The lieutenant – who turns mid-way into 'the adjutant', without explanation – begins by telling the others what has happened to the battalion since Loos:

> *'During dinner the man on leave had delivered an epic. It had traced the adventures of the faithful few who remained over when the regiment marched back in the grey hours of Friday's dawn from the chalk lines before Vermelles, to be flung back to trenches thirty-six hours later. It followed them through the Givenchy craters and Festubert marshes, on marches southward and northward, among shellings and bombings, short rests and heavy labours. It told of the slow welding of the new regiment, when the fresh drafts came rolling in from the Base, of worries and perplexities surmounted. . . . of how the battalion, once more conscious of itself as a unity with history and honourable scars, was being tempered to a fine edge for the next stroke.'*

His hearers, recovering wounded from the battalion, ask him about particular men. The second question leads to the real point of the sketch:

> *'"What exactly happened to that rum old bird in No. 10 platoon, Cockburn, W.J.?" asked the junior listener. The young adjutant took out his cigar and examined the end carefully, with a tightening of his clean-shaven lips. "It's a rotten story," he answered slowly.'*

He goes on to describe how, on the night of 25 September, Cockburn was close to him in Gun Trench. In the early morning, when a shell killed a group of men, *'Cockburn was the only one left alive, and he was up to the ankles in blood.'* Cockburn struggled on through nights of digging and shelling though obviously unwell, *'he was coughing and spitting blood all night, and shivering when the bullets went over. Poor old thing, I was damned sorry for him.'*

After this Cockburn is sent to the Field Ambulance, but he returns on a night when the battalion is being shelled in billets. The lieutenant/adjutant can see how shaken he is, *'but of course 'there's no release from the War' and up he went into the trenches two days later'.* That night the trenches are bombarded. *'It was a pretty fair mess; our traverse was blown clean in and a man was buried under it; in the next bay were two bodies, both smashed up – we never found the head of one – young Henry, that used to be Francis' batman – nice boy he was too.'* They do not find Cockburn so assume he has been killed, until some hours later a ration party finds him wandering near Battalion HQ, saying that he is looking for a shovel. They report him to his company commander; Cockburn says he went to see the doctor. When the doctor denies this, Cockburn is put under arrest pending court martial. The adjutant argues that he was not in his right mind, but the doctor contradicts him.

Cockburn expects to be shot, *'and the swines who were on guard used to twit him about it and say the firing party had been told off to do it.'* They tell him the sound of the pioneers making a sentry box is his coffin being made; in desperation, Cockburn manages to get hold of one of their rifles, intending to shoot himself. But his courage fails, and he shoots himself in the foot.

At this point one of the listeners interrupts; surely this is too far-fetched – it has to be invention. The adjutant says no, Cockburn shot himself in the left foot. He should have been put on a second charge, for deliberate wounding, but the pain and shock made him so ill that he was sent to hospital, where he died a few days later from septic poisoning.

> *'There was a prolonged silence, broken by the youngest: "It's worse to think of the old chap going out like that than to hear of half the battalion getting scuppered in a show."'*

All the background circumstances of this fit Noel Hodgson's actual experience. The actions he describes, the other casualties; even the replacement medical officer whom the old hands thought inefficient. And Hodgson almost certainly did have experience of preparing evidence for a man facing trial: he refers to it again in a later sketch and obviously it bothered him. Both of the 9th Devons' regular diarists, John Upcott and Frank Wollocombe, took part in courts martial, so the duty was not uncommon. But 'Nestoria' has the feel of a constructed story, and it seems unlikely that he would give details of an actual case in a sketch that was intended for publication. It is interesting, though, that he chose to tell a story which highlighted the strain of war and the consequences of a mind pushed beyond its limits. The weeks following its writing were to be a dark time for him too, though never quite so dark.

'Nestoria' was posted to Stella at the beginning of February, so was probably written in the early weeks of 1916. But before that, before the end of 1915, she had the 'Company Mess' articles and something else in hand, and she was actively trying to place them with a publisher on Noel's behalf. This becomes apparent in the letter written just after Christmas. Stella had received a positive response and was going to send it on to him, presumably with the family's Christmas gifts, but forgot: *'How typical of the Hodgson family to forget the enclosure in your letter,'* he writes. *'However I gather it would have been to the effect that the N.W. was willing to take one of my scribbles? If so, then more power to them. Do as you think fit about offering them any more of the same stuff.'*[2]

The first prose sketch by 'Edward Melbourne' to be published in *The New Witness* was 'Friday Afternoon in Flanders', which appeared on 17 February. It is set in a village behind the lines, somewhere in the Givenchy – Festubert area, and it highlights the casual, everyday nature of death in the war. There are bombers in the village unloading grenades from a wagon; a sentry; an ammunition column; an old French woman with her belongings on a cart, all going about their business when suddenly shells begin to fall and everyone takes cover. One soldier attempts to run across the empty street and is killed. As life returns to normal, two stretcher bearers take away what remains of him. The old woman, shaking her head, *'plods away with her barrow and the stain of blood on her sabots'.*

The day after this was published, Friday, 18 February, Noel wrote to Stella, *'The amiable Miss Hedley has sent me a writing-pad and a pencil! Asking for it, what? She'll get it too. We'll go halves on all proceeds.'* Miss Hedley was connected with *The New Witness*: this becomes apparent in a later letter, dated only 'Monday', which begins, *'I see that a small contribution by E.M. appears in the current New Witness. It was one I sat down and wrote on receipt of Miss Hedley's epistle – strike while the iron is hot – what? If she takes Patrol and the poem too it will be A1.'* But which Monday? 'The Patrol' appeared in *The New Witness* on Friday, 9 March. A week before, the paper carried his poem, 'Back to Rest', written immediately after the Battle of Loos. The 'Monday' letter has to have been written on 21 or 28 February, probably the earlier date as he is *'still in the same place'* and on 28 February the battalion moved into trenches. This suggests a very tight turn-around for writing getting into *The New Witness* – which is important when it comes to dating his later work – but there is no other timetable into which all the pieces fit.

From this time onward he was a regular contributor to the paper. He dealt directly with Miss Hedley, leaving it to Stella to offer the pieces of his work she had to anyone who might take them. *The New Witness* pieces were also re-published around the country in local papers. Until the entire collection of the British Newspaper Library is digitised and searchable it will be impossible to say how often this happened. But it is clear already that it did happen, in papers from Aberdeen to Bristol, exposing Edward Melbourne's work to a much wider readership.

The first weeks of January can be a leaden time, the days short, the nights prolonged and dark, as Christmas fades into the past and spring feels very far away. On Monday, 3 January 1916 Noel Hodgson turned twenty-three years old. At 9am C Company – now officially known as 'No III'– paraded and marched to Talmas, north of Amiens, to work under the Royal Engineers. This set a pattern for the rest of the month. A week or so later D Company was also claimed by the Engineers, leaving the rest of the battalion at Ailly-sur-Somme, busy with route marches, rifle practice and attack training until their turn came. Hodgson's Headquarters Company, being specialists, were exempt from the pioneer work and did their own training, much to Thompson's glee, *'I don't think there is any objection to telling you what the bn. is or what we think it is,'* he told John Upcott, *'we train furiously for open fighting – attacks etc; then we dig like rabbits (all except HQ Coy!!!) and they tell us that is Pioneer Training – so you see we don't know what we are. . . I don't think anybody believes we shall be a Pioneer Bn and I don't think anyone wants it.'*[3]

They did march with the rest, though. Sometimes over long distances for no apparent reason. The day after Noel's birthday the battalion trudged nearly 16 miles [25km] to Ailly-le-Haut-Clocher. They were on the road all day, *'from morn to noon, from noon to dewy eve',* as Harold Rayner put it, quoting 'Paradise Lost'. He told John Upcott that he and the other officers of B Company amused themselves on the road by composing limericks about one another, with a blood orange for a prize:

> *This cherubic, diminutive fairy –*
> *With a head that's more brainy than hairy –*
> *Has charms to cast spells*
> *Over French demoiselles*
> *Who all love L.S.R.A.J. Cary*

> *To the rosy-cheeked, long-eyelashed Pridham*
> *They said "You can't possibly kid 'em"*
> *He replied "Though I look*
> *Too demure for a crook*
> *I'm damned if I don't," – and he did 'em.*[4]

The *'Order of the Blood Orange, first class'* was won by Cary, 'little Cary' with the triangle at the Christmas party. This was the march that reminded Hodgson of the circular Alton–Winchester trek of the previous spring, and he was not far wrong. Within days the battalion was marched back to Ailly-sur-Somme and their previous billets.

Harold Rayner had returned to the 9th from his trench mortar battery in December. Then he went on leave. He was expecting to be posted back to trench mortars but it never happened, and he settled happily back into B Company alongside Jack Inchbald. A man of extraordinary ability, strong when it mattered, 'Nibby' Rayner's habitual take on life was laid-back and amused. The limerick competition was his idea. *'Nibby brought back some very nice records when he returned from leave,'* Jack told John Upcott, *'Nibby by the way – who is acting O.C. No 8 platoon now – has developed a novel and all-absorbing passion. . . .. He has covered our walls with pictures and silhouettes of Xmas Number ladies & you can find him snipping away with his scissors almost any time of the day. He's a regular ragtime scissor man is his Nibs now.'*[5]

On 14 January Hodgson's Military Cross was announced in the *London Gazette*. He never received the medal itself, but wore the ribbon on his tunic and slipped it into several of the trench sketches. In 'Nestoria' the lieutenant on home on leave has a tunic *'as weatherbeaten and old as the mauve-and-white ribbon over his left pocket was new and bright'*. There is pride in the way he describes it, also a hint of self-mockery: he is laughing at himself for being impressed by it. His parents hoped the award might mean an extra period of leave and an investiture, but he knew that was not to be: *'Tell Dad that unfortunately there is no chance of my coming to England to be given the Cross, as the King presented crosses on the 15th to a few selected representatives of the huge crowd who possessed that honour; and the others just get 'em when they can. Voilà.'* In the same letter he told Stella that his 'weatherbeaten tunic' had suffered an unfortunate accident: *'A lamentable occurrence is the burning of my tunic owing to the enthusiasm of the adjutant, who made the stove red-hot when my tunic was hanging over it to dry. That marked a step on the downward path; I plunged into a desperate course of gambling to recover my loss – and won seventy francs odd at nap and Van John.'*[6]

It was a relief to their families to know they were out of the line – *'There is no sign of our returning trenchwards yet, so you may rest happy on that score,'* he added in postscript. But the weeks of what seemed rather pointless activity, far from any action, and the uncertainty over the battalion's future, were beginning to tell. As was the emphasis on discipline. There was restlessness in the air. In one letter Thompson proudly tells John Upcott that a man he had promoted to lance corporal after Loos has just been made a sergeant. Soon after, Hodgson lets Upcott know that even as Thompson was writing, the new sergeant was on a charge for drunkenness and has been reduced to the ranks. The man celebrated this by *'utterly bamboozling the earnest young innocent in charge of his platoon'* during a route march. *'Great are the strafings in the days of Milne,'* Hodgson continued:

> *'Today our C.Q.M. Sergeant, one armourer-sergeant and one orderly-sergeant were separately given one of the smartest tellings off of their careers. We shall have discipline at last – de mortuis – You will never again see a Ninth Devon leave the ranks and mount a lorry without permission, – and billets, why you could eat your dinner of the floor – if such Nebuchadnezzarian habits appeal to you.'*[7]

He liked Major Milne, but even he seemed to feel things were going too far. Word had reached them that Captain Mockridge was hoping to return and they feared this might be a flashpoint. *'"Mog" seems to imagine he may be out again soon,'* Thompson commented, *'if he does he will be fearfully strafed by the C.O., who when he does strafe, well, everybody feels sorry for the culprit.'*[8]

Ralph Mockridge did return, with John Upcott. They received their orders at Wareham on Friday, 4 February, sailed the next day, and were in the Rest Camp at Etaples by 2am on Sunday. On Monday they were ordered to rejoin the 9th Devons: *'I was in an awful funk lest we should be packed off to some other regiment,'* Upcott wrote. *'It will be like going home to see the dear old 9th again.'* Jack Inchbald met them at Ville-sur-Ancre and they walked to Battalion HQ beside the ration wagon. Upcott resumed command of C Company and Mockridge D Company, and with their coming the old guard was almost fully restored. Only B Company was not commanded by one of the originals. Captain Muntz, its original commander, had told John Upcott back in November that he was itching to return:

> *'The parade grounds of Wareham and the chalk hills of Dorset for the winter sound to me very concentrated essence of boredom and ennui beside which the water filled trenches of Flanders seem a very garden of Eden. My soul sinks at the thought of another winter's play acting at home. All very necessary, I know, but I'd like someone else to do it.'*[9]

But with a shattered jaw and an open wound under one eye that still required draining, his recovery was going to take much longer.

The other two returned a few days after the battalion moved to Méaulte, just south of Albert. John Upcott captured the scene in his diary:

> *'Méaulte is a long straggling village of the usual type, a broad muddy chaussée with dirty white court-yard farms on either side; here & there a small shop, & a 14th century church in the middle. The country is not unlike our Sussex weald in parts; rolling plough lands, bare February spinneys & wooded valleys. The fighting centres round Fricourt, a smashed up village which the Germans hold: we have got the railway station & between the lines stand a few battered railway trucks. There is a little river too; empty now, as the Hun, in an attempt to achieve Frightfulness, has dammed it higher up & diverted it.'*

This move brought the battalion closer to a sector of the front line to the west of Fricourt that had recently been taken over by 20 Brigade. Seen on a map, the trench lines of what was to become the Somme battlefield run roughly due south, in a meandering line that begins to veer slightly to the east above Albert. Immediately below and to the east of the town the line turns more sharply due east, to run in that direction a short distance before curving back towards the south again and crossing the river Somme. Fricourt lies at the point east of Albert where the line turns, in a valley with a wood rising behind it. To its right on the map and nearby is the hilltop village of Mametz. Both villages were in German hands, both were heavily fortified. Together they formed a salient – a bulge – in the German lines, and a formidable challenge to any hope of a breakthrough.

The immediate task for the 9th Devons in February was the improvement of the British defences facing Fricourt. On arrival at Méaulte the battalion divided. Duncan Martin took his company forward a short distance to garrison the village of Bécordel, closer to the lines. He set up his headquarters in great style:

> *'He occupies a jolly sort of manor farm. The village consists of a few large houses & the Church. The latter is in ruins & Iscariot has the big bell suspended in front of his house as a gas alarm; while his servant has decorated the interior of his billet with statues of saints. In the house almost the only thing remaining is an old library containing some old editions.'*[10]

The reputation of the library spread even to the exalted heights of Brigade Staff. Later B Company joined the garrison. From Bécordel working parties went out to improve and repair the trenches and the redoubts – strongpoints – behind the lines that formed part of the British defences. Martin also provided mining parties to work in the Tambour, a small bulge in the British trenches on a ridge west of Fricourt. The Tambour was a hotbed of mining activity. The lines ran close together there and both sides were constantly vying to mine and undermine one another's positions.

Captain Martin's Headquarters at Bécordel, just as John Upcott described it in his diary.

Battalion Headquarters was at Méaulte, and with it Noel Hodgson and the Headquarters Company. D Company was at Méaulte too, while John Upcott's C Company was all over the place. Two of his platoons were in Bécordel, one was with him in Méaulte – except for a group of trained miners called away to build deep dugouts in the trenches – and George Underhill had taken the remaining two platoons some miles south, across the Somme, to work on railway construction. Upcott had excellent billets, *'in a delightful old farmhouse in the village; my room has bare stone walls, an open chimney & a brick floor. Some of the furniture must be as old as the hills. The chest I use as a dressing table must date from the 16th century.'* But there was little for him to do there and most of his time was spent commuting from one to another of his platoons.

He was not the only one. There was constant coming-and-going between the scattered outposts of the battalion, both official and social. Jack Inchbald, who was Acting Quartermaster and based further from the Front at Ville-sur-Ancre, made daily visits to Méaulte and Bécordel with the ration wagon and other supplies, and was a good source of news. The officers met for meals, particularly in the evening, and Hodgson and Major Milne lunched once with Martin at Bécordel. There was also constant traffic between Méaulte and the trenches. The battalion was not required to hold the front line yet, but the officers were expected to know the layout of the trenches and the approaches to them, so tours of inspection and individual explorations were frequent.

In the second week of February Stella wrote to Noel with exciting news. She was expecting her first baby in June. She had mentioned feeling sick in earlier letters but he seemed not to catch on; his replies only wished her better. Now he was overjoyed. *'Dear old girl, How perfectly splendid'*, he wrote, on Friday, 18 February:

> *'I'm most awfully surprised and delighted. Good luck to you and your 1936 soldier. What do the others think of it? Toby is very proud, isn't he, and frightfully excited. I hope it's a boy, don't you? I don't know why, but a boy seems more thrilling than a girl. Anyway, whatever he or she is, it's quite splendid. I must start saving up to present him (or her) with the most 'normous mug or other useless piece of plate on his (or her) first birthday.'*

'Good luck to you and your 1936 soldier'. With hindsight, that comment is extraordinary. He was just three years off an accurate prediction of the next war, and though there was a lightheartedness to the remark, there was also a shadow. The idea of life going on at home – of a new life beginning – set off an impatience with the course his own life had taken. He missed his freedom and his mountains. He missed being with his family at what promised to be an exciting time. He had found plenty of things to enjoy in soldiering – most of all, the comradeship of the battalion – and he liked taking an active part. He did

not question his or Britain's involvement in the war. He just wished at that moment that none of it had ever happened.

> *'If he's a he I hope he's luckier than his Uncle Bill, and doesn't get involved in silly squabbles of European potentates.*
>
> *'The adversary, as he is now called in the French communiqués, has only put five shells into our little burg since Tuesday, which is a most comforting thought. He placed a few in the trenches, but at the moment I was some distance away, and observed the occurrence through my glasses, with complete sang froid. . . . How are they all at home? Is Mum well, and sleeping better than she expected? The post is very rotten here now. Letters are taking about four or five days to come, and often don't come at all.'*

But slow post or not, the latest *New Witness* reached him in the next few days; probably the issue of the previous Thursday, with 'Friday Afternoon in Flanders'. He had been thinking about the baby, and wrote to Stella again on the Monday to say that he had seen his contribution in the paper. He told her he wanted Miss Hedley to make out cheques for his work to her, so that she could start a bank account for the baby. Then he changed the subject and passed on a recipe – a prime example of officer's mess cuisine:

> *'We are still in the same place, and very comfortable; we have got a stove and plenty of fuel, and we can make ourselves rum punch in the evenings. The C.O. has received a consignment of all manner of potted delights from home, and we have devised a most excellent dish. Take one round of the loaf, toast it, butter it and anoint with anchovy paste. Lay on it two poached eggs and the chopped portions of a sheep's kidney. Place in the oven for one minute and eat immediately. Most succulent I assure you, we eat it whenever the kidneys can be obtained. The bag of kippers and the socks have both arrived. You spoil me, you know, but it is very pleasant to be spoilt.'*[11]

Since the British took over the Somme area the previous year the Germans in the trenches opposite had been alert to the change. It was impossible to hide the trench digging and construction work that unrolled as the months passed, suggesting that some large-scale plan was afoot. The Germans wanted to know what it was. Frank Wollocombe described how a spy was caught in the Tambour masquerading as a British officer; he heard rumours of several others. The area was becoming more active with bombardments and raids, designed to hinder the progress of the work and also to take prisoners – another means of gathering information. On the afternoon of 22 February the garrison at Bécordel telephoned HQ for artillery support as they were being heavily shelled. Around

Bécordel crossroads, March 1916, drawn by John Upcott.

5pm the bombardment lifted onto the front line. The 2nd Borders were actually holding it at that time, but an officer and fifty men of A Company of the 9th Devons were there too, mining in the Tambour. At 5.50pm the 9th Devons from Méaulte were ordered into battle positions. Hodgson and his bombers – 110 men and two other officers – were sent to the Queen's Redoubt, behind the Tambour. Nine men were wounded on their way up by a shell that caught them just to the north of Bécordel.

After about ninety minutes the bombardment lifted from the Tambour to target the communication lines while the Germans attacked in strength, aiming to destroy some new tunnels the Engineers were digging and to capture some of the defenders. They broke through, but the Borders, the mining company of the Royal Engineers, and the Devons' working party, managed to push them back. Just after 8pm, when things fell quiet, Hodgson's men from Queen's Redoubt were sent forward to help repair the damage to the front line. Most of the casualties were from the Border Regiment; one officer and eleven men killed, twenty-two wounded, four admitted to hospital with shell shock and twelve missing altogether, either taken prisoner, blown to pieces, or buried in the bombardment, no one knew.

The next day it snowed heavily, carpeting the whole landscape:

'Last night it was extraordinarily picturesque up in trenches. Great wastes of snow & the black lines of the trenches lying across them, occasionally illuminated by a brilliant flare, & a serene moon over all.

John Upcott's sketch of Company Headquarters at Fricourt, March 1916.

Upcott's drawing of the trenches at Fricourt and new traverse, March 1916.

But it was a wee bit cold; everything was frozen stiff as a doornail. Men were sleeping on the firesteps with snow all over them, but they seemed to sleep all right; they snored anyway, you could hear them all down the line on the frosty silence.'[12]

The 9th Devons took over the front line trenches to the right of their previous position on the night of 27/28 February, and there was no further talk of them becoming pioneers.

This was a positive move for them. Soldiering rather than navvying. John Upcott described an attempted raid on his part of the line on 29 February, which he and Ralph Mockridge spotted in time to frustrate: *'We had a most exhilarating half hour; everybody enjoys a little turn up like this after the ordinary routine of trench life. I never saw any one so bucked as the men.'* In his normal frame of mind Hodgson would have felt the same, but the darker mood that was on him a few weeks before when he heard of Stella's pregnancy had not lifted. Grief was one reason. James Tombs, who shared the fell-walking holiday with him and Nowell Oxland not three years before, had appeared in the casualty lists. Tombs had joined the 7th Battalion of the Border Regiment at Ypres in November. In December he contracted a fever and was sent to hospital but he did not recover. Pneumonia developed and he died on 18 February in No.7 General Hospital in St Omer. For Noel this underlined a growing sense of futility. He was troubled by the fact that his friend had died alone, far from anyone who knew or cared for him: that seemed far worse to him than dying in battle.

To go so far and then die of illness. It must have depressed him even more because he too was nursing a fever and trying to fight it off. On 3 March Major Milne sent him to 22 Field Ambulance, one of three mobile medical units attached to 7 Division (a 'Field Ambulance' was not a vehicle, but a unit of the Royal Army Medical Corps, roughly similar in size to an infantry company). Noel's records state 'PUO' – pyrexia, unknown origin – a blanket term for the many fevers that flourished with men cramped together in poor conditions. He was admitted to hospital in Corbie where 22 Field Ambulance was based at that time. Stella had written to tell him that her husband had a new job as Second Master of the King's School, Canterbury and Headmaster of the Junior School, and on 6 March he replied from his hospital bed,

'Your news is splendid; this is obviously to be an annus mirabilis in the annals of the Bernard Tower family. If only I could put a leg or an arm in the way of a bullet and get home for the summer, to keep Mum & Dad company when you go away. Take care you make yourself agreeable to the Society of the Close or the Palace Green or whatever it is: do not shock or shame them by your juvenility. How is the turret to be named,

have you yet decided. J.C. [Junior Curate, recalling Bernard Tower's early days in Berwick] *ought to be extremely happy now, with a good job and a very good wife and a Turret under construction. . . .*

    'Send anything of mine you have to any paper you like that will have it, I'll keep on scribbling for Miss Hedley. I am to be allowed up to-day for the first time, quite an event; also I had a solid breakfast today. But I am not going to get well too soon, not till the snow's gone. I'd give my M.C. to be home with Mum to look after me.'

He was in hospital almost two weeks, while the weather eased, the heavy snow and biting winds giving way to the first signs of spring. For Noel, comfortably far from the front line in a landscape untouched by the fighting, illness provided a much-needed rest and a chance to think. Once he was well enough to be classed as convalescent he did what he always did – found the nearest hill and climbed to the top. The scene is described in one of his *New Witness* sketches, published in April and, as with most of his war sketches, the details that can be verified match his own experience exactly.

    In 'There and Back' a convalescent officer in *'hard-worn khaki with a small ribbon on the left breast'* – the ribbon having clearly aged since 'Nestoria' – climbs the ridge outside *'a little hospital town in the Somme country. . . . It was one of those incomparable mornings after rain, when every line is clear and every colour vivid almost beyond belief.'* He throws himself down on the grass at the top, lights his pipe and surveys the scene.

    'No sign or sound of conflict broke the spell of that healing quiet; not the echo of a gun, not the distant vision of a hovering 'plane. But all the sounds of the living country mingled: the rippling song of the larks, the chirping grasshoppers, the rumble of a farm cart on the valley-road, and, as it were the motive and spirit of it all, the delicate melancholy of a far-off church bell.'

After a while he knocks out his pipe and walks back down the hill. On his way to the hospital he meets a man from his battalion and learns that his second-in-command and sergeant-major were wounded by a rifle grenade the day before, and have been brought in for treatment. The officer realises that his company needs him. Returning to the hospital, he tells the doctor he is ready to rejoin his battalion.

    It would be impossible now to say how much imagination is woven into this. But it is certainly true that two days before Hodgson returned to the battalion, on the afternoon of 13 March, an officer and a sergeant were wounded by a rifle grenade; it was an accident, which Frank Wollocombe described in his diary. In 'There and Back' the second-in-command's name is Holland; the real-life equivalent was Second Lieutenant Butland, and he was actually standing in as bombing officer while Hodgson was in hospital. The sergeant was his sergeant. Both had leg wounds and would have been taken to the Field Ambulance. And beyond these details, the essential truth of the piece holds. The main character, who climbs to the highest point he can find to drink in the landscape and make his own peace with the future is Noel Hodgson to the life. He had told Stella that he wanted to prolong his illness – his escape – for as long as possible. He would have had to go back anyway once he was passed fit, but in 'There and Back' he explains why going back is a matter of choice, not compulsion. He decides to return because he belongs to the battalion and the battalion needs him.

The issue of *The New Witness* that carried 'There and Back' also included a poem by 'E.M'. Edward Melbourne? The paper did not have had any other contributor using either the initials alone or another name with those initials at that time. And Hodgson did refer to his alter ego as 'E.M.' in letters – *'a small contribution by E.M.'* The poem, if his (and it does sound very like his), is interesting in the context of his other writing because it takes imagery that he did use – the coupling of beauty and sorrow, for example; *'Beauty and sorrow hand-in-hand'* ('The Call') or *'every sad and lovely thing'* ('Before Action') – into the darker mood that affected him in the spring of 1916. It sets the romantic image of battle against the reality of the trenches, implying 'is it worth it?' and finds an answer similar in spirit to the ending of 'There and Back': when every other reason pales, the reason to carry on is the men – or in this case, those who have already died.

A Field

Here sorrow has no beauty, death no greatness,
Where the dumb fields from Heaven to Heaven run
In a dull poverty of desolateness
Under a blind sky, and the rain is spun
In a grey web that long has slain the sun.

To go down reeling in a wild endeavour,
Or take unvanquished in a heart of scorn
The inevitable sword – were well – but never
In these low lands to watch as soon as born
The golden thread in abjectness outworn.

The worth of all things is what men will pay,
And for these mean fields men die every day.[13]

Hodgson returned to the battalion on 15 March, finding them in the front line; their relief came two days later, and they spent the next week in billets and on working parties. While he had been in hospital, Second Lieutenant Eardley-Wilmot (*'I mean to say one can't hit Eardley-Wilmot on the head with a tambourine'*) had died from a chest wound and others had been injured. Several of the men had been wounded and two killed. Méaulte was coming under heavier shelling than before and everyone was on edge:

> *'Being shelled in billets is far more beastly than being shelled in trenches & we are all getting rather nervous. It is quite common to see the whole mess prick up their ears in the middle of dinner & without a word shoot out of the room into the little cellar in the yard, followed by cooks, servants and retainers. In this connection fowls are most unpopular. A hen scrooching to herself makes a noise not unlike the distant approach of a six inch shell. It is very embarrassing to discover half way down the cellar steps, that it is a fowl which has caused the alarm.'*

John Upcott (that was from his diary) could see the funny side of running in fear from an innocent hen, but after the brief respite of hospital Hodgson's mood was once more bleak and disgruntled, quite unlike his normal self. He told Stella:

> *'I got back to duty on Wednesday, luckily in glorious weather. Now I am as fit as can be. We have just come out of trenches for a spell in close billets. Personally I'd just as soon be in trenches as in this mouldy village, but it is a rest of sorts I suppose. The thought of spending another summer on this rotten game leaves me cold. The better the weather gets the more utterly futile the whole business seems. . . . when it's nice and fine and you feel like having a ride or a game of tennis, having to spend your time in a rotten trench and be shelled is utter rot.'*

He was also not as fit as he claimed at first:

> *'The porkpie turned up alright and was eaten happily though I was not in a condition to eat any myself. Up to date (Friday) there has been no sign of any 'special parcel' or any bag of kippers. But the parcel post has been pretty groggy for some time so I expect they're on the way, unless some hound in the A.S.C. has strafed them. I wish I had some news to tell you, but there is simply nothing here. Life is amazingly dull; it's hardly credible that one can do so much work and be so bored at the same time.'*

Comparing the accounts of the battalion's two diarists, Upcott and Wollocombe, for the early months of 1916 suggests that another reason for his bleak mood may have been the comparative isolation of the Headquarters Company. Being exempt from the threat of becoming pioneers and the work that went with it might have seemed positive, but he had not been able to share the mud and the grumbles, or the elation when it ended. And being based at headquarters, close to a very strict commanding officer, seemed to have been rather like having a room next to the headmaster's study: it kept the others away. In one of the four companies he would have been in the thick of things. Their officers were forever meeting for dinner, walking or riding together, sharing and exchanging duties, but he is never mentioned among them and that was a marked change from before and after. He had also lost Thompson and Whiteway to the brigade bombing and machine gun companies.

From 23 March the battalion had another six days in trenches, and on 31 March Hodgson went home on leave. His path might have crossed with three new arrivals heading for the battalion that day. Two were from the 'old 9th', Humphrey Cole and Rowan Freeland, able at last to rejoin the 9th after their long months at Wareham. But Humphrey Cole lasted only four days before being shot by a sniper in the Tambour. *'They have just brought him back,'* John Upcott wrote, *'but I am afraid he won't live. I had a look at his helmet, the bullet had pierced one side, but had only dented the other & was fixed in the lining. Bad luck his first day in trenches.'*

Life was short then and time precious. Noel probably snatched the opportunity to enjoy himself in London on his way through. He had his photograph taken at Langfier's in Bond Street (complete with medal ribbon) and may have met Miss Hedley or Cecil Chesterton about his work for *The New Witness*. There were friends from the battalion in and around town, still recovering from Loos; he certainly saw Frank Worrall during this leave. Frank mentions it in a letter though he does not say where they met: his home was in Devonshire. But Noel's priority would have been Ipswich, his parents, and Stella.

His leave lasted a week but he managed to secure a two-day extension and was able to visit Durham, and the school that still meant so much to him. It might have been unsettling: being there, it would have been hard for him not to be reminded of dead friends. In so small a school community most of the losses were personal. But though there must have been ghosts for him among the new generation of boys, the visit was not a mournful one. Far from it; he was glad to be back and he found real strength in the school's continued existence, strength and a source of hope. He narrowly missed the visit of another returning hero, his friend Robert Parr, fresh from Serbia. Whatever stories Parr told the boys, it made a real impression. Writing from the Somme a few weeks later Hodgson told him, '*You seem to have made a great impression at Durham when you were there; from what filters through I gather that a catchword much used in reply to questions is 'Ask Parr'; indicating a veil of dark and abysmal secrecy surrounding the affair.*'[15]

The day before he had left Méaulte, 30 March, word reached the battalion that there was to be an attack in the near future – they thought by 20 Brigade only – and that they were about to move to a new sector to begin preparations. John Upcott and Frank Wollocombe both knew about this, so it is likely that Hodgson also heard the news and went home on leave knowing that something was in the wind. When he rejoined the battalion, on Tuesday, 11 April, they were in the new line of trenches, facing the village of Mametz.

Chapter 12

'Before Action', April – June 1916

From the Devons' previous positions facing Fricourt to their new line of trenches is no great distance. A few hours' walk in peacetime, no more. From the Tambour the opposing lines snaked southwards, crossing the railway and the Albert–Carnoy road and cutting off Fricourt from its station and cemetery, both behind British lines. Then the trenches climbed the western slopes of the Montagne de Cappy – no mountain, really, but a sizeable hill and an excellent vantage point. The lines drew nearer as they climbed, coming perilously close to one another near the top at the Bois Français, neither side being willing to yield the advantage of the high ground. Like the Tambour, the Bois Français was a hotbed of mining. It was also pocked and cratered by artillery fire where the two sides vied for possession.

Beyond the Bois Français lay Kiel Trench, where Second Lieutenant Siegfried Sassoon of the Royal Welsh Fusiliers was to win the Military Cross in May for bringing in his wounded sergeant in the aftermath of a raid. The trench lines followed the hilltop eastwards a short distance before curving round to the north-east and sloping steeply downhill towards the road and railway line, which ran beside one another in the valley. Then, crossing road and railway at right angles, the trenches curved away to the east up a more gentle slope, skirting the defences of Mametz and passing out of sight and out of the Devons' ken.

The part of the line that concerned them most was the downward slope of the hill as far as the road, its most prominent feature being an L-shaped patch of woodland on a raised bank near the hill's foot. The Army called this 'Mansel Copse'. With one arm of the L running parallel to the trenches on the slope and the other parallel to the road, Mansel Copse formed a natural corner. It forced the British front line trench back on itself at right angles to follow the tree line along the top of the bank, before turning to resume its course where trees and bank ended, so doubling the width of no man's land at the point where the opposing lines crossed the Albert–Carnoy road. There was also a second, smaller road, little more than a track, which branched off near the corner of the Copse and hugged the foot of the bank before turning south to climb the hill. The trees of the Copse towered over this secondary road; in places the bank was as sheer as a cliff.

Once it would have been a lovely spot. After one of the hardest nights the Devons spent in the Mansel Copse trenches, John Upcott drew breath as the light returned, briefly glimpsing the landscape as it must once have been:

'I have seldom seen day break more beautifully. Daybreak is wonderful in trenches; the guns & rifles stop & the larks & the thrushes begin all along the line, especially in poor little Mansel Copse, that stands at the corner of my line & once overhung a shady country road. Here the blackthorns & anemones still flower after two years of war. Out towards Carnoy stretches a park-like valley, dotted with rounded copses which throw long shadows in the early morning light. Seen through the early morning haze, one might imagine it an English park, but for the black gashes that mark the line of some past barrage.'[1]

On the slope of the hill the copse bank was also steep. The opposing lines running down the hill were divided by a dip in the ground, closer to the British trenches than the German and deepening as it descended, forming a natural hollow at the foot of the copse. After months of shelling the wood was a poor shadow of its peacetime self and offered little cover. Every movement close to the front line was open to view from the Germans on the hillside, while those entrenched across the valley could see the whole sweep of the hill laid out before them. *'Luckily the Boches do not take their chance in sniping, or they could get half the Company in a morning'*, Frank Wollocombe wrote, his first time in, *'We are on the side of a hill.'[2]*

On 27 March, in the early stages of planning for the Battle of the Somme, Brigadier General Deverell of 20 Brigade set out a detailed proposal for an attack by his brigade across the slope of the hill, to push the line forward to Hidden Wood, which lay in the next dip on the hillside below the Bois Français. From their front line his men would have to advance downhill into the dip, more steeply on the right through Mansel Copse than on the left. Then would begin the climb to the German front line, *'higher than our own'* and on rising ground. On the right it was possible to see three lines of German trenches rising one above the other, 100 yards apart on the hillside: well-built, deep trenches, protected by barbed wire. His men's advance would only be steep in the centre, where the German front line lay behind a bank overgrown with bushes and protected by barbed wire. He estimated the height of this bank at between 12 and 18 feet and *'in parts a sheer drop from the top'*. There were also three hostile saps running out to the bank. Saps were used for listening and observation; Deverell believed that one of these was also a machine-gun post. As it stood, he said, this bank was *'impracticable to attacking infantry'*. He suggested that trench mortars might be used to demolish it or, better still, *'if this bank could be mined by shallow mines and blown up at the moment of assault it would be most helpful'*. He wanted the trees and undergrowth of the copse on the hill slope to be cleared, and recommended that the attack should take place at night, to protect the advance from direct observation by enemy artillery.

Details of the plan would change, but this document describes the ground the 9th Devons had to cross on 1 July, the trenches they had to take. Reporting on the state of the British trenches, Deverell was unimpressed:

> *'Our trenches are at present unsuitable. They run up the side of a hill and are badly traversed, and in many places troops in them are entirely exposed to view from the high ground to the East. From personal experience I know that hostile field guns can and do enfilade the front line trench traverse by traverse from Mansel Copse to the Craters. . . . The whole area allotted will require to be cleaned, deepened, traversed, machine gun emplacements constructed, communication trenches opened up, H.Q. shelters made, suitable bomb proof stores for ammunition and grenades built, telephonic communication lines buried and reorganised, and dressing stations established.'* [3]

So the Devons had their work cut out when they took over these trench lines, ten days after the report was written. They were not impressed with them either. A first inspection left Frank *'very disgusted, there is no room for half a Company, no firesteps or any sign of traverses, parados or anything'*. John Upcott complained that the front line was too narrow and the support trenches too wide. When the digging started he found it *'very filthy work as below our duck boards, we came on old French boarding & indescribable filth below that'*. Given the cramped conditions and lack of cover, half of the men had to spend daylight hours in Wellington Redoubt, the strongpoint at the top of the hill where the battalion had its headquarters. The Somme may have been quiet before the British took over, but the dangers of this small corner of the battlefield soon became apparent. There were old French bodies on the German wire, and when Frank Wollocombe's men set about rebuilding the line they made an unnerving discovery: *'A lot of dead men's feet stick out of these trenches which hinders work rather.'* And all the while they faced a steady bombardment: *'If this ever was a quiet sector,'* John Upcott said, *'it is wakening up.'* Four of Frank's men were wounded by a rifle grenade one morning and Major Milne had a lucky escape, happening to be in the same part of the trench. On 12 April Brigadier General Deverell came to see the work in progress and lost himself in a maze of disused French trenches behind the front line. [4]

Noel Hodgson rejoined the battalion on Tuesday, 11 April. It was a noisy day, Frank Wollocombe said, with a lot of shelling and trench mortar fire. Frank believed he had shot a sniper on the railway embankment – another danger point not identified in the brigadier general's report. The next evening a German patrol reached as far as the wire close to John Upcott's C Company. They threw bombs into a listening post injuring three men, one of whom later died. It was a warning of worse to come.

The Devons left the trenches on Friday, 14 April for rest billets at Bray-sur-Somme, a few miles to the south. Harold Rayner rejoined them there after two months in hospital and was posted back to C Company. The rest was not entirely restful: they had still to send working parties in the line, and at first the weather was disappointing. Later it brightened. One morning Duncan Martin and John

The road to Bray (by John Upcott).

Horse lines in Bray (by John Upcott).

Upcott rode out on the downs, *'with such clouds as you only get in April & the Somme marshes sparkling far below'.*[5] And Noel Hodgson had hills to climb and the sort of conditions he loved: *'a peculiarly spring sunshine, a vintage sunshine, dry and stimulating, drenched the hills. Infinitely distant in the clear heavens, no larger and no louder than silver dragon-flies, had flown the 'planes. . . and now peace seemed to fall with the dusk like a mantle upon the tired slopes under an opaline sky.'* This passage sets the scene for one of his trench sketches, 'The Raid', surely based on the events of Wednesday, 19 April, when the peace of what had been *'an unnecessarily perfect day'* was shattered at dusk by the sounds of a violent bombardment on the British lines around Mansel Copse. The 2nd Borders were in the trenches, but as the 9th Devons in Bray were

John Upcott's drawing of Bray Church in April 1916.

ordered to stand to, John Upcott's thoughts went straight to Harold Rayner, who was up with a working party.

Rayner was probably Hodgson's *'subaltern of impressionable mind'*, through whose eyes we see the horror of the bombardment. One moment he is enjoying the evening's peace and quoting the *Aeneid* to himself, the next:

> *'Death, in every degree of horror, sudden and unseen, with a voice of unbearable violence, took men up and dashed them lifeless, bags of blood and bone, upon their comrades . . . . The subaltern was flung upon his back by the first salvo, and picked himself up from a débris of earth and timber. His hands he noticed were bloody, and the idea "I am hit" occurred to him. Then he noticed that he was alone in the wrecked bay. The sentry had disappeared, and looking at the ruin from which he had crawled, he realised whence the blood had come.*
>
> *'He walked round the traverse, and found one man firing frenziedly to his front, while all that remained of another was pitifully attempting to bandage a shattered leg with a field dressing.*
>
> *He said afterwards that the act of checking the man from wasting ammunition alone helped him to retain his reason. Certainly one of the most startling features of the horror known as a heavy bombardment is that men will carry out the rules of "the book" and find comfort from so doing, though death is taking both the calm and the distraught equally.'*

In the real world as in Hodgson's sketch, the bombardment was only the prelude to a raid on the front line. A German raiding party about twenty strong had made their way unseen into the hollow below the copse. In places the wire had been cut; in others the force of the explosions had thrown it clean over the trench. At about 8.15pm the barrage lifted onto the support trenches and the raiders attempted to enter the front line. Repulsed at the corner of Mansel Copse, they were successful further up the slope and got away leaving three officers and sixty-two men dead or wounded, and a further eight missing. Harold Rayner was unhurt, but several of his working party were injured. It was a serious affair. Serious enough to warrant a formal enquiry at brigade level, though all concerned were found to have done everything that could be expected, and were praised for their actions. The commanding officer of the 2nd Borders was adamant that the missing men had not been taken prisoner, and the enquiry agreed. But the bombardment had undone weeks of work on the trenches; when the 9th Devons took over on Good Friday, 21 April, all the digging had to be done again. John Upcott, taking over the copse section of the line, was asked to dig for the missing men. *'The state of my trench line passes all conception,'* he wrote:

'The whole line had been blown in during the raid, except for a few square yards at the corner, where the line bends back round Mansel Copse. The rain of the last two days has turned the loosened soil into a pulp; one wades along them knee deep in liquid mud – literally. I hold nearly 400 yards of line & it takes me well over an hour to get from one end to the other, so slowly can one move in this morass.'

It worried him that there was so little wire left in front, but rewiring could only be done safely in the brief window of darkness before the moon rose. On the night of 23/24 April a small German patrol spotted one of his wiring parties and followed them back to the trench unnoticed. They hid by the parapet until the wiring party dispersed; then slipped quietly into the trench and captured the first sentry they found, while two of his companions ran for help and the other was knocked out. By the time anyone could reach the place, raiders and sentry were gone.

'There will be the devil of a row about this', Upcott noted in his diary, and he was right. Major Milne sent for all his company commanders the next day, *'me in particular. . . . I got what I expected, but of course he has had it hot from the Brigadier'*. The companies in the front line were ordered to put two officers and all their men on duty at night in future, cooks and orderlies included; to have every fire bay manned with double sentry groups (which in C Company's case required more men than John Upcott actually had, and exposed the entire company to enfilade fire from German positions on the right). And all four companies were ordered to send out wiring parties to rewire the whole front that night. Putting so many men into no man's land increased the risk of attracting enemy fire, but without adequate wiring the trenches were too vulnerable.

It was a 'grisly' night, John Upcott said. The Germans were expecting wiring parties and began shooting and putting flares up as soon as the Devons entered no man's land. Frank Wollocombe was shot in the shoulder – *'It felt like a hard bang with a round thing. . . I wasn't quite sure if I was wounded or if some stone had hit me.'*[6] Six other men were wounded and one killed. He came from C Company; when they realised he was missing, Harold Rayner went out under fire to look for him and brought him in, but *'He was dead, poor chap, shot through the mouth. One of the jolliest chaps in No 12.'*[7] Private John Martin from Bow in Devon, aged nineteen, was buried just over the hill in what is now the Citadel New Military Cemetery.

The next night was grim too, with an aborted enemy raid and even more casualties from the bombardment that came with it – eighteen, with two dead: *'one sentry group just above Mansel Copse had got a shell right among them, a sergeant of A Company killed, amongst others, & most of the rest wounded. Beyond this point the trench was very badly damaged, with dead & wounded lying in the bottom. . . . Shells kept whistling through the half light, shaking the ground with the violence of their explosions & filling the trench with reeking smoke.'* John Upcott's men bore the brunt of it – not for nothing was the line of trenches running through Mansel Copse known as 'Blood Alley' – and after four days with no more than four hours sleep, he was so exhausted he fell asleep standing up. When the battalion was relieved a few hours later he had to be left sleeping in the doctor's bed in Wellington Redoubt, because he was in no fit state to move.

In their two spells in the Mansel Copse trenches the 9th Devons had learned a lot about the ground over which they were to attack. They had experienced its dangers, most of which arose from the lie of the land itself, with its rises and hollows and steep wooded banks, and its vulnerability to enemy observers on three sides. Being based at headquarters Noel Hodgson was cut off from the routine of holding the front line. If a raid had broken through in force his bombers would have come into their own, and some were positioned in the front line trenches in case. But for him, apart from supervising the bombing sections, the main tasks were getting to know the ground and overseeing the building of bomb stores. The bombers had their own agenda, and when Frank Wollocombe was taken to Wellington Redoubt to have his wound dressed he found Hodgson there talking to two other bombing officers, Second Lieutenant Prynne from his own Headquarters Company and Charles Cecil Thompson, now part of the Brigade Bombing Company. But in and around Battalion HQ there was never any shortage of other jobs that needed doing. Sometimes Noel acted as

Grovetown camp in April 1916. It was at Grovetown that Captain Martin's model was on display for the last ten days before the Battle of the Somme. (Sketch by John Upcott)

messenger, on one occasion carrying orders to the front line during a heavy bombardment – suggesting, perhaps, that the relative safety of his position irked him while friends were in danger.

Once out of the line he became close to John Upcott, who caught up with the battalion in the tented camp at Grovetown, still exhausted from his experiences. They put him straight to bed in a pair of Hodgson's silk pyjamas (silk being a 'must have' at the Front because it discouraged lice), and he slept for almost twenty-four hours. When he awoke, he and Hodgson rode to Bray-sur-Somme in search of a bath. They shared a tent at Grovetown with Ralph Mockridge, and Hodgson also provided reading matter for Upcott in the form of Hilaire Belloc's *The Path to Rome*, an account of a walking pilgrimage from France to Italy across the Alps, *'which I am reading with considerable amusement'*. Belloc's books were in favour that spring: in a letter written a few weeks later Rayner told his brother that he, Upcott and Hodgson were enjoying *Hills and the Sea*.

On Sunday, 30 April, Upcott and Hodgson attended an open-air service on the hillside above the camp. The chaplain gave *'one of his inimitable sermons – if you don't stop a bullet — bon* [good]; *if you do & get a blighty — très bon* [very good]; *but if you get killed it is more bon still — for though you may not realise it, you give your life for others.'* This was a good sermon, John Upcott said, because the men understood it and it helped them to fight; also *'It gives an answer to the eternal question which every man of us asks himself out here; — If I get killed — what next?'* After the service, he and Hodgson walked back down the hill with the chaplain in the gathering dark.

The Rev Ernest Courtenay Crosse had joined 20 Brigade after Loos, the previous chaplain, Frederick Hewitt, having been killed on the battlefield while attending to the wounded. Hewitt had been in parish work before the war and was in his mid-thirties but Crosse was a younger man – of an age with the junior officers. He identified closely with them and several in both Devon battalions became his friends, Noel Hodgson among them. Before long, Crosse would be inextricably bound with their story.

The first two weeks of May had a holiday feel. The weather was fine and it was spring:

'We are encamped in a shallow valley, worn dry between undulating slopes of green wheat. Some fifty tents, splodged with patchwork paint for concealment, a number of horses & mules tethered about, & a brace of archies [anti-aircraft guns] *up in a little copse full of cowslips complete our surroundings. We do as little work as we can & mostly lie about in the sun & dust, hoping the authorities have forgotten us. I am writing this sitting in my tent, drinking a little white wine. From over the hill comes the intermittent rumble of guns; sometimes they are still;*

sometimes for no apparent reason they will fire all day. For the time being we are in the war but not of the war.'[8]

On May Day morning Upcott and Hodgson rode over the downs to the reserve lines to reconnoitre a route in case they were called in to support. Other mornings they took early rides for the joy of it; one afternoon they played at target practice, shooting oranges balanced on glass bottles. On 4 May they had a very early breakfast before riding three miles over the downs to the Bois des Tailles,

> *'which contains among other useful & ornamental things, Iscariot, nightingales & the prospect of a second breakfast — also bluebells. So, riding slowly along woodland paths, which remind me of Gudgeon Woods at Canterbury, we arrive at his Nissen Hut by the side of a clearing full of bluebells, where Iscariot & his officers reside. Here we tie up our horses where there is grass, & indulge in eggs & bacon & Oxford marmalade, the latter being the real reason for the ride, since we have only the Keiller's variety here. Breakfast over we race back to camp to be in time for the 8 a.m parade, Meickie leading off in an excited scramble which he calls a gallop & Dolores, alias Our Lady of Sorrows, alias The Decker, lolloping along behind.'*

Racing back to be in time for parade. It has irresistible echoes of Hodgson's schoolboy exploit with Nowell Oxland. Meickie (or Mickie) was the horse John Upcott had ridden ever since their training days in England, while Dolores *'an enormous mare, with a most dejected cast of countenance (hence her soubriquets)'* had wandered into the Devons' lines during the winter. As no one owned her Hodgson took possession and she had been his ever since.

The next day they left Grovetown with the rest of the battalion to join the two companies already camped in the wood. A few days later the whole battalion marched some miles to the west, to train over two areas of practice trenches, at Heilly and at Vaux, where the trenches were supposed to be a replica of the German lines facing Mansel Copse, built on Brigadier General Deverell's orders.

The Devons encamped in tents in Treux Wood, which was *'rather like a large Sussex copse with most of the underwood cut. It is carpeted with bluebells, bugle & yellow nettle.'* Upcott and Rayner *'even found bluebells growing in our newly pitched tent & arranged for the space to be fenced off as a sort of indoor garden.'* John Upcott was so keen to preserve the bluebells that first night that he slept outside the tent, *'& was much worried by a beast variously described as a badger or a fox; anyway I woke up to find him nuzzling at my air-pillow – with which he eventually made off & I had much ado to find it again behind a bush.'* The wood was idyllic, with *'one of the most glorious views in France;*

John Upcott's sketch of Treux Wood, 12 May 1916.

at the foot of the hill . . . lies the little village of Treux, its gardens pink & white with blossom. Beyond flows the little Ancre between its poplar trees; across the valley the blue downs with ribbon-like roads zig-zagging up them; far away on the horizon one can see with glasses the distant trenches & watch the white puffs of smoke by day & the flash of guns by night – the sight of which just gives sufficient contrast to our present bliss.'

Their first full day was a Sunday, and Ernest Crosse held an outdoor service in the wood. It was an Easter service, to make up for their miserable Easter spent in the line. That afternoon – the last of comparative freedom before the serious business of training began – was damp, but undaunted, Hodgson, Upcott and Duncan Martin set out on a mission, *'ostensibly to look for a parade ground,'* John Upcott said, *'in reality to take tea in the little château at Heilly, which is kept for officers by two French girls of a beauty reported to be surpassing.'* Later he added a note in his diary, *'The ride was ripping. We didn't get very wet; the tea was reasonable & one of the girls really pretty. They are refugees from Liège & this was their holiday house. We walked all around the garden, round which the little Ancre goes singing on its way to join the Somme. Tomorrow work begins; intensive training in the attack— 8 hours a day. So I shall be busy.'*

They would all be busy, but the chance to relax in untouched countryside, bursting with the new greens of spring, had brought back the atmosphere of the early days, before Loos and the onset of winter. *'Mud will kill anything,'* John Upcott wrote, *'it gets into your soul, just as it oozes into your boots & hair & under your clothes. One becomes just a sticky machine, which carries on because it has got to. Now in these sunny days I find myself thinking the same way as I used to in the splendid days before Loos.'*

For Noel Hodgson too this was a restorative time, not least because he was among friends again, in a way he had not been for some months. As training began in earnest, he still spent free moments with Upcott, Harold Rayner and Duncan Martin, the old hands tending to stick together. News came from home that his sister, in her eighth month of pregnancy, had left Canterbury for Worcester to escape the risk of enemy air-raids. Noel was on mischievous good form when he replied, writing,

> *'Dear Star, I am greatly relieved to think of you as safe from German beastliness for a bit, though it must be rotten to be among aliens, however agreeable, at such a time. . . .*
>
> *We dwell now in tents like Arabs, and have an intense dislike of rain, of which we get much at present. But when the rain is not raining we find it very pleasant, the wood where we now dwell being full of bluebells, anemones, nightingales and other aesthetic paraphernalia.*
>
> *There is not far from here a chateau and a hostellery of outstanding merit, to which we lately repaired one evening and dined. Our ride back was an epic event, which I duly celebrated in immortal verse, and a copy of the opening stanzas are enclosed for your edification together with my latest lucubration in the press, as you say the paper was sold out – the run of course was immense, naturally.'*

The 'latest lucubration' was 'The Raid', published in *The New Witness* on 4 May. The 'immortal verse' was this:

The Tale of Four Men

> *This is the tale of Four Stout Men*
> *Who mounted their stark steeds there and then*
> *And rode to Heilly o'er moor & fen,*
> *Clanrobert, Cuchulain and Curgenven*
> *(Not to mention Gaukrodger) – remarkable men.*
>
> *And the number of things they didn't discuss*
> *From Aristotle's De Partibus*
> *To Marie Corelli and even wuss*

Dalhousie, Defoe and Decius Mus
(Not omitting S.M. Grubb) astonishes us.

They feasted like men of Homeric mould
And drank as much as their guts would hold
And sang good songs like the men of old,
Bunyan and Barnum and Charles the Bold
(Not forgetting Barabbas) those hearts of gold.

Then into the saddles the four did vault,
And their spirits soared like the E in alt,
If their horses bolted it wasn't their fault,
Genghis, and Grettir and Edwin Gault
(And of course John Silver, the excellent salt.)

And as they carolled a man of sin
Exploded a horrible culverin
But in spite of the state those four were in,
Disraeli and Daniel and Gunga Din
(Together with Micawber) survived the din.

John Upcott gives a more prosaic account of the adventure: *'Smiler, Nibby, Iscariot & I to Heilly in the evening, where we dined excellently & drank a bottle or two of excellent Sauterne. We rode home by moonlight. As we neared Ville "a monstrous piece of ordinance" as Smiler put it, bolted all four horses, Mickie swerving in his usual way clean across the road.'*[9] He adds later that they planned to dine out again on their last evening in Treux Wood, but the battalion Sports Day overran, and they had no time. Still, 'Smiler' was back, and very much his old self. His Headquarters Company challenged B Company to a rugby match and beat them 4-0. On 19 May he had a letter from his old headmaster inviting him to play cricket – how the Rev Budworth thought he could manage this, goodness alone knows. Writing to Robert Parr a few days later, Noel smiled at the absurdity of it:

'Two days ago I received a letter from Dutton, an invitation to play for his eleven v. the School on the 29th of June! Think of it; white flannels, drinks, and delightful smooth-haired children with brown faces; what an irony. . . .

How are all at Herrington? It is a long time since any correspondence passed between myself and any of your family. But not long ago, one evening when I & another had accomplished a very terrible ride, and were enlarging on it to others, I told them all of the matter of CRAGGS, and filled their hollow hearts with fear. Truly that night was among the greatest of nights, only to be linked with the night when the Gunner was sick on the level-crossing before the Paris express.

'Do you know that in a few weeks I expect to be an uncle – my sister is introducing a Turret into the world; rather interesting, though unpleasant for her at the moment. Other news I have none.'[11]

By this time the battalion had moved back to the Bois des Tailles and to the routine of night-time working parties. Henry Innes Storey, now a lieutenant colonel, returned on 22 May and resumed command. Jack Inchbald came back the same day. He contracted measles at the beginning of April – one of a number of cases in the area that spring – and had spent several weeks in the Base Hospital at Le Tréport. He probably missed seeing John Upcott, who left on leave on 22 May, looking forward to a reunion with Renée Motte in Brittany. Upcott knew that on returning he would go straight to a course at the 4th Army School in Flixecourt; in fact, he had timed his leave around this because he expected the attack to begin soon after and anticipated leading his company. It may have crossed his mind in the circumstances that the leave might be his last chance to see Renée; he could not have imagined when he set out for Brittany that he would never see Noel Hodgson, Harold Rayner and Duncan Martin again.

The Devons were in the Bois des Tailles five days before marching back to Treux Wood. They spent just over a week there practising attack techniques. For Hodgson it was a time to make sure the bombing sections were thoroughly prepared; later his friends would pay tribute to the time and effort he put into their training. Work apart, his mood was becoming reflective, stimulated, perhaps, by hearing from the Rev Budworth and writing to Robert Parr; also by an unspoken awareness of the battle to come. Through 1916 almost all his published output had taken the form of prose sketches of things that were happening around him. Now he turned again to poetry. On 1 June *The New Witness* carried a short Edward Melbourne poem entitled 'Renunciation':

> *Take my love that died to-day,*
> *Lay him on a roseleaf bed,–*
> *He so gallant was and gay, –*
> *Let them hide his tumbled head,*
> *Roses passionate and red*
> *That so swiftly fade away.*
>
> *Let the little grave be set*
> *Where my eyes shall never see;*
> *Raise no stone, make no regret*

> *Lest my sad heart break, – and yet*
> *For my weakness, let there be*
> *Sprigs of rue and rosemary.*

This was a slight variation of something he had written before; probably in the summer of 1915. A manuscript survives on the same scrap of paper as a fragment of *'Ave Mater – Atque Vale'*, which his father dated 'At Durham, 1915'. But the earlier manuscript opens differently – *'Take my Youth that died to-day'* – and it was this line that Henry Hodgson chose when he included the poem in *Verse and Prose*, with the title 'The Death of Youth'.

A week later came the publication of the poem 'Durham', which Henry called 'Durham Cathedral', the early workings-out of which survive in the little pocket notebook Noel had carried from the beginning. 'Durham', like so many of his poems, speaks of the healing power of time and the endurance of stone and river, set against the transience of individual lives. He played with several ideas for a closing line but settled in the end for something gentle and very far from the Somme: *'God's kindness dwells about these courts of peace.'*

Another poem of the spring of 1916 would not see publication until it was included in later editions of *Verse and Prose*. 'God's Hills' is Noel Hodgson's last love song to Cumbria and the fells:

> *In our hill country of the North,*
> *The rainy skies are soft and grey,*
> *And rank on rank the clouds go forth,*
> *And rain in orderly array*
> *Treads the mysterious flanks of hills*
> *That stood before our race began,*
> *And still shall stand when Sorrow spills*
> *Her last tear on the dust of man.*
>
> *There shall the mists in beauty break,*
> *And clinging tendrils finely drawn*
> *A rose and silver glory make*
> *About the silent feet of dawn;*
> *Till Gable clears his iron sides*
> *And Bowfell's wrinkled might appears,*
> *And Scawfell's clustered might derides*
> *The menace of the marching years.*
>
> *The tall men of that noble land*
> *Who share such high companionship,*
> *Are scorners of the feeble hand,*

Contemners of the faltering lip.
When all the ancient truths depart
In every strait that men confess,
Stands in the stubborn Cumbrian heart
The spirit of that steadfastness.

In quiet valleys of the hills
The humble grey stone crosses lie,
And all day long the curlew shrills,
And all day long the wind goes by.
But on some stifling alien plain
The flesh of Cumbrian men is thrust
In shallow pits, and cries in vain
To mingle with its kindred dust.

Yet those make death a little thing
Who know the settled works of God,
Winds that heard Latin watchwords ring
From ramparts where the Roman trod,
Stars that beheld the last King's crown
Flash in the steel grey mountain tarn,
And ghylls that cut the live rock down
Before kings ruled in Ispahan.

And when the sun at even dips
And Sabbath bells are sad and sweet,
When some wan Cumbrian mother's lips
Pray for the son they shall not greet;
As falls that sudden dew of grace
Which makes for her the riddle plain,
The South wind blows to our own place,
And we shall see the hills again.

His longing for his own landscape aches through every line. The war is present too, but not his war: France in spring was hardly a 'stifling alien plain'. He was thinking of Nowell Oxland at Gallipoli, recalling his friend in the timeless landscapes they had shared. Landscapes with long memories and legends – like the story he mentions of the 'last King', Dunmail of Cumbria, killed in battle, whose crown is said to lie in Grisdale Tarn awaiting his return.

Returning after death in battle was very much on Hodgson's mind. 'God's Hills' is his answer to a poem Nowell Oxland wrote on the troopship to Gallipoli, which was published anonymously in *The Times* shortly after his death. The editor gave it the title 'Outward Bound' but Oxland had called it 'Farewell'. It evoked his beloved Cumberland: *'There's a waterfall I'm leaving/ Running down the rocks in foam,/ There's a pool for which I'm grieving/ Near the water-ouzel's home.'* If he died, the poem said, the wind would carry him home: *'Mixed with cloud and wind and river,/ Sun-distilled in dew and rain,/ One with Cumberland for ever,/ We shall not go forth again.'* When Hodgson saw the poem is unknown. That he did see it, and realised or was told who had written it, is clear in 'God's Hills'. The meeting of minds is there, the need to be buried at home, even, at one point, the same phrase, *'the dust of man'*. And his reassuring echo of Oxland's *'We shall not go forth again,'* is clear in the closing lines, *'The South wind blows to our own place, And we shall see the hills again.'*

In 1916 Ascension Day fell on 1 June, and that too brought Nowell Oxland to Hodgson's mind. It also gave him a subject for his last prose sketch of the war. In 'Ascension Morning' the narrator is riding beside a column of marching men. An overheard remark about the day stirs the memory of another Ascension Day, at school, when he and a friend climbed out of the study window before sunrise and set off across country bird-nesting. Recalling that distant morning in vivid detail brings back all the excitement it gave him at the time: he turns to a friend remarking on the joys of memory, and finds the man in despair. For him too a memory has been revived. He describes a walking holiday in Cumberland with two close friends, up the Sty Head Pass to the Gable, over the Gable and across Ennerdale to Buttermere, *'and it was a great, still, clear evening as we came singing by the lake; and we talked and smoked late that time under a great night of stars'*. One of the friends is already dead, killed at Gallipoli, and he has just learned from a casualty list that the other has died in hospital among strangers. Remembering them brings only pain, and the very idea of Ascension Day seems a cruel irony.

Hodgson used 'Ascension Morning' to pose the question: is memory a gift because it allows the double joy of reliving past happiness, or a curse, because the pain of remembering makes it harder to carry on. But knowing that both memories in the sketch were real, and his own, gives it a deeper meaning. The two characters in 'Ascension Morning' are both Noel Hodgson. They voice the tension in his mind between the calm faith in something stronger and more enduring than present troubles, which he had expressed so often before, and a nagging fear of futility and darkness. He sensed that the first was still true, but to the second he could offer no answer.

The battalion was at Treux Wood until 4 June. Then they moved back to the Bois des Tailles and resumed working parties in the line. New drafts of men arrived; officers too, most of them very young and new to France. A few days before the battle, Duncan Martin wrote to Frank Wollocombe, telling him how much A Company missed him and wished him back. *'Of the present Platoon*

Commanders, none have ever been in trenches before, with the exception of Webber, who had one tour.'[12] But one of them was older. Second Lieutenant Cyril Shepard, an underwriter's clerk at Lloyds in peacetime, was thirty-eight – eight years older than Martin, whom Jack Inchbald had classed among the battalion's 'old men'. Shepard was a sensible man, whom the others seemed to take to. He arrived at Treux Wood on 24 May and was placed in C Company under Harold Rayner,who had taken over in John Upcott's absence.

In a letter to his brother two weeks later, Cyril offered his impressions of the 9th Devons. (His brother, Ernest, an artilleryman for the duration, was already a gifted and successful illustrator. But he had yet to draw the much-loved images of Pooh, Christopher Robin, and their friends, for which he will always be remembered.) Cyril told him, *'the men are a capital lot, N.C.O's young & want watching but are good, especially in trenches I am told. Three other officers came out from the 3rd with me, but I don't care much for them. However most of the others are very good chaps. The C.O. & many of the other officers were through Loos, so have seen some service. The C.O. & 2nd in command are regulars & several others were through the S. African war. Altogether I am very lucky.'* He ended with a typical put-down from an older brother to a younger, from the infantry to the artillery: *'if you happen to be behind us be careful of the angle for I don't want to be crumped by your ruddy guns.'*[13]

The battalion spent four days in the Bois des Tailles. On 9 June they moved to Grovetown and then, after a day's training, marched back into the line, but not to the Mansel Copse trenches from which they would attack. From 11 to 20 June they held a completely new sector of the front line, looking towards Mametz on the open ground between the village and Carnoy. Whether by accident or design, they were being given a completely different view of the hillside – the view shared by the German lines to the right of Mansel Copse. From this sector they were also able, did they but know it, to see the enemy positions that would be most dangerous to them in the battle to come, positions hidden from the lines around Mansel Copse.

Their days in this sector were almost unnaturally peaceful, the Battalion War Diary simply noting *'Bn in trenches'* day after day, with nothing else to report. There were cornflowers growing on the trenches; Cyril Shepard sent some home in letters to his fiancée. With little else to do, Noel Hodgson's mind was also focused on home. Stella's baby was due during the week. Just before going into the line he found time to pencil a quick note, *'Dear old girl; a word in haste to wish all luck to you and the BIT, this week; your loving brother, Bill. I think much of you.'*

It seems likely, though it can probably never be proved, that it was at this time, with the downward slope of the Montagne de Cappy stretched out before him, that he wrote the poem that would make his name. *The New Witness* pieces follow the order of his documented experiences precisely and 'Before Action' was the last. 'Ascension Morning' appeared in the paper on 22 June; if he had written or completed 'Before Action' in this new sector of trenches between 11 and 20 June it could easily have reached Cecil Chesterton in time for publication on the 29th: his February trench sketches show how fast a turn-around of material was possible. He might even have requested publication that day, the day the battle was due to start. The poem was, in effect, his farewell letter. In it he took the conventions of lyric poetry, the sunrises and sunsets and beauties of nature, the lovely cadences of language he handled so well; he took his memories and hopes and set them down in front of the machine guns he knew would be waiting. He did not ask for a way out. All he said, very simply, was 'I'm not a soldier, I'm too young for this, but I will go through with it,' and that resolve struck a chord with readers in his own time that has never ceased to resonate.

Before Action

By all the glories of the day
And the cool evening's benison,
By that last sunset touch that lay
Upon the hills when day was done,
By beauty lavishly outpoured
And blessings carelessly received,
By all the days that I have lived
Make me a soldier, Lord.

By all of all man's hopes and fears,
And all the wonders poets sing,
The laughter of unclouded years,
And every sad and lovely thing;
By the romantic ages stored
With high endeavour that was his,
By all his mad catastrophes
Make me a man, O Lord.

I, that on my familiar hill,
Saw with uncomprehending eyes
A hundred of thy sunsets spill
Their fresh and sanguine sacrifice,
Ere the sun swings his noonday sword
Must say good-bye to all of this;–
By all delights that I shall miss
Help me to die, O Lord.

Chapter 13

'Goodbye to all of this'

On 20 June the 9th Devons marched back to Grovetown, where 20 Brigade had set up its headquarters. A new draft of sixty men was waiting to be assigned to their companies, and the company commanders busied themselves inspecting clothing and equipment. For Noel Hodgson there was also the welcome news that Stella had a baby daughter, born at their parents' home in Ipswich on 16 June – Henry had written immediately to tell him. Noel was overjoyed, and in quite a silly mood when he sent his congratulations:

> 'Dear Star;–
> The great news has just arrived. Splendid, old lady, I am tremendously bucked; heartiest of all welcomes to the wee maid, and I hope I may not be long before I see her myself. Her beauty won't be apparent yet, but of course she will be beautiful, and she cannot help being good.
> What is her ladyship to be called? I suggest Audrena as one of her names, and Baldwin has its merits. Thomasina I cannot recommend honestly, nor Tookey, but you may be of a different opinion.
> She isn't as big as mother yet, I suppose, nor as intelligent of course. Dad asserts her to be dark haired but I accept it with reserve.
> Anyway, best of luck to you and her from
> affect. brother
> and Uncle
> Bill'

Uncle Bill. He must have talked a lot about the baby and his new title: so much that he acquired yet another nickname, 'Uncle'. His letter was written on a Wednesday – it would have been 21 June, the day after their arrival at Grovetown. While the battalion sorted itself out and working parties were sent back the line, the officers were introduced to a new visual aid to increase their understanding of the battlefield. On 21 June Brigade Major Foss wrote about it to all the units in 20 Brigade, to the other infantry brigades of 7th Division involved in the coming battle, and to Divisional Headquarters:

> 'A contoured model in plasticene has been made by Captain Martin, 9th Devonshire Regt. showing the whole area to be attacked by the 20th

Infantry Brigade also Fricourt Wood, Fricourt Farm, Railway Alley, Fritz Trench, Bright Alley. The model may be seen at any time on application to 20th Infantry Brigade HQ Grovetown after 9 am on 22nd June. Officers commanding Battalions will arrange for all officers to inspect this model. The officers of a Company should all arrange to see it together.'[1]

Captain Martin's model is part of the folklore of the Somme. For over forty years the story has been handed down and embellished, and Martin – Duncan Martin, 'Iscariot' to his friends – has become an emblematic figure, a lone voice raised against the blinkered arrogance of high command. Martin, it is said, went home on leave worried about the danger his men would face. He studied the map, becoming convinced that a machine gun sited at a shrine in the village cemetery would cut down his battalion as they advanced through Mansel Copse. So he made a relief model of the battlefield to demonstrate the danger, took it back to France and showed it to his fellow officers. But when he attempted to tell his superiors they dismissed the idea, secure in their belief that the British bombardment would obliterate everything in its path. And Martin and his men died just as he predicted.

The immediate source of this story is Martin Middlebrook's classic *The First Day on the Somme*, published in 1971 and still in print. Middlebrook's source appears to have been a letter in the correspondence files of Brigadier General Sir James Edmond's *History of the Great War* – the British Official History. As each of the twenty-nine volumes neared completion, drafts were sent for comment to selected individuals with personal knowledge of events. Ernest Crosse was one. He was teaching in New Zealand in April 1930 when the draft reached him, and illness prevented him from dealing with it until October. Then he responded. He had few comments about the draft itself, but added, *'There is a rather pathetic story in this connection, but I do not suppose you could insert it.'* He went on to outline the familiar tale; Martin's leave, a plasticene model of the German trench system based on a 1,5000 map. *'Having made the model he came to the conclusion that there must be a great concentration of enemy fire just in front of Mansel Copse. This is just what happened. Capt. Martin & most of his company fell just here'.*[2]

Martin did go home on leave, the details are in his service records. He left from the Bois des Tailles on 7 June and returned nine days later, either joining the battalion in the 'cornflower' trenches facing Mametz or waiting for them at Grovetown. If the first, he would have gained a new perspective on the terrain and seen features invisible from Mansel Copse. The second would have given him four days to set up (or make) the model at Grovetown. But the existence of Brigade Major Foss's letter should begin to raise questions about the familiar story. Far from ignoring Martin, the letter indicates that his superiors in 20

Brigade took him so seriously that they wanted his model and its findings to be seen and studied before the battle by every single officer in the attacking brigades of 7th Division – and that they gave him credit for its making. The letter also proves that the scope of the model was far broader than one machine gun pointed at one battalion – or, for that matter, one trench system. It included ground that was no part of the Devons', or even of 20 Brigade's, objective.

It was Crosse, in all good faith, who introduced the exclusive focus on the shrine machine gun which now dominates accounts of the 9th Devons on 1 July. Edmonds' draft mentioned the battalion coming under artillery and machine gun fire; Crosse's only remark on the content was to question this. *'It was, I believe almost entirely machine guns which did the damage & in particular one machine gun stationed at the Shrine, the gunners of which I believe were all killed at their post, (I believe in the afternoon by Lt Duff).'* In fact there was an artillery barrage but Edmonds accepted the correction. He also added a brief footnote about the model. He did not, however, include a shrine machine gun in his account of what happened to the Devons or take up Crosse's final point. After telling the story of Martin's model and saying that there had indeed been a concentration of enemy fire just in front of Mansel Copse as Martin predicted, Crosse continued, *'when on the following day I started to collect the dead I buried them at Mansel Copse because (speaking from memory) I sould say more than half the dead of the 9th Devons lay at this point. . . . I believe it was this one machine gun at the Shrine which killed nearly all these'.* Edmonds did not take up Crosse's point about a machine gun at the shrine, but Martin Middlebrook did.

It seems unlikely, though, that 20 Brigade HQ would have gone to so much effort to point out the danger of a single machine-gun position on an elevated site which could be seen from the ground, and could have been targeted by the artillery at any time. The Danube Trench bank with its three saps and machine-gun post, which Brigadier General Deverell identified in March, was bombarded with heavy trench mortars on 26 June. But brigade clearly did think that the model was worth the effort. In fact, Martin's model was considered so important that in August a returning Frank Wollocombe found Martin being credited on all sides with 20 Brigade's achievement of its objectives on 1 July: *'they all say the success of the whole show was chiefly due to him, especially his wonderful model of the country. No one knew what it was like until he made it.'*[3]

No one knew what it was like. The first value of Martin's model if it was accurate – and the evidence is unanimous that it was – was that it allowed the officers leading the advance to study the ground beforehand in a way that was impossible from the trenches or from a two-dimensional map. It showed them the lie of the land. Brigadier General Deverell's insistence on having the trench theatre at Vaux replicate the layout of the German lines facing Mansel Copse demonstrated how much importance he attached to an understanding of this

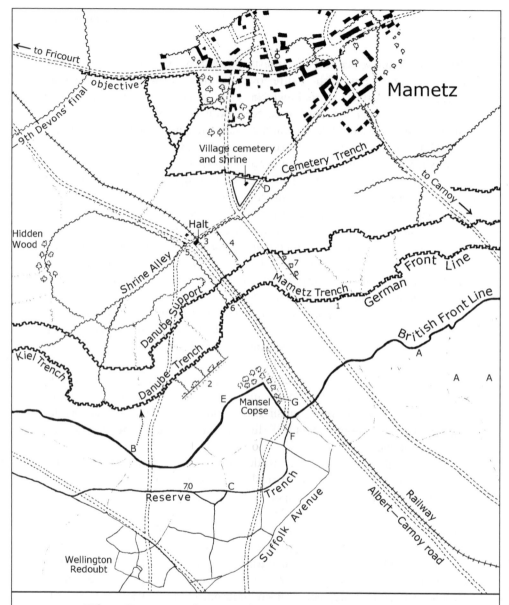

The Devons' attack on 1 July 1916

The first wave went over from Reserve Trench with its left-hand platoon at the junction with 70 Street (70). Second and third waves from the trenches behind.

Danger points:
1. German positions on the right 2. Steep bank described by Brigadier General Deverell
3. The Halt 4. The railway embankment 5-6. The Halt bank 7. The 'scrubby' bank

Other important sites:
A. Machine gun positions to cover the advance B. Intended site of flame projector
C. Battalion HQ D. Captain Davidson's position on sunken road E. Viewpoint used by Wide and Storey F. Captain Martin's body found G. Blood Alley and Devonshire Cemetery

particular patch of ground, but his life-sized replica could only go so far. It could not possibly show every hill and furrow, ridge and bank. Only a scale model could do that – and Deverell may well have discussed the model with Martin in advance. He certainly became its custodian afterwards.

But studying the shape of the landscape would naturally lead to discussion of potential dangers. Setting the shrine aside for the moment, was there anything else Martin's model might have revealed – anything not easily apparent on the ground? There was.

Facing the British front lines on the slope of the hill was the German front line, Danube Trench, its name changing to Mametz Trench on the right, beyond the road and railway line. Behind it on the hillside was Danube Support – the 9th Devons' first objective. Behind that, Tirpitz Trench and then Shrine Alley, part of which was their second objective. Shrine Alley was a very long trench, running right down from the German front line at the top of the Montagne de Cappy and crossing the road and railway line just behind the Halt, the village station. From there it continued up the facing hill to Mametz, passing several metres in front of the cemetery. The shrine itself was a prominent feature in the cemetery. In Army photographs it appears to have been a typical wayside shrine with a pillar topped by a gabled roof.

The Germans had concentrated their defences where Shrine Alley crossed the road and railway line. A machine-gun position at the Halt had an unimpeded view down the road towards British lines. On the Mametz side of the railway line was the embankment Frank Wollocombe identified as a favourite with German snipers. And on the other side of the road, facing this, was a steep bank similar to the Copse bank. It ran beside the road for some distance, invisible along most of its length from the British lines on the slope of the hill and from the hilltop. General Deverell's report did not mention it, but it turned out to be formidable. It was in the middle of 20 Brigade's area and its defenders could direct enfilade fire in two directions; up the slope of the hill or across the road to the open ground below Mametz. *'Also, the traverses being firestepped, they could shoot down the valley to our lines.'*[4]

This 'Halt bank' sat on top of a well-built network of dugouts and tunnels, dug deep into the chalk and safe from bombardments. It even had its own aid post. Effectively it was a small fortress tucked away at the foot of the valley. Another scrubby bank, just beyond the railway embankment and behind Mametz Trench, had a commanding view of Mansel Copse, and the Germans in Mametz Trench could see the whole sweep of the hillside. So any troops attempting to advance through Mansel Copse and beyond would indeed face *'a great concentration of enemy fire'*, potentially coming at them from three sides at once.

These defences clustered round the road and railway line have a far better claim than the shrine to be the dangers highlighted by Martin's model because 20 Brigade actually did something about them. Early orders for the advance included the road and the railway line, with the 9th Devons moving up the road, and the Gordon Highlanders on their right taking the railway. But in 20 Brigade's 'Report on Operations' after the event it is stated that the road and railway line were purposely left as a gap in the line, *'owing to the heavy machine gun fire which the enemy could bring to bear up the valley from the direction of the HALT – FRICOURT WOOD and VILLAGE'.* In these revised orders the two battalions were not to join until the Halt was taken. The task of clearing the Halt bank fell to the 9th Devons.[5]

The enigma in all this is Duncan Martin himself. On paper he did not tick any of the boxes which normally recommended a man to the Army. Not a university or public school man, no previous military experience or training, yet here he was giving high-ranking staff officers his assessment of the battlefield and commanding their respect. He must have had exceptional presence. Ernest Crosse's letter refers to him an artist. Artistic he certainly was, but at the same time creating an accurate relief model from the contours on a map is a precise skill few artists would have or need.

But whoever, whatever Martin was, he made the model and the model made its contribution to preparations for the battle. It may have come a little too late to have played any part in the apprehension Hodgson displayed in 'Before Action', though it is possible that he wrote and sent the poem after seeing the model. And if Martin had rejoined his fellow officers in the cornflower trenches, with the whole sweep of the hillside, including the Halt bank, laid out before them and his discoveries fresh in his mind, that would certainly have added weight to Hodgson's realisation of just how slender their chances were.

The battalion spent just over a day in Grovetown. On Thursday, 22 June, they marched west to billets in Bonnay, and for the next two days they practised on the trenches at Vaux. The date of the battle had been decided the previous Saturday. The advance was to begin on 29 June, preceded by five days of heavy bombardment, to wear down the enemy's nerves, obliterate his defences, and give the attacking battalions an easier passage across no man's land. It began on 24 June with a concentrated barrage each morning lasting 80 minutes, followed by a steady barrage through the day. The intensity lessened at night when half the guns were rested. The sound could be heard from south-eastern England but behind the lines it was possible to ignore: just a dull, thudding accompaniment to the day's work. Only at night, when flashes from the guns lit the sky and other sounds were quiet, did it begin to pervade the senses.

The next day, Sunday, 25 June, was fine, warm and cloudless. The battalion left Bonnay and marched to the Bois des Tailles, passing a large new dressing station by the roadside: rows and rows of camouflage tents set up to receive the expected flood of casualties. At 7 that evening Ernest Crosse held a church parade in evening sunlight beside the wood. *'It was rather picturesque,'* Harold Rayner told his mother in a letter the next day, *'the Padre had raised a small Union Jack for the occasion, and a miniature oak screen and two vases of poppies. We in khaki made up three sides of a four-sided figure, it wasn't actually a square, and the Padre was the fourth. . . . Afterwards there was Communion, to which some ten officers and twenty men stayed. It was rather a striking moment when the officers were kneeling to receive the Sacrament, the men behind were singing, "And now O Father mindful of the Love." '*

He went on to quote two verses of the hymn, adding, *'It may have proved to be the last Communion for some of us there.'*[6]

With John Upcott still away, Rayner and Hodgson were often together. 'Ascension Morning' had been published in *The New Witness* on 22 June and good news of its critical reception must already have filtered back. Rayner wrote to his brother as well that Monday, telling him, *'Smiler (of the House, you remember) is some lad, and has a well-received Parody of Belloc, called "Ascension Morning" over the pseudonym Edward Melbourne.'*[7] This seems to be the only surviving evidence that anyone in the battalion knew that Hodgson was writing for publication, or had heard the name Edward Melbourne. Others, like Ernest Crosse, would say afterwards that they had no idea. But in referring to the sketch as a 'Parody of Belloc', Rayner suggests that even he did not know how personal to Hodgson, and therefore how serious the sketch was.

That same day, Monday, 26 June, Hodgson wrote a last note to his sister, sending small presents for her and her husband. She had written, referring to the baby as his godchild, and he was taken aback by this, and endearingly humble in his response:

'Dear Star,
A little gift of no intrinsic value for you or your daughter just to show I think of you, and a cigarette-lighter for Toby made by some industrious French 'poilu'. I could wish to have found better things, but there was no chance of it. Use any of the N.W. money you want for your own purposes won't you?

I feel very proud to be an uncle – but you say 'goddaughter', surely a lady baby doesn't have two godsires, and Winnington Ingram was to be the one, wasn't he.

Haven't time for more at present,
Bill'

Of the situation in France and the battle to come he said nothing – but by this time had sent a message home in the form of 'Before Action', which as yet they had not seen. Also around this time he wrote to the Rev Budworth, sending a cutting of the poem 'Durham' from *The New Witness*.

Heavy summer storms set in that day, continuing through Tuesday and soaking the trenches and the roads going up to the line. During the night of

From John Upcott's sketchbook, showing 'Smiler' in May 1916. This is almost certainly the last picture of Noel Hodgson.

27/28 June, patrols had gone out from each of the attacking battalions to examine the German wire and listen for signs of activity in the trenches behind it. The 9th Devons were *'not very successful'*, but as to how, or what happened, no clue is given.[8] One company from each battalion went into the front line trenches in the morning; from the 9th it must have been Captain Mockridge's D Company. There is no mention of this or of the raid in the Battalion War Diary, but Ralph Mockridge was badly injured on the night of 27/28 June with bomb wounds in his back and kidney. There is also a note that the brigadier was *'very pleased with the good work done in trenches by 2nd Lt. W. Riddell,'* who was one of Mockridge's subalterns.

Meanwhile, to reduce the danger from German positions to the right, in Mametz Trench, and give the advance through Mansel Copse its best possible chance, 20th Company of the Machine Gun Corps was ordered to establish strongly defended machine-gun posts far out to the right behind British lines, in 91 Brigade's area, *'in order to cover the advance on the LEFT of our line in front of MANSEL COPSE.'*[9] On top of the Montagne de Cappy there was to have been a Livens flame projector, a enormous contraption housed in an underground tunnel, which would fire a jet of burning petroleum over the German trenches. The range of this was up to 100 yards and it was intended to terrify rather than kill, keeping the enemy pinned in his dugouts and so buy a few precious minutes for the crossing of no man's land. It might have made a lot of difference. But as sections of the machine were being carried into place in the early hours of 28 June, a heavy bombardment put an end to the work and buried vital parts of the flame projector itself. They were uncovered by an archaeological dig in 2010; in 1916, the battle had to go on without them.[10]

For Hodgson and the others, waiting in the Bois des Tailles, the last days were uneventful, a time for last-minute preparations and light training; even some physical exercises and drill, probably intended to keep the men occupied. On Wednesday 28 June their packs were put into store and a last group of young officers joined. Around mid-day orders went out for a 48-hour postponement of the battle. Some say this was done to give the ground time to dry, others that the combined evidence of raids, patrols and aerial observation suggested that the bombardment had not done its work. Perhaps both factors played a part. Either way, the Battle of the Somme was now to begin on 1 July.

Granted this sudden reprieve, Harold Rayner settled down to read his *Times Literary Supplement*, newly-arrived from home. *'At the same time "Smiler" Hodgson read his Odyssey in the original, just as he and I read his Iliad a few weeks ago in a wood near by,'* he told his brother. But with the steady drum beat of what was to come never far from their minds, they also went a little crazy: *'After dinner a spirit of skittishness came over the officers, and we indulged in various rags, the most brilliant being to try running up to the top of a bell tent. When done by several at once from all sides it has a terrifying effect on the inmates of the victimised tent.'*[11] The battalion spent the last day resting in the wood and Ernest Crosse gave Communion. In the evening the officers built a bonfire and sat around it exchanging stories. Rowan Freeland would later describe the scene in a letter to Stella; he was with her brother, he said, *'we were all sitting round a fire of old boxes, in the Bois des Tailles where we were in bivouac. We were all very cheery and singing'*. Echoes of a school outing or boy scout camp linger round accounts of their last few hours before the battle;

deliberately so, perhaps, as these things would have been comfortingly familiar. Before they left for the line the men were issued with sandwiches and told to make sure their water bottles were full, but they were strictly forbidden to eat the sandwiches or drink the water on the way to the line. Watering points were provided along the route and the sandwiches would be their breakfast: a long day lay ahead of them, and it was something to do in the final hours.

They left the wood at 10.30pm, 22 officers and 753 men, leaving the rest in reserve. Noel Hodgson was with his bombers. It would be their task to 'mop-up' after the first lines of the attack, dealing with pockets of resistance and strongpoints, and countering enemy bombers and machine guns. Hodgson, as bombing officer, answered directly to the Lieutenant Colonel Storey and had his own copy of battalion orders.

> *'When we marched out. . . that night he was with his Bombers, who were simply devoted to him, and absolutely worshipped him, as we all did.'*

The front line trench had been badly damaged by enemy shelling in the last few days, forcing a late change of plan. Instead of using it, the 9th Devons and 2nd Borders on their left, further up on the hill, would advance from new forming-up positions in the reserve trenches. This possibility had always been envisaged. It was safer, given the accurate fire the Germans regularly directed into the front line. The disadvantage was that the two battalions now had 250 yards of extra ground to cross.[12] The change also caused some confusion and delay as the carefully planned timings and routes through the trenches no longer applied, but by 2.35am everyone was in place with a few hours ahead to snatch whatever sleep they could. Gaps had been cut in the wire over the previous three nights, and once the men were in position, bridges and trench ladders were put in place.

At 6.25am the bombardment became intense. The air vibrated with the sound and the ground shook. Rowan Freeland told Stella that he was with her brother *'when we were in assembly trenches waiting to "go over". He and Capt. Martin and I were watching the bombardment of Mametz village. Then we sat on the fire step and ate some sandwiches. We were all very cheery & I don't hesitate in saying that dear old "Uncle" was the cheeriest of the lot.'* German shells were also falling in the front line trench; a worrying sign, since it showed that the bombardment had not silenced all resistance. But the men watching from Reserve Trench – now the Devons' first line – were probably just thankful for the change of plan that meant they were not sitting in the front line at that moment.

Battalion orders had the bombing sections going over with the third and fourth lines of the attack. Rowan Freeland was positive that Hodgson went with the second line, but that too may have been a last minute change of plan. He told Stella that while they were eating her brother was called away by Lieutenant Colonel Storey, *'with whom he talked for some time in Bn Headquarters'.* They must have been discussing the attack. *'I saw him again when he came out,'* Freeland continued, *'& I remember him asking me if I had any rum left from my platoon's issue I could spare for his bombers. But unfortunately my issue was short, & some didn't get any: but I went round the whole Company & several others to try and get some for him, but couldn't. I didn't see him much after that, except now and again in the trench.'*[13]

All along the British front line, zero hour was 7.30am, but the 9th Devons and 2nd Borders, with extra ground to cover, went over the top three minutes before the barrage lifted. At 7.27am, Captain Martin with two platoons of A Company and Captain Pridham with two platoons of B Company, one of which was led by Rowan Freeland, climbed out of their trenches and began to move forward. Behind them, in the second line, the other two platoons of both companies and the first of the bombing sections; in the third line, Harold Rayner leading C Company, probably flanked by the remaining bombers, all three lines going over the top and moving forward simultaneously towards Mansel Copse, across the lower slope of the hill.

If the War Diary of 2nd Gordon Highlanders is correct in saying that their own advance did not begin until 7.30am, then for three minutes the 9th Devons were the only moving target near the road. They came under heavy fire immediately from the open ground to the right. As they drew nearer no man's land they also came into view of the German lines just ahead and the firing increased, both from there, and in the distance from Fricourt Wood. According to the Adjutant, Lieutenant Hearse, there was also an intense artillery barrage: *'Our Devon men walked through it in perfect line.'*[14]

At the top of the hill where a mine had been blown the Borders had a relatively easy start, and did not meet any serious opposition until they reached the upper end of Shrine Alley. Reginald Pridham's company on their right were also successful at first, but lower down the slope the combined effect of machine-gun fire from several directions was devastating. The Official History estimated that half of the battalion's casualties occurred before they reached Mansel Copse. Duncan Martin was among the first to die. One of Hodgson's bombers, Private Jack Owen, saw him go down:

> *'Capt. Martin was the first to fall. He had gone 15 yards when he was shot through the head above the right temple. He turned his head to the left, flung out his right arm and fell dead on his back.'*[15]

This sounds like sniper fire rather than a machine gun and 15 yards is no distance. Even allowing a margin of error, it leaves no possibility that Martin could have reached no man's land. In his diary – surely more accurate than his recalling of events fourteen years later – Ernest Crosse described finding Martin's body on the little track road, which was invisible from the shrine but a horribly easy target from Mametz Trench.

These events were out of sight of Battalion HQ, in a dugout at the junction of two trenches further up the slope. At 7.40am Lieutenant Colonel Storey ordered William Riddell to lead D Company to the hollow at the foot of the Copse *'and to be prepared to reinforce if necessary'*.[16] D Company lost all its officers before reaching the hollow. Riddell was shot in the head within minutes; one of the men saw Raymond Holcroft, who was also the Lewis gun officer, hit in the leg as he bent to help a wounded corporal. When the same man crawled back, wounded himself, Holcroft was dead. John Upcott's uncle asked him later about another D Company officer, Cecil Hirst, because he knew the family: *'You ask after Hirst,'* came the reply. *'He was shot through the head early in the advance on July 1st, while his Company (No.4) were going through the machine gun barrage. I liked Hirst & I think he was a good officer. I used to be with him in trenches a good deal back in the winter.'*[17]

Within fifteen minutes Lieutenant Colonel Storey had committed all the men at his disposal. There is no further comment in the Battalion War Diary until 9.30am, almost two hours later, but a brigade observer, Captain Compton-Smith, in an observation post far out on the right behind the cornflower trenches, was watching movements on the hill and sending back regular reports. At 7.32am he saw some of the 9th Devons reach the German front line, slightly behind the 2nd Borders. At 8am he reported *'9th Devon Regt. a bit behind'*, though five minutes later he saw, or thought he saw, some of them walking in Hidden Wood.

Between 8 and 9am the surviving 9th Devons became increasingly isolated in the German trenches that were their first and second objectives. They had not been able to keep pace with the battalions to their left and right, or to make contact with them. Captain Davidson of 2nd Gordon Highlanders was in a good position to see what was happening. Pinned down through the morning in a sunken road just below Mametz, occupied by his men from Cemetery Trench, which defended the village, to the shrine, he sent a series of messages back to his battalion. On the right he was in contact with men from 91 Brigade. On his left there was no one but Germans. The ground stretching out in front of him as far as the road and beyond was dominated by the *'enemy's Machine Guns in the valley W of SHRINE'* – in other words, the lower part of Shrine Alley and the railway embankment, the Halt and the Halt bank. He could not make contact with the two left-hand companies of his own battalion. According to 2nd Gordons' War Diary, the right-hand company of the 9th Devons – Martin's Company – was *'wiped out'* in the initial advance.

It is Davidson's evidence that throws the largest question mark over the 'shrine machine gun'. The shrine was a prime site for a machine gun with a commanding view of the valley. It seems entirely likely that there would be a machine gun there: according to the Official History a machine gun at the shrine caused heavy casualties among the 2nd Gordon Highlanders. But if this was so, it was strange that Captain Davidson, at most a few metres away from the shrine and pinned down from 8am until the afternoon, appealing for reinforcements, did not mention such a clearly identifiable gun site once in his many messages to his battalion. Nor, for that matter, is there a single reference to a machine gun at the shrine any of the diaries of the attacking battalions.

By 9.30am Lieutenant Colonel Storey knew of the gap between his men and the Borders. He could not know how many of his men were still in the battle. He sent a runner to Harold Rayner, ordering C Company to fill the gap between the 9th Devons and the 2nd Borders. But Rayner was already dead. Private Owen saw him *'killed by a machine gun fire in a German sap in their front line trench.'*[18] He had been leading his men up the Danube Trench bank and his servant Private Lawrence, also dead, was said to have been killed by the same bullet. Second Lieutenant Travers Adamson of C Company was seen by Private Ralph Jones in no man's land, wounded but sitting up. *'He told the Sergt. to carry on. I got back to the lines & saw no more of him.'* Adamson may have picked himself up and gone on: Private Owen reported seeing him killed instantly on reaching the German trenches.[19] And Cyril Shepard also died somewhere in the German lines; Lieutenant Hearse told Ethel Shepard, Cyril's sister, *'He reached the most advanced point of any of our company officers except one, who survived.'*[20] By around 8am that 'one', Second Lieutenant George Edward Porter of B Company, was the only officer left standing.

So if Storey's orders did not get through, it was no wonder. At around the same time a message reached him that his men in the German trenches were being pushed back by bombers coming from Mametz. His telephone line to Brigade Headquarters was down so he sent a verbal message, and he was given a company of the 8th Devons to reinforce his right, with a second if necessary – the 8th, as brigade reserve, had moved into the assembly trenches after his men left them. There seems to have been a failure of communications at this point. Captain Davidson's messages should have alerted someone to the danger of attempting to reinforce close to the road. It seems that they did not; perhaps they were taking too long to get through. Between 10 and 10.30am – the timings in the War Diaries differ – two companies of the 8th Devons were ordered to reinforce on the right, advancing through Mansel Copse in the direction of the Halt. Both lost all their officers within minutes. The survivors of the first company pushed on and nothing more was heard of them for several hours; the second took cover in the hollow at the foot of the copse. Two further platoons of the 8th Battalion were ordered in on the other side of the road, to reinforce the Gordon Highlanders, but were held up by uncut wire.

Later in the morning Lieutenant Colonel Storey moved forward to Mansel Copse. With no telephone lines and no runners coming in, he needed to see what was happening. The higher end of the copse bank was an excellent viewpoint, across the full sweep of no man's land to the road and the ground below Mametz. From a shell hole somewhere in that area one of the battalion's Lewis gunners, Private Howard Wide, watched the first two hours of the battle unfold. *'I had a clear view of The Gordon Highlanders advance and I noted how they were mown down by machine guns at a terrible rate.* '[21] Looking back from that position, Storey would also have been able to see most of his own early casualties, but his focus had to be on the battle still being fought. He noticed survivors of D Company in the hollow below the copse and sent a lance corporal to gather them up and lead them forward.

Somewhere ahead in the maze of German trenches on the hillside, Second Lieutenant Porter was gradually collecting survivors of the 9th Battalion. He was awarded the Military Cross for the coolness and efficiency with which he took over as the only remaining officer. His captain, Reginald Pridham, had been hit in the left arm and stomach on reaching the German lines and lay in a shell hole for seven hours, seeing no one and praying not to be taken prisoner. And Rowan Freeland was shot through the chest in an amazing feat of courage which also won a Military Cross, *'when he himself was responsible for the capture of a machine gun, which was in action against his men, he personally accounting for three of the enemy.'*

'The Boys are Proud to be in the Platoon, and to have you as Platoon Commander,' one of his men told him afterwards, *'they were all Astonished when they saw you jump forward into the Second German Line and Put out that Machine Gunner and Bomb Thrower, which is the talk of the Platoon from them that is Left.'* [22]

Around mid-day 7th Division command took stock and issued revised plans. The 9th Devons were to collect up stragglers and push on towards their final objective; also to make contact with the 2nd Borders. But they were still scattered, fighting their own battles. At 2.30pm a staff officer of 20 Brigade saw a party of about sixty 9th Devons in the Halt bank. An hour later the cluster of strongpoints round the road was still deadly. C Company of the 8th Devons, the last company not yet committed to the battle, was ordered to advance through Mansel Copse. Two platoons went ahead and suffered heavy casualties. Seeing this, their officer diverted the rest further up the hill and they were able to cross safely into the German trenches. Just after 4pm the Gordon Highlanders reported that Mametz had fallen.

At the same time, Major James of the 8th Devons sent one of his officers to round up survivors and take them forward. Just after 5pm this officer, Second Lieutenant Duff, reported that with a mixed force including some 9th Devons he had successfully cleared the Halt bank: the Halt bank, not the shrine as Ernest Crosse believed in his 1930 letter. Duff took a number of prisoners in the bank and the tunnels below, including the officer commanding the German 109 Reserve Regiment, who was in the aid post with a broken leg. *'A machine gun was found at the Halt which had fired a great quantity of rounds,'* Major James reported, confirming how lethal these positions had been. In his view the high number of casualties came as a result of the 9th Battalion's 'disregard' of the Halt bank.[23]

It was a harsh word to use, but Major James had not been told when the first two of his companies were ordered to advance, and this sharpened his sense that things had been handled badly. In fact, the survivors of the 9th Devons had not so much disregarded the bank as been completely unable to get anywhere near it; once Mametz fell it was isolated and easier to deal with. Lieutenant Colonel Storey sent for nine of his officers who had been kept out of the battle and seventy-two NCOs and men, and together they advanced across the hillside to join George Porter and the remnants of the 9th Battalion. Since the morning ten of its officers had been killed outright or died of wounds; seven more were wounded and 463 men were dead, wounded or missing.

But what of Noel Hodgson? There are two conflicting accounts of what happened to him. In 1919, in E.B. Osborn's *The New Elizabethans*, he is said to have reached as far as the third German line, keeping his men supplied with bombs, '*and was then mortally wounded, a bullet passing through his throat. His last words, addressed to his sergeant, were: "Carry on; you know what to do."*' Osborn had Henry Hodgson's co-operation, and that should lend his account some weight. An undated letter from John Nind Smith, Noel's friend from Christ Church, tells Stella, '*I got a letter from your father asking for some particulars about Bill for a book that is to come out*'. Smith's memories are quoted at length in Osborn's book; Osborn also quoted a sentence from Ernest Crosse's letter to Henry, assuring him that his son had taken Communion before the battle.

Versions of this account of Hodgson's death persist to this day. Its origin must have been in something Henry was told; it was almost a given that families would try to find out more about how their men died. Stella certainly asked Rowan Freeland and Frank Worrall to make enquiries in the battalion. On 10 July Frank wrote from his home in Devon:

> '*I've sent all the news I could collect to your Father I've only just got back. As I knew he was magnificent. It is grand to hear the men speak of him even those who never served under him.*'

This may be the source of the account but it is impossible to say now what Frank sent. The only letters from the Front among Stella's papers are handwritten copies of Lieutenant Colonel Storey's letter to Henry and Ernest Crosse's, and they would have written anyway. Frank must have passed on something from other officers and men. And there was nothing unlikely in the idea that Noel had led his bombers through to the German third line. It described the role he played at Loos to win the MC, the role they expected him to play. After nearly a year at the Front without injury he seemed to have a charmed life. '*Poor old Smiler Hodgson's death was awful,*' John Pocock wrote to Frank Wollocombe, from Wareham. '*Somehow I thought he would come through.*'[24]

The account was likely. It was even comforting to think he played his part and died in the thick of battle, but other evidence tells against it. Lieutenant Colonel Storey's initial report to brigade, hastily hand-written on 2 July, names Noel Hodgson as one of three officers to be killed right at the start in the initial barrage of machine-gun fire, with Duncan Martin and William Riddell. To Henry, Storey wrote, *'He had just left me and was taking up his party of "Bombers" whom he had so thoroughly trained when they came under a heavy machine gun fire,'* suggesting something immediate – as if he actually saw what happened, or at least heard it. And Osborn did not quote, perhaps did not see, the rest of Crosse's letter. First, it defines where the body was found: *'I buried him afterwards within 50 yds of the spot where he was killed.'* [25] In letters to other officers' families Crosse was more vague; here he attempts precision, and even if he was out by 10 yards, or 15, Noel still died within the area bounded by the two arms of Mansel Copse, before he could reach the British front line, never mind the German third.

Second, Crosse's letter implies a narrative of how he died:

> *'I found his body together with that of his faithful servant, Weston, in the afternoon of the battle in what was the hottest corner of the battlefield. He was hit in the neck & leg by bullets, probably from a machine gun.'* [26]

This suggests that Noel was hit first in the leg and went down, then, as Private Weston tried to help him, a second round of bullets firing at the same height took them both. This was the account his mother, Penelope, accepted. She told Robert Parr,

> *'He was shot in the morning charging across with his bombers & his faithful servant was found by his side, also shot, with a half-opened bandage in his hand.'* [27]

Earlier in the year Alfred Frederick Weston, alias 'Pearson', had been the subject of one of Noel's *New Witness* sketches. *'He is my servant, and if he were Commander-in-Chief the war would be over in a week. But I should get no baths, so I'm glad he isn't.'* 'Pearson' could manage anything, he said. *'There are many like him, I am sure, though I prefer to think of him as supreme.'* Now the tribute had been well paid.

It was a matter of fierce pride to the survivors that they had achieved the day's objectives. The litany of deaths, however searing, had a purpose. No one expressed this more forcefully than John Upcott, writing to Harold Rayner's mother, whom he knew:

> *'I cannot tell you how much we miss him, especially the men whom he so splendidly led. I cannot tell you what his help has meant to me; he and I*

have been in so many tight places. But I would like you to know this – that there was no other Battalion in the Army that attacked so magnificently or was so heroically led as the 9th Devons. They went into and through fire that could hardly have been more terrible, and everywhere they won through to their objective even when the officers were gone. '[28]

Ernest Crosse said much the same in letters to bereaved families. After the first rush of injured men able to crawl or drag themselves off the battlefield ended, he had fretted for a chance to go out and look for men to help, but Lieutenant Colonel Storey wanted him to stay in safety. As soon as he could, Crosse made his way down the nearest communication trench to the front line, found four wounded men in a dugout, and helped bring them back. Around 3.30pm, he and the Medical Officer set off down the little track road to the back of Mansel Copse. As they neared the bottom of the hill, the tragedy of the first few minutes was laid out before them. *'The road was strewn with dead. Almost the first I looked at being Martin.'*

As Crosse's diary is written, it appears that he went immediately from here to explore no man's land, but at this time of the afternoon the slope side of the copse was still a death trap. It seems more likely that he and the Medical Officer did what they had gone to do and searched the bodies on and around the road first to make sure they were all dead, so that some time would have elapsed before Crosse moved forward. By 5pm Mansel Copse was safe, and he continues from a vantage point overlooking no man's land:

'In every shell hole all across the valley and up to the German saps were badly wounded who feebly raised a hand or cried out lest they should not be seen. I bandaged up a few as best I could and then went with Gertie [the Medical Officer] *to collect the S.B.s* [stretcher bearers].'

He spent the remaining hours of daylight searching the ground as far as the German front line and organising the evacuation of the wounded on stretchers and trench ladders, fearing a German counter-attack during the night. Inevitably in doing so he recognised the dead, but the living had to come first.

The next day he was out again with his team searching the shattered wreck of the German trenches; it was only on 3 July that he was able to attend to the dead (not the previous day as stated in his 1930 letter). With a working party of fifty men, he began to bring the bodies in to the foot of Mansel Copse, where their identity discs and personal effects were collected.

An officer from the divisional staff gave Crosse permission to bury them in the stretch of Blood Alley running parallel to the main road, and over the next two days he and his men brought in all the dead they could find from the two Devon Battalions – 163, according to Crosse, though present-day records give 161, with two later burials from the Royal Artillery. Crosse included Second

John Upcott's sketch of Blood Alley, Mansel Copse, April 1916. This is the section of trench running along the top of the Copse bank parallel to the road – the Devonshire Cemetery, when it was the front line trench the Devons held. Along the top of the drawing Upcott has added, 'Nibby, Smiler & Martin were buried here afterwards'.

Lieutenant Percy Gethin of the 8th Devons, who was killed in the shelling of the front line on 28 June. Gethin was Irish and a gifted painter, engraver and illustrator. Aged forty-two on the outbreak of war he could have avoided military service but chose to volunteer. Apart from him, all the men in the cemetery died on 1 July. This was Crosse's part in preserving the memory of the Devons at Mansel Copse. He held the funeral on the evening of 4 July, and in the days that followed he drew up plans for the cemetery. Twelve crosses were hammered into the ground in two rows, each with a group of names, and a simple notice: *'Cemetery of 163 Devons, Killed July 1st 1916.'*[29]

This was Crosse's job, of course, but it was personal too. It had been his first battle, his first large-scale burial, and he was burying friends. He told Rowan Freeland:

> *'The total loss is heavy, Martin, Hodgson, Holcroft, Rayner, Riddell, Adamson, Hirst, Shepard, have all gone to their long home. Pridham, Butland, Dines & others are wounded. Nearly all the casualties were just by the Magpie's nest. I buried all I could collect in our front line trench the following day.'*

And two weeks later, after more fighting, more loss,

> *'Despite all the horrors & terrors of it. . . . I wouldn't be elsewhere for worlds. All I want is the society of those I loved like yourself & Cameron who were wounded & Tregellis & Haywood, & Martin & Hodgson who were killed. I daren't let myself think too much of them & yet I can't tell you how I miss them.'*[30]

John Upcott was not recalled to the battalion until 10 July. Other officers at Flixecourt had gone sooner; when no orders came for him he hoped it was a good sign. But he was still anxious. On the afternoon of 10 July he was on the lorry taking the last officers back to their units when he saw Ernest Crosse. Forgetting completely about his pack, he jumped down to ask what had happened, never suspecting how awful it had been:

> *'His news was ghastly – everyone I care for gone: all four officers of my company killed: dear Harold died most splendidly before the German lines. He was shot through the stomach & Lawrence killed behind him by the same shot. Iscariot was shot through the heart below Mansel Copse & all his staff killed round him; Smiler killed about the same place, getting his bombs up. He was smiling in death when they found him. No single officer got through untouched. The men did grandly – going on without officers & reaching all objectives. . . . They were beyond all praise.'*[31]

In August he visited the cemetery and told his mother:

> *'I went to see the grave of Nibby & the others last Sunday. The padre has made it all look very nice. I have so often stood with him in the exact place where he is buried. I used to watch the sunrise from there most mornings. You used to get a lovely view even from the trenches. Or I suppose it appeared lovely after the night & mud.'*

The fighting moved on and the cemetery was left to itself. Cornflowers grew there too: in August Ernest Shepard sent one each to his sister and to Cyril's fiancée. He was based nearby for the rest of the year and used the Albert–Carnoy road on his way to rest billets, passing below the copse. Often he would climb the little track road where Duncan Martin died, to visit the cemetery and his brother's grave. In a letter written in December he told his wife that it seemed oddly home-like and he sensed that Cyril welcomed him.[32] No sinister shadows lingered there: when Ernest had the time he took his art materials and drew the cemetery. Some sketches he sent home, but in the 1970s his biographer Rawle Knox saw one that was still in one of his wartime sketchbooks, showing five plain crosses beneath the shell-torn remains of the trees. [33]

Years later Ernest recalled that on the day he first found his brother's grave he stood by the roadside afterwards and watched a battalion of Welsh Fusiliers marching to the Front, singing the hymns his nursemaid once sang to him, Cyril and their sister. In that setting the familiar tunes took on a new meaning, becoming a requiem for Cyril and the men buried with him.[34]

Climb Black Sail for Me

On the night of 2 July, when the bodies still lay out on the battlefield, Henry and Penelope Hodgson and Stella were together in the Bishop's House in Ipswich when the baby's nurse came to them. She was worried because she could smell tobacco smoke in the nursery and could not tell where it was coming from. So they followed her and they could also smell it, especially near the cradle. But they looked round and could find no explanation. The room was secure, the baby sleeping peacefully, and everything was just as it should be; they reassured the nurse and returned downstairs. Stella had recognised the smell as Noel's favourite tobacco but she thought no more about it; it was only days later when the telegram came announcing his death that she remembered, and wondered. *'I hope I may not be long before I see her myself,'* he had written. For the rest of her life she believed that Noel had come back that night for a glimpse of the baby whose birth delighted him so.

Experiences like this were not uncommon at the time. In a world overwhelmed by untimely deaths people talked about the distinctions between life and death becoming blurred. *'Death is such a frail barrier out here. . .one cannot feel it as a severing in any way,'* Lord Desborough's son Billy Grenfell wrote from the Front, after his brother was killed.[1] Wilfred Owen's brother described seeing him before the news came of his death and J.M. Barrie's play *A Well-Remembered Voice* pictured a father visited by his dead son – *'I say, don't be startled or anything of that kind.'*[2] Stories of soldiers being helped at moments of crisis by their dead friends were legion, in life and in fiction. Noel Hodgson may have scorned the idea of ghosts as a boy, but in April 1916 he wrote a short story, *Half and Half*, based on this idea.

The telegram with news of his death was sent on 5 July. These telegrams had become so much a matter of routine that there was an ink stamp for the words 'regret to inform you that'. The clerk who wrote in the details softened the brusqueness of this by adding 'Deeply', so the message read,

> *'Deeply regret to inform you that Lieut. W.N. Hodgson Devonshire Regiment was killed in action 1 July. The Army Council express their sympathy.'*

And with these words a world ended, for his family as for tens of thousands of others. Life would go on but it would not be the same life, and they would have to find their own way forward. *'At times it seems impossible,'* Penelope Hodgson told Robert Parr, *'& I feel I must see him again, so full of life & vigour & charm & then again the sense of loss & the heart-ache seem unbearable, but it is of no use talking about it. I wish you would write to me sometimes, I don't want to lose sight of his friend.'*

Death in battle was curiously intangible for families at home, its only evidence a piece of paper. With no body, no funeral, none of the normal rituals of mourning, it was hard to grasp the reality that they knew was all too real. The first published notice of Noel Hodgson's death was placed by the Hodgsons themselves in the 'Death' column of *The Times* on 8 July. With over 57,000 killed, wounded or missing on 1 July alone, and more in the days that followed, it took time for the full lists to be compiled, and the newspaper had appealed for information from families. The 9th Devons, Noel among them, did not appear in the published casualty lists for another four days.

But members of the regiment had their own ways of finding out. On 6 July Frank Worrall wrote to Stella from Devon:

> *'I'm just fearfully sorry for you, and you all. "Bill" was everything to me and more that a fellow could wish a pal to be. Perhaps you knew, he was so fond of you, what friends we were.*
>
> *'I just loved him and I am only a hard case man and am not effusive at any time but he was such a loveable old thing, such a straight liver but up to anything, that a real man would think right. Always keen, but never at the expenses of others, for his men. Always to me my "Smiler".'*

Letters from France started arriving in the days that followed. From Lieutenant Colonel Storey:

> *'I can truthfully say that he is the greatest loss the Regiment has sustained. Always cheerful & full of spirits & at the same time thorough & reliable in his work. It is difficult to say who will miss him most in the Regiment, the officers or men, he was so popular with all.'*

From Ernest Crosse:

> *'I joined in the love & admiration which all who knew him felt for him. His sound common sense, his wonderful presence of mind, & his real courage made him an ideal officer. I don't think there was anyone in the Battalion we could less have afforded to miss.'*

And to Stella, from Rowan Freeland:

> *'In losing your brother, I have lost my very best friend. It was an awful blow to me, and to everybody in the Brigade. He was beloved by everybody.'*

And as late as the spring of 1918, Penelope Hodgson received a letter from a Mr J. Evans of Treherbert in South Wales, requesting a photograph of her son.

> *'The Boys was all very fond of him & They told me how he got killed & I was so sorry to hear. . . . Mr Hodgson was my officer when I first enlisted & he was so very kind to us giving us sweets & smokes & we chaps thought the world of him.'*

The life of Lieutenant William Noel Hodgson of the 9th Battalion, The Devonshire Regiment, had ended, but what of the poet and writer Edward Melbourne? Was he simply to disappear, until some researcher in later years, exploring the lesser-known recesses of First World War literature, might stumble across his work and, trying to fathom out who he was, might fasten on Edward Melbourne of the East Kents, or Edward Melbourne of the Royal Army Medical Corps, or perhaps Edward Henry Melbourne of the Queen's Own, who died in September 1916? There would be no path back to the true story, and Henry Hodgson was not about to let that happen. *Verse and Prose in Peace and War* was his act of remembrance. He wanted to lift his son's name from the endless lists of dead and give him something that would last. Whatever future Noel might have had as a writer was gone. It was time for what he had already achieved to be acknowledged under his own name.

Henry must have given Cecil Chesterton permission to disclose the real identity of Edward Melbourne. On 13 July *The New Witness* informed its readers of the death of, *'Lieutenant William Noel Hodgson, who was a frequent contributor to this paper over the signature of "Edward Melbourne". Though only twenty-three years old, he had already a brilliant military record behind him, and seemed destined to have an equally brilliant literary career in front of him. . . . Of the vigour and charm of his poetry, and the vivid humour and observation of his sketches, our readers can judge as well as we.'* The piece ended with the last verse of 'Before Action'.

By August Henry had selected the poetry and prose he wanted to include in the book, and he approached the publisher Smith, Elder & Co for a price. He chose to have an edition of 1,000 copies printed for £50. Many families who had the means and the ability chose to finance memorial books for their dead sons. It was a tangible focus for their grief and a way of preserving a life cut cruelly short. And with a son who was already a published writer, Henry had a head start. All he needed to do was source and edit the work, with a brief biographical note and a photograph. Parents with no published work to draw on usually used letters. On 25 July Harold Rayner's widowed mother Louisa wrote to the War Office to ask for the return of his kit: *'I am anxious to have his things before my other son's. . . leave expires, on Aug 8, that we may go through his letters together.'*[3] She turned Harold's letters into a book: *Letters from France, July 26 1915 to June 30 1916, Selected by his Mother* was printed privately in 1919.

Verse and Prose in Peace and War came out earlier, in November 1916. The thousand copies sold out in two months. In January 1917 the publisher approached Henry for permission to produce a second edition. He agreed, adding 'Youth's Immortalities' and 'God's Hills' and requesting changes to the order of the poems. By June this edition too was exhausted. Smith, Elder & Co had been taken over by John Murray, who approached the Bishop for permission to reprint. Once again he agreed, adding corrections. On the first anniversary of Noel's death a third edition was under discussion and Henry asked for a brief postponement to allow him to read another prose sketch: at the end of the month he sent it in. *'As many people, including the Poet Laureate, have spoken very highly indeed of his prose work, I send this for your judgement. Should it be included in the 3rd edition?'*[4] It was. The sketch was Noel's account of Loos, edited to remove real names. References to throwing a body over the back of the trench and to taking a waterproof coat from a dead man were also removed; there were some parts of the experience that people at home would never really comprehend.

The book was reviewed in the national and local press, often in conjunction with other volumes of war poetry. Most reviewers assessed Noel in terms of potential. *The Observer*, for example, writing in January 1917: *'There are signs of immaturity in his work. . . but the charm of the lyrics and the vividness of fancy eagerly expressed gave a promise that can now never be realised.'* And his name steadily gained currency, testifying to a growing reputation. He was cited regularly in general and incidental references to the war poets, alongside Brooke, Sorley and Grenfell, and later Owen and Sassoon. John Murray received a steady flow of requests to publish musical settings of the poems, and to include them in anthologies.

The coming together of 'Before Action', with its *'Help me to die, O Lord'* ending, and Noel's death on the Somme so soon after, provided the emotional engine which drove his fame forward. It gave the poem a context and a story. In a world where so many were grieving, so many longing to reach out to a son or brother, lover or husband, and know how he felt at the end, the knowledge that this was actually a last poem written in the face of death in battle, gave it immediacy and power. The following summer, when Vera Brittain's brother wanted to tell her he was about to go into battle and may not survive he quoted 'Before Action' in a letter. No other explanation was needed.[5] In time the story overtook the facts. The publication date Henry added to the poem was taken as a date of writing; successive writers would imagine Noel sitting in the trench just before the advance, penning his final thoughts. The poem's familiarity may even have helped to inspire the title of one of the war's classics, Robert Graves' *Goodbye to all That*.

Grief, and the need to remember, rippled out from the small circle of family through the communities which had shaped the war dead, the worlds which owned them. All boys' schools were hurt by the war and Durham was no exception. At first war seemed like an interesting side-show which barely touched the daily life of the school, except to see the introduction of an OTC. Some social events were curtailed and there was pride in the lists of Old Boys serving in the forces. When the first deaths were reported they were met with quiet stoicism: *'We know, and understand, what their loss means to their families, and we share, so far as we may, their sorrow.'*[6] But steadily the war swallowed everyday life. The casualties mounted and became younger – well within the memory of masters still teaching at the school, if not the boys:

> *'As the shadow of the war becomes darker and darker, and as our Roll of Honour becomes longer and longer, it is becoming increasingly difficult to turn our attention to the little things of School life'.*[7]

When James Dingle, who had gone back to the school to teach after leaving Oxford, died at Gallipoli, the magazine included a selection of his letters. And one loss bit deeper still. Boys who were in the school on the day the Rev Budworth announced Noel Hodgson's death never forgot the sight of their gruff and taciturn headmaster breaking down as he read that particular name. A memorial poem to Noel appeared in the school magazine: *'Well might your friends and comrades, noble soul,/ Be outraged at the theft of such a friend,/ And vow to lose the world to have you whole / And keep you to the end!'*[8] Henry reprinted it on the title page of *Verse and Prose*. Anonymous, it is generally agreed to have been Budworth's work.

The school's first war memorial was a brass panel in the parish church, but something more was wanted. The Rev Budworth invested his considerable energy and a large sum of his own money into the creation of a memorial chapel, built on a hill overlooking the school. Each of the steps leading up to it was said to represent a life lost in the war. The names of the dead were engraved on the pillars in the nave, and Noel Hodgson was also commemorated on one of the stained glass windows. Of 536 Old Dunelmians who served in the War, 212 became casualties and 104 are now known to have died.[9] But Robert Parr was one of the survivors. He emerged from the fighting in Serbia with several medals and the recognition of the British Army, which had at first turned him down. He went on to carve out a distinguished career in the Consular Service; in the 1940s he was one of the first British diplomats to recognise the importance of General de Gaulle.

War affected the universities more quickly than the schools. All their members except the older teaching staff were of military age, and from 1914 onwards the intake of new undergraduates fell away dramatically. Like the schools, universities kept lists of members serving in the forces, and of those who died. Dean Strong of Christ Church, who interviewed Hodgson and many of his other undergraduates personally for their commissions, felt their fate keenly. In a pamphlet issued in the first year of the war he expressed its essential dilemma. On the one hand, he said, the war represented *'a failure on a tragic scale of peoples professedly Christian, to live up to their principles,'* yet on the other, *'I do not mean that we were not right to go to war; we should have failed hardly less completely if we had refused.'*[10] Week by week, casualty lists were published in the *Oxford Magazine* and obituaries were included in Christ Church's Annual Report.

It was in the process of tracing his own College members that the Rev. F.J. Lys, Bursar of Worcester College, chanced on details about Nowell Oxland and his writing that make a nice counterpoint to Hodgson's story. At school and at Oxford the two friends were well-matched in ability and ambition to write. They also shared a tendency to keep their writing secret from all but those they chose to tell. Lys himself had known only vaguely, despite the interest he took in Oxland. In October 1915 he had just written a brief obituary notice for the *Oxford Magazine* when he received a letter from Canon Rawnsley in Carlisle, (*'until I thought of Rawnsley and pulled myself together'*), asking for information about Oxland. Rawnsley referred to Oxland's *'poetic gift'* and this prompted Lys to write a hasty amendment to the obituary, adding reference to Oxland's poetry. That he also gave Rawnsley information, including the circumstances in which Oxland was sent down from Durham, is evident from Rawnsley's next letter. The Rev Lys had asked for some examples of Oxland's poems: *'Dear Mr Lys,'* came the reply:

> *'Thank you for your most kind letter. I knew he had left Durham under a cloud but what it was I did not enquire.*
>
> *About the poems I am unable to send them, they were lent me in strict confidence . . . . I had asked the person if I might in writing a short paper about him have used a poem but I got no answer & I take it as meaning that she refuses her consent.*
>
> *How little it was known that he had the poetic gift is clear from the fact that his own parents knew nothing about it. But you must not say so.'*[11]

That was a key difference. While Hodgson's family knew about his writing and encouraged him, and were responsible for making his name public at the end, Oxland's knew nothing. Even when he had a poem published in the *Saturday Review* they knew nothing; perhaps they would not have approved. The 'person' Canon Rawnsley referred to, Miss Amy Hawthorn, was a friend of the family, a schoolmistress, whose unmarried sisters lived in Alston.[12] Rawnsley had been put in touch with her by the editor of *The Times* after seeing 'Outward Bound' in the paper and enquiring about its author. Amy had submitted the poem: in October she joined in the correspondence with Lys, having seen the obituary in the *Oxford Magazine*. She hoped he could tell her more about what had happened to Nowell Oxland than she or his parents knew: at first even the date of his death was uncertain, and none of his possessions was ever returned.

> *'Mr Nowell Oxland spent all his vacations at Alston where I saw a great deal of him,'* she told Lys, *'and he gave me all his manuscripts, poems and stories from time to time. It was because of our long & close friendship that I wrote to you; for though it is hopeless to expect news, one longs to gain definite information.'*

The Nowell Oxland Amy Hawthorn knew was not the self-possesed boy who dominated the debating society, and whose disregard for the rules saw him sent down from school, nor the undergraduate of the Lovelace Club who liked to provoke with his views. She saw a different side to him:

> *'Mr Oxland was extremely reticent about his work and never thought them worth publishing, with the exception of one which appeared in the Saturday Review on March 28th 1914 – "The Secret of the Hills". I believe I was the only one who saw all his work & believed in his powers; he gave me leave to publish anything I liked that he wrote after leaving England; that is how I sent "Outward Bound" to* The Times *– it was sent to me in the last letter he ever wrote.'*

Knowing her only through her letters, Lys assumed that Amy Hawthorn was a bereaved fiancée. That she loved Nowell Oxland is clear from the way she wrote about him; *'at present,'* she told Lys, *'the gap is almost unbearable'.*[13] But given the circumstances of their friendship and the difference in their ages – Amy was over fourteen years older, and single – it seems far more likely that hers was an unspoken love, finding expression in encouraging his writing and its only return in the trust he placed in her. When Oxland died, that trust left her with a dilemma. She had his manuscripts and was keen to do for his work what Henry had done for Noel, to give Oxland the recognition she felt he deserved. He had given her the right to publish but she was close to his parents, how would they feel? His father was in failing health and no longer capable of performing his parish duties. In 1917 she turned the manuscripts into a book for private circulation only; had it not been for the poem published in *The Times*, reprinted and identified in later anthologies, Nowell Oxland's writing would be forgotten. His parents remembered him in a pair of portraits on either side of the parish church altar, one showing Oxland as St George, the other as St Pancras of Rome, with a sword and the palm branch of martyrdom.

The 9th Devons returned to the trenches on 11 July and for the next few months would often pass by the ground they fought over on 1 July, and the cemetery with its memories. At some time, someone who knew the story wrote an epitaph for the men buried there: *'The Devonshires held this trench: the Devonshires hold it still.'* Variously said to have been written on a lost board or a wooden cross, it was given permanent form for the seventieth anniversary of the battle on a stone at the cemetery entrance.

The losses continued. Cary – little Cary with the triangle at the officers' Christmas party – was killed in the early hours of 20 July near Bazentin-le-Grand. In early September George Underhill and Bertram Glossop – who returned to the battalion in May after being wounded at Loos – died in an attack on Ginchy. Frank Wollocombe, who rejoined in August, spent two days there in a shell hole with leg wounds and died from the resulting infection after he was brought in. John Pocock, also recently returned, was badly shell-shocked.

Ginchy was a desperate affair: John Upcott, who lost the use of his right arm in the attack, compared Ginchy to the Charge of the Light Brigade. Jack Inchbald escaped it because he was on a course, and returned to find half the battalion gone. An irrepressible character at first, Jack betrays an increasing sadness in letters to John Upcott, though to his own father he was always brisk and upbeat. At the start of 1917, with the battalion still under strength, he writes,

> *'I'm left with practically nobody to help me, and a company almost entirely consisting of 'draft' men to run. Most of our present subalterns are of negligible utility having not the vaguest notion of how to comport themselves much less their men. At times I could lie down and cry almost when I compare the present with the past, and yet the Battalion has done damned well.'*[14]

John Upcott had returned to teaching and offered to find him a job, but it was not to be. Jack was killed in action at Ecoust-St-Mein on 2 April 1917. As for Upcott himself, he married Renée Motte, and in time became a housemaster at Eton.

Another survivor, Martin's model, ended its days in the museum of the Royal United Services Institute in the Banqueting House at Whitehall, the gift of Brigadier General Deverell. It had done its work so well that the reserve officers who carried the battalion on after that first day were confident that Martin would be decorated. In fact, in November 1916 he was given a posthumous mention in despatches. In 1932 the model was described in the museum catalogue:

> *'Model of the attack on Mametz, July 1st, 1916: This model was made by the late Captain D.L. Martin, the Devonshire Regiment, previous to the attack, and was used for instructional purposes by all taking part. After the completion of the attack the model was found to be very accurate.'*

It was on display well into the 1950s; probably until 1962 when the museum was closed and its exhibits dispersed; after that, who knows? Plasticene does not last forever.

After the Armistice came the memorials. Noel Hodgson is remembered on the House of Lords memorial, as a bishop's son; in the Regimental chapel in Exeter Cathedral, and on the town memorials of Thornbury, and of Berwick, where the memorial uses an amended quotation from 'To a Friend Killed in Action'. It was unveiled in 1923, but in September 1920, a few weeks after visiting his son's grave, Henry Hodgson was in Berwick for the dedication of the memorial in the parish church. This must have been extraordinarily painful for him, with so many small ghosts moving among the packed congregation. Boys he prepared for confirmation, cheered on at Church Lads' Brigade and Sunday school, saw in the pews week on week, growing up. One boy most of all.

In his address, Henry asked the congregation to remember that the 126 men named on the memorial were not special:

> *'They were not without their faults and failings, many in the first flush of life and passion. The saying that love is blind to the faults of those we love is not true. Love is unusually sensitive to the faults, but in spite of them loves on. These lads, just the ordinary young men to be met with in the towns or on the country roads, possessed something greater than we imagined, something of the stuff of which heroes are made. They deserve that we should remember them.'*

He summed the stuff of heroes up in five words: cheerfulness, brotherhood, courage, tenacity and kindness.[15]

The vicar read the names, Noel among them and his friend Frank Smail. Another childhood friend, Francis Cowen, commanded the company of Northumberland Fusiliers that attended the service. It was an intensely emotional occasion and the congregation, still devoted to Henry as their former vicar, felt they could see a change in him. When he died six months later following an operation, the local paper reported, *'Dr Hodgson never really recovered from the shock of Noel's loss and it was noticed that he was not in full health on his last visit to Berwick.'*[16] William Oxland, admittedly a much older man, also died soon after his son. And whether just coincidence or a reflection of something deeper, so did James Tombs' father – he had lost two sons in the war – so did Louisa Rayner. She too had lost both her sons. Penelope Hodgson lived on into the 1940s, as quietly stoical as the mother Noel imagined in 'England to her Sons'. Stella kept a poem in her mother's handwriting, 'Remembrance Day, To W.N.H':

Does our world's clamour reach them, where
Bitterness laid aside,
They think ungrudging of the years
When they were crucified?

Or does our silence cry aloud,
Once every passing year?
Startled by that compelling call
They turn, and drawing near

Bend close and look into our eyes
By memory blinded – wet
Grave for the nonce, each turns to each,
"All's well – they don't forget."

Memorials in wood and stone; memorials in ceremony and in silence. In 1915 Noel Hodgson had looked forward to a time when he might climb the fells again, over the passes and hills he knew so well, remembering his friend. *'So if in happier times I climb Black Sail. . .'* A year later Frank Worrall told Stella, *'To-morrow, I'm taking all the men out of the Hospital here on to the hill, it is all I can do in memory of the "best pal" a fellow could have – it is what he would wish & my thoughts will be more than ever with him - & he'll know.'* That love of the heights was so deeply ingrained in Noel Hodgson's being.

Stella, who was probably closer to him than anyone, had found her own ways of remembering. Her two children were named for him; Penelope Noel, whose godfather he would have been, and William. *'If he's a he, I hope he's luckier than his Uncle Bill, and doesn't get involved in silly squabbles of European potentates,'* Noel had written during his sister's first pregnancy. But his nephew and namesake William, Sub-Lieutenant William Tower RN, was lost at Dunkirk in 1940 while helping with the evacuation. After two days in charge of a motor yacht, ferrying men from the beaches to the waiting ships, his propellor shaft broke on the final run. Last seen heading for the harbour in search of a vessel to use as a tug, he received a posthumous mention in despatches *'for great courage and inspiring devotion to duty.'* [17] His uncle would have been saddened but not surprised; he never expected his war to be the last.

Stella herself lived on into the 1980s. She was a published novelist under the name 'Faith Wolseley', occasionally echoing her brother in her characters. She remembered him in her own ways but she also remembered in his. Through the 1920s, year on year, she retraced the route of his 'Farewell Walk' on or near its anniversary, 22 August: climbing from Rosthwaite over the Sty Head Pass to Wastwater, taking a day to explore the Screes and the little church at Wasdale Head, continuing next morning back up Sty Head to the gully he described and the path, and up to the top of Great Gable, his favourite summit. And that was a remembrance he would have understood, and enjoyed.

Notes

Hodgson family:

WNH (William Noel); HBH (Henry Bernard); PMH (Penelope Maria);
SMH/SMT (Stella Mary); HBT (Henry Bernard Tower)

JDU – from the papers of John Dalgairns Upcott

Freeland – from the papers of Bryan and Rowan Freeland

TNA – The National Archives

Worcester – Worcester College, Oxford, Archives

Illinois – Special Collections Research Center, Morris Library, Southern
Illinois University Carbondale, Inchbald Brothers Collection: 1/7/MSS 240

Shepard Archive – Shepard Archive, University of Surrey

Leeds: Liddle Collection – Leeds University Library, Liddle Collection, GS
1282 J W Pocock and ITA 20 H L Wide

Westminster – Westminster School Archives

John Murray – John Murray Archive, National Library of Scotland.

BNO – British Newspaper Archive Online

Chapter 1: From God's Hills to Gloucestershire

1. HBH to SMT; dated only 'Friday'
2. PMH to SMT from Albert; postmark [?] August 1920
3. *The Times*, 6 Jan 1919; 23 Jan 1919; 8 June 1920
4. *The Times*, 12 Sept 1919
5. *The Times*, 8, 11 and 12 June 1920
6. From *Labantur Anni*
7. Letter from Susan Ashmore, 11 June 1986
8. PMH to SMT, 13 June 1921
9. SMH to HBT, 28 March 1909
10. *The Times*, 3 January 1893
11. SMT to HBT, 10 June 1909
12. *The Dursley, Berkeley & Sharpness Gazette*, 7 January 1893
13. Letters from Canon John Cornwall.
14. *The Bristol Mercury,* 29 June 1895; http://www.thornburyroots.co.uk
15. *The Bristol Mercury,* 19 Feb 1890, BNO
16. WNH to SMH, end Feb/beginning March 1916
17. From *The Hills*; published in *The New Witness*, 23 August 1913
18. WNH to SMH, 12 May 1916

Chapter 2: Berwick-upon-Tweed

1. SMH to HBT, 17 Nov 1908
2. *Berwick Advertiser*, 17 Sept 1897
3. ibid
4. SMH to HBT, 18 Nov 1908
5. *Berwickshire News*, 28 May 1901, BNO
6. *Berwickshire News*, 16 April 1901, BNO
7. *Berwickshire News*, 18 Oct 1904, BNO
8. SMH to HBT, 14 Nov 1908, 3 March 1910
9. SMH to HBT, 29 Oct 1909
10. SMH to HBT, 10 Sept 1908
11. *Berwickshire News*, 11 Nov 1902, BNO
12. *Berwickshire News*, 25 Aug 1903, BNO
13. *Berwickshire News*, 10 Nov 1903, BNO
14. SMH to HBT, 17 March 1909

Chapter 3: Durham

1. SMT, 1943
2. *The Pocklingtonian*, 26 March 1904
3. Information about life at Durham School, unless otherwise acknowledged, comes from his nearest contemporaries still living in the 1980s; R.F. Kirby, who grew up at the school, his father and stepfather both being masters; Frank Youngman, who started as a pupil in 1919 and returned as a master, serving under the Rev. Budworth, and C.W. Surtees, another of Budworth's boys and later the school archivist.
4. *The Dunelmian*, 6 March 1906
5. Vera Brittain, *Testament of Youth*, Virago, London, 1978, p.89
6. *Uppingham School Magazine*, August 1914, no. 412, vol.liii, pp.162-169; quotation on p.167
7. From 'England to her Sons', August 1914
8. *The Dunelmian*, July 1913
9. From 'Ave Mater – Atque Vale' and 'Durham', both 1915
10. Letter from the Rev. F.A. Youngman, 16 June 1989
11. E.B. Osborn, *The New Elizabethans*, John Lane, the Bodley Head, London 1919, p.250
12. *The Dunelmian*, 29 June 1908
13. *The Dunelmian*, 1 August 1916, pp. 316-7. The later title was 'Youth's Immortalities' and the poem had one extra verse; eight, as compared to Fisher's seven.

Chapter 4: 'We learned and grew'

1. *The Pocklingtonian*, Michaelmas, 1909

2. SMH to HBT, 14 Nov 1908
3. SMH to HBT, 30 Jan 1910
4. SMH to HBT, 13 May 1909
5. SMH to HBT, 11 Feb 1909
6. SMH to HBT, 9 Aug 1909 (all three quotations)
7. SMH to HBT, 13 Sept 1909
8. *The Dunelmian*, Easter 1911
9. *The Dunelmian*, Summer 1911

Chapter 5: Oxford, 1911 – 1913

1. E. B. Osborn, *The New Elizabethans*, John Lane, The Bodley Head, London, 1919, p.254
2. Serge Obolensky, *One Man in his Time*, Hutchinson, 1960, p.97ff
3. Worcester College Archives: Nowell Oxland, Student File, ref. DM
4. Quoted in Philip Ziegler, *King Edward VIII*, Collins, 1990, p.35
5. *One Man in his Time*, p.98
6. *The New Elizabethans*, p.256
7. ibid, pp. 255, 256
8. ibid, p.257
9. Worcester: Nowell Oxland, Student File, refDM: 24 June 1912, from the Rectory at Alston
10. Worcester: WOR/JCR 6/1/5 – Minutes of the Lovelace Club, 19 October 1912
11. Various references in Worcester: WOR/JCR 6/1/6 – Minutes of the Lovelace Club, November 1913 – March 1914
12. *The Dunelmian*, Summer 1912
13. Lavinia Talbot (ed.) *Gilbert Walter Lyttelton Talbot*, Sidgwick & Jackson, London, 1917, pp.105-6
14. PMH to SMT, 31 July 1912
15. Nowell Oxland, *Poems and Stories*, printed privately in 1917; 'Ilicet' means 'It is over'
16. ibid: 'In the "Radcliffe"'
17. It was Oxland, in his poem 'Cumberland'.
18. *The New Elizabethans*, pp. 254-5
19. John Murray to HBH, 21 July 1919

Chapter 6: 'Time Stands Waiting', April 1913 – August 1914

1. *The New Elizabethans*, p.255
2. PMH to SMT, 11 June 1921. 'These be but toys' means 'these things don't matter.' In her novel *Old Mrs Warren*, Stella included a character almost certainly based on her brother, a young lawyer, who speaks in a deliberately archaic language and is constantly quoting *Hymns Ancient and Modern* – except when things become serious.

3. Based on F.W.H Myers' poem 'On a grave at Grindelwald'
4. *The Dunelmian*, Easter 1914
5. Last two verses only
6. PMH to SMT, [5 February 1914] Only dated 'Thursday, 6.30' – the news broke on Friday, 6 February.
7. *Newcastle Daily Journal*, Friday, 6 March 1914, BNO
8. *Berwick Advertiser*, 24 April 1914
9. John Murray to HBH, 21 July 1919
10. Horace Odes, Book II, poem 14; final lines of 'Labuntur Anni' only.
11. *The Dunelmian*, Summer Term 1914
12. May Wedderburn Cannan, *Grey Ghosts and Voices*, The Roundwood Press, 1976, p.70.
13. *The Dunelmian*, Oxford Letter, Summer Term 1914
14. *Aeneid* Book 2, line 325ff, translated by Mr N. Hammond
15. *The New Elizabethans*, p.255

Chapter 7: 'The Work of Men', September 1914 – July 1915

1. JDU Diary, 31 May 1916
2. TNA: WO339/17743
3. TNA: WO339/12298
4. UK census returns, 1891 and 1901
5. TNA: FO655/68/ passport no.23027, 7 August 1903
6. TNA: WO339/13105
7. Westminster School Archives: *The Grantite Review*, Election 1909,VIII/12 and Play 1909, IX/1
8. TNA: WO339/8737
9. Freeland, Diary. Bryan Freeland's diary fills in details of the 9th Battalion's movements in this period that are not recorded elsewhere.
10 JDU: from WNH, 9 January 1916
11 Illinois; Inchbald Brothers Collection: 1/7/MSS 240, Folder 4
12. Concluding verses only. 'Old Simeon's passing hymn' is the 'Nunc dimittis', *'Lord, now lettest Thou Thy servant depart in peace'*, always sung in the Anglican service of Evensong.
13. All names from Durham School. 'Dutton' was the Rev Budworth's middle name. The quotation is from Vergil, *Aeneid* VIII.560.
14. JDU: to his uncle, 31 March 1916
15. Illinois; Inchbald Brothers Collection: 1/7/MSS 240, Folder 4

Chapter 8: 'Interminable Land', July – September 1915

1. JDU, Diary, 19 July 1915. The official war diary does not begin until 17 September, so the unpublished diaries of JDU and Bryan Freeland are invaluable in piecing together details of the first weeks in France.

2. JDU, Diary, 1 August 1915 (also the two preceding quotations and the next)
3. WNH to SMT, 5 August 1915
4. JDU, Diary, 8 August 1915
5. ibid, 11 August 1915
6. ibid
7. JDU to his uncle, 5 August 1915
8. Freeland, Diary, 19 August 1915. Freeland was wrong about Kitchener being C.I.G.S (Chief of the Imperial General Staff). In August 1915 that was the soon-to-be-replaced Sir James Wolfe-Murray.
9. JDU, diary, 22 August 1915
10. SMT to WNH, 30 August 1915
11. Illinois, Inchbald Brothers Collection, 1915-1916 1/7/MSS 240 Folder 4
12. JDU, Diary, 5 September 1915
13. JDU names the place as Verquineul; but Freeland gives Fouquereuil and the Battalion War Diary confirms this.
14. There are two copies. Hinshelwood's is captioned 'WNH by ASH, 20 September 1915'

Chapter 9: 'The Grime of Battle': Loos, September 1915
1. JDU to his sister, 9 September 1915
2. Battalion from his Medal Index card; the War Diary of the 9th Devons has '2nd Warwicks'.
3. Illinois, Inchbald Brothers Collection, Folder 3
4. Harold Rayner, *Letters from France, July 26, 1915 to June 30, 1916*, Privately Printed, 1919, p.81
5. Illinois, Inchbald Brothers Collection, Folder 3
6. JDU, Diary, 11 August and 22 September 1915
7. ibid, 24 September 1915
8. ibid
9. Information from Mr Darren Jones
10. JDU: from Major Anderson, 24 October 15
11. JDU: from W.E. Martin
12. *Letters from France*, p.78
13. JDU: from Inchbald, 18 Oct 15
14. W.N. Hodgson, 'Nestoria (2)', in *Verse & Prose in Peace and War*, John Murray, 1920.
15. Quoted by Davies's father in a letter to the War Office, TNA: WO339/25309. Said to be from *'the only company officer left and who was near at the time'* which can only refer to Hodgson.
16. *Letters from France*, p.80
17. 'Nestoria (2)', p.62
18. TNA: WO95/1652

19. ibid
20 JDU: from Inchbald , 18 October 15
21. *Letters from France*, p.81

Chapter 10: 'The Old 9th', October 1915 – January 1916
1. JDU: from Thompson, 28 Dec 1915. This chapter is written around the collection of letters John Upcott received from fellow officers and other members of the Battalion after he was wounded at Loos. Unless otherwise indicated, the quotations are from his papers and the senders are identified in the text.
2. Leeds: Liddle Collection GS1281; Pte. W. Hedden to J.G. Pocock, 29 December 1915,
3. R.H. Wollocombe (ed), *In the Trenches with the 9th Devons: Frank Wollocombe's War Diary*, privately printed, Bath, 1994, entries for 5 and 6 Oct, pp.6 and 7
4. TNA: WO95/1652
5. Wollocombe, pp.16 – 17. The handler was probably Leutnant Heinrich Stennes of the Reserve-Infanterie-Regiment Nr. 25, then serving in the Givenchy area. [Information from Robin Schäfer]
6. JDU: WNH to Martin, 27 Oct 1915
7. JDU: quoted in a letter by Pocock, 31 Oct 1915
8. Wollocombe, pp.20-21
9. Illinois, Inchbald Brothers, Folder 3
10. Wollocombe, p.22
11. WNH to SMT, 27 Dec 1915. There was a Private Harry Gay but he was wrong about the number: 11630 Private William Harry Gay, 9th Battalion, Devonshire Regiment

Chapter 11: 'There and Back', January – April 1916
1. John Murray Archives: HBH to John Murray, 31 July 1917
2. WNH to SMT, 27 December 1915
3. JDU: from Thompson, 24 January 1916
4. JDU: from Rayner, 5 January 1916
5. JDU: from Inchbald, 13 January 1916
6. WNH to SMT, 24 & 27 January 1916
7. JDU: from WNH, 9 Jan 1916: *'de mortuis'* (of the dead) probably short for *'de mortuis nil nisi bonum'* (of the dead, nothing but good). Otherwise 'not to speak ill of the dead'; he's being ironic here.
8. JDU: from Thompson, 24 January 1916
9. JDU: from Muntz, 16 November 1915
10. JDU, Diary
11. The continuation of the 'Monday' letter above, almost certainly 21 February 1916

12. JDU, Diary, 25 February
13. *The New Witness*, 20 April 1916
14. JDU, Diary, 19 March 1916
15. WNH to Robert Parr, 21 May 1916

Chapter 12: 'Before Action', April – June 1916
1. JDU, Diary, 25 April 1916
2. Wollocombe, p.80
3. TNA, WO95/1653
4. Wollocombe and JDU Diaries
5. JDU, Diary, 20 April 1916
6. Wollocombe, p.87
7. JDU, Diary, 25 April
8. JDU, Diary, 1 May 1916; At this time JDU refers to the Bois des Tailles as 'Bois des Rossignols' [nightingales]. A map in Harold Rayner's *Letters from France* identifies a southern tip of the wood, below the Bray road, by this name.
9. WNH to SMT, 13 May 1916
10. JDU, Diary, 11 (or 12) May; his dates become confused around this time
11. WNH to Parr, 21 May 1916; the second of the 'Michael' to 'Nestor' letters.
12. Wollocombe, p.97
13. Shepard Archive, EHS/C/15/4, postmark 7 June 1916

Chapter 13: 'Goodbye to all of this'
1. Quoted in W. J. P. Aggett, *The Bloody Eleventh*, The Devon and Dorset Regiment, Wyvern Barracks, Exeter, 1995, vol.III, p.44
2. TNA: CAB45/132 f.673-674 (with thanks to Mark Banning and Paul Reed)
3. Wollocombe, p.104
4. TNA: WO95/1653
5. ibid
6. Rayner, *Letters from France*, pp.215–216
7. ibid, p.215
8. ibid, June. Unless otherwise acknowledged, all details in this account are taken from the War diaries of 20 Brigade [WO95/1653]; 9th Devons [WO95/1656]; 8th Devons [WO95/1655]; 2nd Gordon Highlanders [WO95/1656]
9. TNA: WO95/1653
10. http://jeremybanning.co.uk/2011/04/13/the-time-team-special-dig-at-mametz
11. Rayner, *Letters from France*, p.216
12. Some sources have all 20 Brigade advancing from the support lines, some

the whole 7th Division. But the diary of 2nd Gordon Highlanders places them in the front line trench, going over at 7.30am.
13. Rowan Freeland to SMT, 30 August 1916
14. TNA: WO95/1656
15. TNA: WO339/13105
16. TNA: WO95/1653
17. TNA: WO339/933 (Riddell); WO339/18678 (Holcroft); JDU to his uncle, 29 July 1916
18. TNA: WO339/17743
19. TNA: WO339/4694
20. Shepard Archive: EH5/C/15/3/4
21. Leeds: Liddle Collection: ITA 20
22. *London Gazette*, 25 September 1916; Freeland: A.E. Norman to Rowan Freeland, 21 August 1916
23. TNA: WO95/1653 and WO95/1655
24. Wollocombe, p.98
25. Storey to HBH, 9 July 1916;
26. Crosse to HBH, 8 July 1916
27. PMH to Robert Parr, 14 August
28. *Tonbridge School and The Great War of 1914 to 1919*, Whitefriars Press, Tonbridge, 1923, p.274
29. IWM Documents 4772: Diary of Rev E. C. Crosse.
30. Freeland: Crosse to Rowan Freeland, 7 & 22 July 1916. The reference to the 'Magpie's nest' also helps place the largest number of casualties close to the corner of the Copse. There was a real magpie which Crosse mentions elsewhere, carrying on with her life in one of the last remaining trees, oblivious to the shells. In an Army panoramic photograph of October 1915, before the area had become active, it is even possible to see two trees with what could easily be nests in them.
31. JDU, Diary, 10 July 1916
32. Shepard Archive, EHS/C/8/17/6
33. Rawle Knox, *The Work of E. H. Shepard*, Methuen, London, 1979, p.28
34. E.H. Shepard, *Drawn From Memory*, Methuen, London, p.144

Epilogue: Climb Black Sail for Me
1. Lady Desborough, *Pages from a Family Journal*, Eton College, privately printed, Spottiswoode, Ballantyne & Co, 1916, p.594
2. Quoted in Andrew Birkin, *J. M. Barrie and the Lost Boys*, Constable, London, 1979, p.276
3. TNA: WO339/17743
4. John Murray: HBH to John Murray, 31 July 1917
5. Alan Bishop and Mark Bostridge (eds), *Letters from a Lost Generation:*

First World War Letters of Vera Brittain and Four Friends, Little, Brown & Co. London, 1998, p.362. The editors of the book do not identify this quotation but the source is unmistakeable.

6. *The Dunelmian*, 16 December 1914

7. ibid, 18 December 1915

8. ibid, 1 August 1916; third of five verses

9. Figures from *Floreat Dunelmia, 1414 – 2014*, Durham School, 2013, p.131

10. Anson, *T.B. Strong*, p.137

11. Worcester: Nowell Oxland, Student File, ref. DM

12. She signed herself 'F. Amy Hawthorn' and came from Newcastle. UK birth and census records yield one candidate. Frances Amelie/Amelia Hawthorn, born 28 May 1876, one of seven children of a Newcastle doctor. The 1911 Census lists her as 'Amy', and a school teacher, and shows her sisters Eleonore and Lilian living in Alston.

13. Worcester: WOR/BUR 8/25/53 18 Dec, 27 Dec, 10 Jan

14. JDU: from Inchbald, 9 Jan 1917

15. *Berwick Advertiser*, 10 September 1920. The address is given in reported speech

16. *Berwick Advertiser*, 4 March 1921

17. Wellington Roll of Honour, 1939-45, p.319; *London Gazette*, 21 August 1945.

Bibliography

NEWSPAPERS AND PERIODICALS INCLUDING:
The Times
The Observer
The New Witness
The Saturday Review
The Spectator
The Bristol Mercury
The Bristol Gazette
The Berwick Advertiser
The Berwickshire News
The Western Daily Press
The Western Morning News
The Aberdeen Daily Journal
The Newcastle Daily Journal
The Burnley Express
The Hull Daily Mail

BOOKS
Adcock, A. St. John, *For Remembrance, Soldier Poets who have Fallen in the War,* Hodder & Stoughton, 1918

Aggett, W.J.P, *The Bloody Eleventh: History of the Devonshire Regiment*, vol. III 1915 – 1969, The Devon and Dorset Regiment, 1995

Anson, Harold, *T. B. Strong: Bishop, Musician, Dean, Vice-Chancellor*, S.P.C.K., 1949

Atkinson, C.T., *The Devonshire Regiment 1914 – 1918*, Eland Brothers, Exeter, 1926 [Naval & Military Press reprint]

Barker, Dudley, *G. K. Chesterton*, Stein & Day, 1973

Barton, Peter, *The Battlefields of the First World War*, Constable, 2008

Barton, Peter, *The Somme: a new panoramic perspective*, Constable, 2006

Bishop, Alan and Mark Bostridge (eds) *Letters from a Lost Generation: First World War Letters of Vera Brittain and Four Friends*, Little, Brown & Co. 1998

Blagden, C.M. *Well Remembered*, Hodder & Stoughton, 1953

Brittain, Vera, *Testament of Youth*, Virago edition, 1978

Cannan, May Wedderburn, *Grey Ghosts and Voices*, The Roundwood Press, 1976

Cherry, Niall, *Most Unfavourable Ground: The Battle of Loos 1915*, Solihull, Helion, 2005

Cowe, F.M., *Berwick upon Tweed*, [J.D. Cowe, Ravensdowne, Berwick upon Tweed, 1984]

Crosse, Ernest, *The God of Battles*

Curthos, Judith, *The Cardinal's College: Christ Church, Chapter and Verse*, Profile Books, 2012

Farrar-Hockley, A.H. *The Somme*, Batsford, 1964

Gardner, Brian, *Up the Line to Death: The War Poets, 1914 – 1918*, Magnum Books, 1976

Hibberd, Dominic, and John Onions, *Poetry of the Great War*, Macmillan, 1986

Hodgson, Courtenay, *Heats of Youth*, Herbert Jenkins Limited, nd

Hodgson, W.N., *Verse and Prose in Peace and War*, Smith, Elder & Co, 1916; John Murray, 1920

Lewis-Stempel, John, *Six Weeks: The Short and Gallant Life of the British Officer in the First World War*, Weidenfeld & Nicolson, 2010

Lloyd, Nick, *Loos*, The History Press, Stroud, 2006

Malden, John, *Floreat Dunelmia 1414-2014*, Durham School, 2013

Malden, John, *Let Durham Flourish,* The Friends of Durham School, 1996

Masterman, J.C. *On the Chariot Wheel*, Oxford University Press, 1975

Middlebrook, Martin, *The First Day on the Somme*, Allen Lane, 1971

Osborn, E.B, *The New Elizabethans*, John Lane, 1919

Saunders, Tim, *West Country Regiments on the Somme*, Leo Cooper, 2004

Sewell, Brocard, *Cecil Chesterton*, St Albert's Press, 1975

Thompson, Captain A. Broderick & Captain E. Watts Moses, *The War Record of Old Dunelmians, 1914 – 1919*, privately printed, Sunderland 1919

Wollocombe, R.H (ed), *In the trenches with the 9th Devons: Frank Wollocombe's War Diary*, [privately printed, RH Wollocombe, 1994]

Wolseley, Faith, *Old Mrs Warren*, Dorothy Crisp & Co., 1939

Index